THE CAT

A COMPLETE GUIDE

THE CAT

A COMPLETE GUIDE

Claire Bessant

The Cat – A Complete Guide
was conceived, edited and designed by
Team Media Limited, London

Copyright © Team Media Ltd

Published by
SILVERDALE BOOKS in 2001
an imprint of Bookmart Ltd
Registered Number 2372865
Trading as Bookmart Ltd
Desford Road
Enderby
Leicester LE9 5AD

Authors
Claire Bessant: What is a Cat?
Caring for Cats
Bradley Viner: Your Cat's Health
Paddy Cutts: Cat Breeds

Consultants
Bradley Viner, Julia May

Project Editor: **Jinny Johnson**
Editors: **Simon Hall, Rupert Matthews**
Fiona Plowman, Gwen Rigby
Art Editor: **Dave Goodman**
Designer: **Darren Bennett**
Design Assistants: **Max Newton**
  Zoe Quayle
Picture Research: **Veneta Bullen**
  Elizabeth Loving, Julia Ruxton
Illustrators: **Wildlife Art; Michael Woods**

Team Media
Editorial Director: **Louise Tucker**
Managing Editor: **Elizabeth Tatham**
Art Directors: **Eddie Poulton**
  Paul Wilkinson

Illustrations front cover,
John Daniels, back cover
PhotoPress, Stockdorf (2)

A CIP catalogue record for this book is available from the British Library.

ISBN 1 85605 619 8
Printed in Czech Republic

Claire Bessant is the Chief Executive of the Feline Advisory Bureau, an organization dedicated to cats and their health and welfare. Claire is the author of a number of books, including *How to Talk to Your Cat*, and a regular contributor to pet magazines.

Bradley Viner runs a highly respected three-centre animal practice. He writes for a number of pet magazines and has written several books about pet care. He is also a regular contributor to radio programmes and frequently appears on television.

Paddy Cutts is an established expert on cat breeds and has bred prize-winning Burmese cats. She has written a number of books on cats and contributes to pet magazines. She is a successful animal photographer and runs her own picture agency.

Julia May is a veterinarian specializing in small animals. A confirmed cat lover, she breeds Oriental, Siamese and Angora cats. She is a member of the committee of the Governing Council of the Cat Fancy in the UK and show manager of the Supreme Cat Show.

Contents

Introduction

Cat lovers the world over know how special their pets are. In fact, in a great many countries, cats are more popular than man's original best friend, the dog.

But at one time, the cat was seen as a somewhat second-rate pet. Cheap and easy to obtain, the cat lived mostly outside the home and was occasionally given food to supplement what it was expected to catch in its role as pest controller. Dogs, too, had to work for their keep, but their specialized tasks, such as hunting, protecting or fighting, gave them a respect that was not generally afforded to cats.

The dog's obedience was also appreciated by its owners, but humans had little control over the cat – how it behaved, where it went, or how it looked. It was seen as rather disrespectful by those who enjoyed the dog's slave-like devotion.

In the 19th century, this situation began to change. In Europe and North America, people started to import cats such as the long-haired Persian and the exotic-looking Siamese from other countries, and to breed different types of cat. As it became acceptable to treat these 'special' cats with care and indulgence, the ordinary domestic cat or 'moggie' also became more treasured as a pet.

THE WORLD OF THE CAT

The position of the cat in our homes and hearts is now without question. However, the adaptability of the cat to most domestic situations can make us complacent as to its needs and true nature. We could be in danger of forgetting the cat's origins as a highly successful predator.

Cat – The Complete Guide aims to illuminate the qualities, behaviour and senses that make the cat such a special creature and to help owners choose a cat to suit their needs, keep it content and understand how to tackle any problems that arise.

Part 1 examines the natural cat – its structure, body systems and senses. We discover how the cat sees the world, how it communicates, and examine its normal life cycle and pattern of daily activity.

Part 2 looks at the cat as a pet: how to choose the right cat for each owner and family, how to prepare for the arrival of a new cat, and how to deal with practical matters such as feeding and grooming. Advice is given on what to do if a pet cat develops behavioural problems, such as scratching or spraying indoors.

Part 3 explains how to keep a check on a cat's health, what vaccinations it needs and when and how to deal with parasites. It looks at more serious problems and advises on what action to take if a pet cat does become ill.

Part 4 looks at the range of pedigree breeds of cat and helps the owner decide which might make the right pet. The history, appearance and temperament of each breed is described and a brief assessment lists key factors such as grooming needs.

A COMPREHENSIVE GUIDE

The book ends with an engaging and informative look at the cat's role in myth and legend, literature and art. Finally, a resource section lists addresses of useful organizations and gives suggestions for further reading.

For people who already have a cat, this book will be the perfect reference. For new owners, it will be an inspiration and a source of valuable information. Only by understanding the cat's natural behaviour, physical make-up and needs can you be sure of looking after your pet properly and helping it enjoy the long and happy life it so richly deserves.

CATS IN THE WILD

Cats, large and small, are among the most beautiful of all animals. From lions to domestic cats, all are supremely well-adapted predators, equipped with speed, strength and stealth. And in even the most pampered pet, the instincts of the wild cat remain. There are about 36 species of wild cat. These include the big

cats, such as the lion, tiger, leopard and jaguar, as well as numerous smaller species, such as the ocelot, margay, lynx and the African wild cat, believed to be the ancestor of our domestic pets. Sadly, because their beautiful fur has long been coveted by humans, many of these magnificent creatures are now rare.

Tyger! Tyger! burning bright
In the forests of the night,
What immortal hand or eye
Could frame thy fearful symmetry?

WILLIAM BLAKE, THE TYGER, 1794

The animal kingdom came
faultily...
Only the cat issued wholly a cat,
intact and vainglorious:
he came forth a consummate
identity,
knew what he wanted, and
walked tall.

PABLO NERUDA, CAT, 1961

Dozing, all cats assume the svelte design
of desert sphinxes sprawled in solitude,
apparently transfixed by endless dreams

CHARLES BAUDELAIRE, CATS, 1857

We were not ever of their feline race,
Never had hidden claws so sharp as theirs
In any half-remembered incarnation

ROBERT GRAVES, FRIGHTENED MEN, 1975

PART I

WHAT IS A CAT?

Cats, large or small, are perhaps the most beautiful of all creatures. As a group, their variety of coat coloration and pattern is unsurpassed, and individuals, such as the tiger, snow leopard and clouded leopard, are among the most spectacular animals on the planet. Add to this the grace, suppleness and regal poise of cats, and you have the true kings and queens of beasts.

There is no doubt that our pet cats belong to this group of top predators. Watch even the most friendly domestic cat stalking in the garden and the ruthless nature of the hunter is obvious. The cat is untainted by its close association with humans; its inner being is unaffected by our soft ways. It can and will survive alone if it has to. A combination of wild animal and loving small pet, which chooses to be our companion, the cat is on a level footing with humans and earns a respect we give to few other creatures.

The Unique Cat

Independent cats ◆ Domestication ◆ Changing looks ◆
Wild relatives ◆ Successful carnivores

What is it about the domestic cat that humans find so appealing? Is it its independence and self-contained nature? Or is it the mysterious way in which this beautiful feline has managed to marry its self-determination with a relationship to people that is not one of servitude? How does the cat juggle its two lives as pet and hunter?

DOMESTIC ANIMALS

Humans have domesticated many creatures over thousands of years, generally exploiting them for food, labour or protection. The cat does not fit into any of these groups. It does do a 'job' of vermin control, but it is not under human direction, like a working dog. The cat's role as rat- and mouse-catcher is a useful by-product of its natural hunting tendencies and of its own exploitation of humans as a source of food and shelter.

The unique relationship began when the cat gradually lost its fear of people and moved closer to human communities – a process sometimes referred to as self-domestication. This is quite different from the dog's long association with humans, which has succeeded because of the canine need to be part of a pack. The pack lives and hunts together, so belonging is vital to the survival of wild dogs.

Domestic dogs compromise their behaviour to keep their place in the human pack or family, which is equally vital to their survival. The cat, in contrast, is by nature a solitary hunter and does not need to make such compromises to ensure success.

Humans have manipulated the looks of the pet cat only slightly. Although a century of cat breeding for specific traits has produced distinct types of cat, this is nothing compared to the variation 10,000 years of human selection have produced in the dog.

Dogs have been selected for specific tasks in the past, such as guarding, and hunting, and their form has altered accordingly. Similar variation

Above: Selective breeding has produced cats with particular features, such as long, luxuriant fur. Such fur is purely decorative and serves no useful purpose. This pampered Persian has the air of a cat who knows its beauty is appreciated by its owners.

Above: Most experts believe that today's domestic cats are descended from African wild cats, which were first 'domesticated' by the Ancient Egyptians. African wild cats have tabby-like markings and are slightly larger than domestic cats.

Left: The look of the non-pedigree cat, or moggie, is remarkably consistent the world over. Adaptable and easy to care for, non-pedigrees are still probably the most popular choice for pet owners.

The dog is a pack animal. Its behavioural repertoire ensures that it fits into a group, and it happily takes a subservient role in the human pack, too. This means that working relationships with humans are generally successful. In the main, dogs depend on their owners to take them out and bring them home again. They require much more human control than cats do.

Below: Like dogs, cats share our homes and our lives – but strictly on their own terms. Although they like attention, cats are generally far more independent than dogs. Most domestic cats are able to come and go to suit themselves.

in form has not occurred in cats. Cats have not been bred for any specific purpose, other than for beauty and companionship. Apart from changes to its coat length and colour and some differences in its body shape, the domestic cat has remained a constant size and is always recognizable. Yet within this small range there is always a type of cat to suit everyone's taste.

WILD RELATIVES

There are 36 different species of cat in the wild, ranging from the familiar big cats, such as the lion, tiger, leopards and cheetah, to the smaller cats rarely seen by humans, including the fishing cat, pampas cat, black-footed cat and jaguarundi. The lion,

tiger, jaguar and leopards can all roar. Their vocal apparatus is able to move freely, enabling them to make this most impressive of sounds. The scientific name shared by all the species in this group is *Panthera*. All the other cats (bar the cheetah) cannot roar and are grouped as *Felis*. These are commonly called small cats, even though the puma is as large as a leopard.

While most wild cat species are finding it hard to survive in natural habitats that have become more and more disrupted by human activities, domestic cats are thriving. Ferals (domestic cats gone wild) have proved adaptable almost everywhere humans have taken them in their exploration of different lands. Individual cats not only survive in new or even harsh

The Unique Cat

Above: Large or small, wild or domestic, cats of all kinds are remarkably similar in their looks and behaviour. Most cat owners will have seen their pet stretching just like this mighty lion or sitting in much the same pose as the tiger. Common to all cats is the finely tuned body structure of a top predator.

environments, but, as long as there are plentiful supplies of food, they breed rapidly and are known for their fecundity. In theory, one female cat can be responsible for as many as 20,000 descendants in a period of five years.

SUCCESSFUL CARNIVORES

Cats are such good hunters that their bodies have not needed to adapt to make use of 'lower grade' foods. They rely on a diet of energy-rich meat, which enables them to eat what they need in a short period and then conserve their energy by sleeping. They are obligate carnivores – their whole structure is geared to catching, eating and digesting meat, and they cannot survive without it.

Omnivores, such as dogs, must have the ability to break down the lower-quality food that they scavenge as well as anything they can kill in a hunt. Herbivores, such as antelope and zebra, living alongside lions on the African savanna, must eat almost continuously to obtain sufficient energy to go and find more food, to reproduce and to outrun their main predators, the big cats!

FAMILY FEATURES

The look of each species of cat depends on the environment it lives in and its own particular lifestyle, but most members of the cat family have a number of characteristics in common.

✦ Male and female cats look similar (with the exception of the maned male lion).

✦ Cats walk on their toes, their steps cushioned by pads, which aid silent hunting and enable them to move swiftly when they need to pounce. Only the cheetah is fast enough to abandon stealth and ambush and rely solely on speed, keeping its claws unsheathed at all times to maintain friction for turning.

✦ All cats have a fine sense of balance, which enables them to leap and pounce with ease.

✦ All cats have acute hearing and sensitive sight.

✦ Most cats are solitary (except lions, which live and hunt in groups).

The pet cat, *Felis catus*, below, shares all of these features and could truly be said to be the tiger on the hearth.

The cat is independent, beautiful, and athletic, but it is its behaviour with us that cements human/feline relationships. The cat on your lap is vulnerable and wanting human attention. Its weapons sheathed, it pats you with a silken paw and purrs – a sound that relaxes and pleases. Even now, scientists do not know how cats make this unique sound, which is usually a signal of contentment.

Cat owners care for, and get to know, a creature that is still, genetically, an African wild cat. We build up a relationship that may last 15 years or more. During this time we learn a mutual system of communication, based on vocal and body language, with an animal that is not tied to us on a lead or fenced in but that simply chooses to remain at our side.

Above: Despite their origins in harsh desert habitat, domestic cats have taken to a life of comfort in our homes with great enthusiasm. Most cats like nothing better than a cosy chair by the fire or a cushion in the sun, with a loving owner on hand to provide food and attention on demand.

CAT. A domestick animal that catches mice, commonly reckoned by naturalists the lowest order of the leonine species.

SAMUEL JOHNSON,
A DICTIONARY OF THE ENGLISH LANGUAGE,
1755

FOSTER MOTHER

◆

Wild and domestic cats have close genetic links. Just how close is evident in the photograph below. This female house cat fostered an orphan kitten of a Geoffroy's cat, a wild South American species. Once the mother had accepted the kitten, she fed and cared for it as one of her own.

Structure of a Cat

Supple skeleton ✦ *Bones and muscles* ✦
Teeth and claws ✦ *Skin and fur*

The cat has been crafted by 35 million years of evolution to become the almost perfect hunter. It has come to look and act in the way that it does because both its physical attributes and behaviour have been hugely successful and have ensured the cat's survival.

The cat is extraordinarily supple and agile. Its skeleton consists of 244 bones – 40 more than a human skeleton. Most of the extra bones are in the cat's spine and tail. More than 33 differently shaped vertebrae form a long, pliable arc along the back from the neck to the tail. There are usually seven cervical vertebrae, which make up the neck; 13 thoracic vertebrae that are connected to the ribs; seven lumbar vertebrae, which form the lower back; three sacral vertebrae, which are attached to the pelvis, or hip bones; and a number of tail vertebrae.

The tail, or caudal, vertebrae play a vital part in balance. They can vary in number from just a few in the Manx cat to 19 to 28 in most other cats. They have very rounded surfaces, so the bones can rotate easily and smoothly. Even the muscle and ligament attachments to these allow for much greater movement than in other animals.

FLOATING COLLAR BONE
The cat's collar bone, or clavicle, is slender and does not attach to the shoulder joint in the way that it does in humans. It lies unattached in the muscle and allows the shoulders to move with little restriction. The cat

can, therefore, squeeze through small spaces or place its front feet one behind the other to walk along a narrow ledge without difficulty.

Watch your cat hunting or study the next television programme on big cats. When the cat is stalking prey, its shoulderblades, or scapulae, rise and fall, while the spine and head remain almost motionless. Unlike the human shoulderblade, which lies flat on the back of the rib cage and moves little, the cat's shoulder swings along with

its leg, giving it a greater range of movements and lengthening the leg. Dogs, too, are made in this way, but they do not have the flexibility of cats. Unlike dogs, cats can also turn their wrists and thus use their paws effectively for climbing, grasping, swiping and, of course, washing.

MUSCLES AND TENDONS
On top of this mobile and specially adapted skeleton lie the muscles and tendons. It is in the muscles of the

Skull

Like all mammals, the cat has a system of muscles linked to its skeletal structure which enables it to make movements. The cat has about 500 skeletal muscles and its body is particularly flexible and supple. The most powerful muscles are in the cat's hind limbs, allowing it to jump and pounce. The jaw muscles are also extremely strong so that the cat can bite and kill its prey.

Tail muscles

Back muscles

Leg muscles

Jaw muscles

Chest muscles

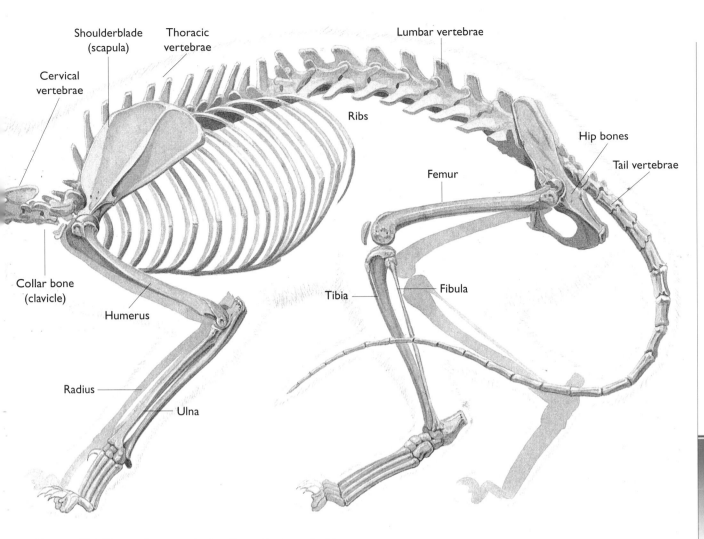

Shoulderblade
(scapula)

Thoracic
vertebrae

Cervical
vertebrae

Lumbar vertebrae

Ribs

Hip bones

Femur

Tail vertebrae

Collar bone
(clavicle)

Humerus

Tibia

Fibula

Radius

Ulna

Above and left: The small, compact body of the cat is strong, flexible and finely controlled. Its skeleton and muscles are adapted for silent, smooth but lethal hunting. The role of the skeleton is to support the body and protect it, and to anchor muscles that work to lever strong light bones for movement. Note the short, compact skull, the long, flexible backbone and the slender legs.

Below: A cat can leap up to about five times its own height – the human equivalent of 9m (30ft) – without turning a hair or twitching a whisker. Before taking off, the cat assesses the height of the jump and then springs into the air, using the powerful muscles in its back legs.

rear quarters that the cat's power for short sprints lies. These muscles also give the cat its ability to leap away from danger and spring upwards. But the cat is not a good endurance machine. It is built for stalking until close to its prey and then pouncing, not for pursuing prey over long distances. Even the cheetah, which is built for speed, must rest and recover after about a minute of sprinting.

These physical attributes, perfected as they are for fluid movement, are no use unless they are controlled extremely efficiently. The cat's nervous system is as complex as that of humans, but it is concentrated on the fine control of movement and the all-important coordination of its actions.

Body systems

In a cat's skull, the two most obvious features are the huge eye sockets and short, strong jaws lined with sharp teeth. Large eyes are vital for successful hunting in low light at dawn and dusk (see page 30), and strong jaws are an essential part of a carnivore's armoury.

TEETH, PAWS AND CLAWS

The cat has 16 teeth in the upper jaw and 14 in the lower – fewer than any other carnivore but obviously enough to do the job required. Like humans, cats cut their first teeth after birth. These baby, or milk, teeth are replaced by adult teeth when kittens are four to six months old.

Other remarkable features of the cat's structure are its paws and claws. Compare the dog's rather clumsy foot with that of the cat and it is clear why the cat is so much more adaptable than the dog. The claws themselves are equivalent to our fingernails but much more useful.

A cat's paws can be padded slippers for silent stalking, crampons for climbing, razor-tipped nets for catching prey, lethal weapons in a fight, washing sponges for face cleaning, and, occasionally, spoons for lifting food to the mouth.

INSIDE THE BODY

Modern pet cats have retained many of the characteristics that were essential to their wild, desert-carnivore ancestors, including a urinary system geared to the consumption of large quantities of protein and the conservation of water. Cats also produce relatively concentrated urine.

Because the cat is such a successful hunter, it can survive by eating just

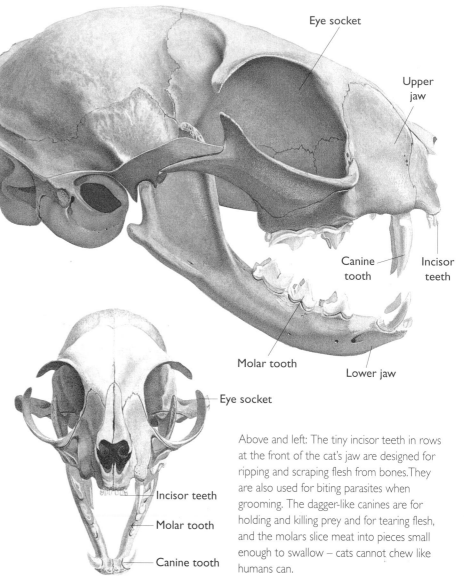

Eye socket

Upper jaw

Canine tooth

Incisor teeth

Molar tooth

Lower jaw

Eye socket

Incisor teeth

Molar tooth

Canine tooth

Above and left: The tiny incisor teeth in rows at the front of the cat's jaw are designed for ripping and scraping flesh from bones. They are also used for biting parasites when grooming. The dagger-like canines are for holding and killing prey and for tearing flesh, and the molars slice meat into pieces small enough to swallow – cats cannot chew like humans can.

Right: Desert-living wild cats have the ability to conserve water and live on a high-protein diet. Pet cats still retain these physical adaptations. If cats are fed on a diet of canned food, containing a high proportion of water, they may rarely take extra liquid.

meat. It does not need some of the chemical enzymes required by other animals to build certain nutrients from plant foods. Dogs and other scavengers must be able to make use of meat and vegetable nutrients because they must survive on both.

The cat has cut plant material out of its diet almost completely. Hence it has lost the ability to use some of the nutrients vegetables can provide if metabolized in a certain way. This also means that nutrients, such as taurine and arginine, which the cat cannot manufacture in its own body as other animals do, must be available directly in its diet. For this reason cats cannot be vegetarians. Plants do not contain these nutrients.

One advantage of feeding solely on the bodies of other creatures, is that cats do not have to deal with the toxins that may be found in food which has begun to decay – they leave that to their prey to deal with. But there is also a disadvantage to this in that their livers do not have the enzymes or pathways that enable them to detoxify certain chemicals. This leaves cats vulnerable to poisoning from manmade chemicals, such as creosote, paracetamol and organophosphates. Thus cats must be treated quite differently to dogs when it comes to veterinary care.

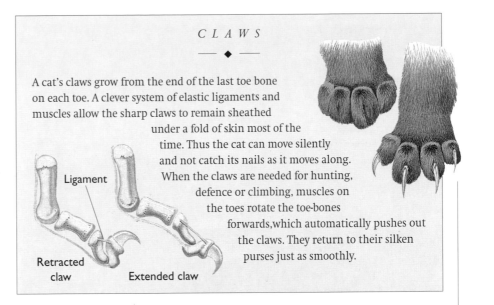

C L A W S

A cat's claws grow from the end of the last toe bone on each toe. A clever system of elastic ligaments and muscles allow the sharp claws to remain sheathed under a fold of skin most of the time. Thus the cat can move silently and not catch its nails as it moves along. When the claws are needed for hunting, defence or climbing, muscles on the toes rotate the toe-bones forwards, which automatically pushes out the claws. They return to their silken purses just as smoothly.

Ligament

Retracted claw

Extended claw

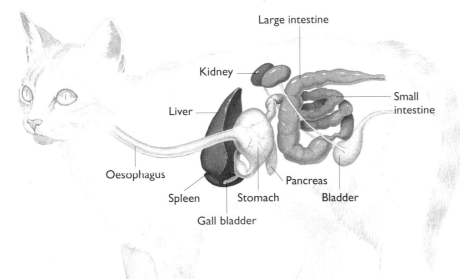

Large intestine

Kidney

Liver

Small intestine

Oesophagus

Spleen

Stomach

Pancreas

Bladder

Gall bladder

Above: Cats do take in some vegetable material when they swallow their prey's gut and its contents. They also sometimes nibble grass and other herbs. Even indoor cats should always have some grass at their disposal.

Left: The cat's digestive system is adapted to its diet of meat. Glands in the stomach secrete strong hydrochloric acid and enzymes break down the food for digestion. Few bacteria enter or survive the system. This is partly because cats rarely eat stale food, preferring it so fresh it is still warm, and also because the stomach is so acidic. Cats rarely suffer from stomach problems or from stomach ulcers.

Skin and coat

Cats have a range of hair types. The longhair, or Persian, (far right) has a long, dense coat, with guard hairs up to 12.5cm (5in) long and a thick undercoat of down hairs. A typical short-haired cat (below left) would have guard hairs about 5cm (2in) long. In semi-longhairs (right) and non-pedigree longhairs, the undercoat is less thick and the guard hairs are long and silky. The Devon Rex (below right) has a soft, wavy coat with no guard hairs. The wave in the hair is caused by the natural curl of the awn and down hairs. Even the 'hairless' sphynx has a thin covering of downy fur on its skin.

Semi-longhair

Shorthair

Rex

The largest organ of the cat's body is the skin. As in all animals, the skin needs to be healthy and intact to provide a firm foundation for the coat and to protect the inside of the body from external elements, such as heat, cold, chemicals, invading microorganisms and physical damage.

Cats have thinner skin than other domestic animals but, like many features of feline anatomy, it is very flexible. On the inside of the thigh, the cat's skin is less than half a millimetre (1/64 inch) thick. At its thickest, at the back of the cat's neck, it is up to two millimetres (1/16 inch) thick.

SKIN STRUCTURE

The cat's skin, like that of humans, has several layers – the outer epidermis, the dermis and the subcutis, the deepest layer. Hair follicles, tiny pits in the skin from which hairs grow, run from the surface epidermis and are anchored deep in the dermis.

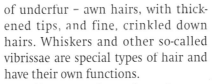

Each hair has several mechanisms working around it – sebaceous glands, apocrine sweat glands, muscles, nerves and blood supply.

The sebaceous glands secrete sebum, an oily substance that forms a waterproof film on the fur and makes it shine. Apocrine sweat glands secrete a milky fluid that has a role in sexual attraction – watery sweat, as we know it, is secreted only from glands on the cat's feet.

Muscles associated with the hairs contract to make the fur stand up if the cat is cold or frightened. Nerves from the skin and hair allow the cat to detect pressure, heat, cold, pain and itchy sensations.

TYPES OF HAIR

Like human hair, the cat's fur grows about two millimetres ($\frac{1}{16}$ inch) a week. Once a hair has attained its full length, it stops growing but remains in the follicle until a new hair starts to grow, causing the old one to moult.

There are about 200 hairs per square millimetre (130,000 per square inch) on the cat's belly and about half this on its back. Several types of hair grow from two types of hair follicle. Primary or guard hairs form the coarse top coat and grow from individual follicles. Softer, finer underfur grows in clusters and provides the cat with insulation. There are two types of underfur – awn hairs, with thickened tips, and fine, crinkled down hairs. Whiskers and other so-called vibrissae are special types of hair and have their own functions.

Pedigree cats have short, long or semi-long hair. There are also other coat types that are made up of combinations of the different hair types. Rex cats, for example, lack guard hairs and have fur that has a thin, wavy appearance.

COAT COLOUR

The coat of the African wild cat, ancestor of domestic cats, is light brownish grey, a colour called agouti, which is seen in many animals such as wild rabbits. On its legs are tabby-type markings. In the wild, the agouti part of the colouring helps the cat blend into the background; the tabby pattern disrupts or breaks up its shape, making it more difficult to see. The stripes of the tiger, the rosette-like markings of the jaguar and the

The coats of most wild cats are coloured and marked, which helps to camouflage them in their surroundings. A lion's golden fur makes it hard to see on a parched savanna plain. The thick, pale fur of this lynx helps it blend into its snowy habitat – and keeps it warm.

spots of the leopard have a similar camouflaging purpose. Each animal is in tune with the environment in which it hunts, whether grassy plains or a dense jungle.

The appearance of the coat, like all characteristics, is controlled by genes. In fact, every cat is still really a tabby at heart. The genes for other colours and patterns do not remove the wild, tabby genes; they simply mask them so that they do not show. Gradually, different mutations of colour and pattern have occurred in the domestic cat. Non-pedigree cats are varied enough, but it is within the breeds over which humans have control that the range of coats is particularly wide.

Cat Senses

Sensitive whiskers and hairs ✦ Heat sensitivity ✦ Hearing ✦ Sight ✦ Taste and smell

Cats are extremely sensory creatures, always finely tuned in to what is going on around them. When domestic cats hunt, they do not rush into the chase. They wait patiently for just the right moment to make that brief dash or pounce. This is when a cat's acute senses of hearing, sight, smell and touch are on red alert and its sensitivity is critical.

TOUCH RECEPTORS

Like humans, cats have pressure and touch receptors on their skin. These can distinguish between sensations such as stroking, tickling or brushing. Temperature and pain receptors also give the cat information about how its environment is affecting it.

Hairs, too, sense movement, and certain hairs have developed special characteristics essential to the cat's ability to feel what is going on around it. The cat's whiskers and other specialized thickened hairs (called vibrissae) are acutely sensitive. They penetrate three times deeper into the skin than normal hairs and have a greater neural network at the roots.

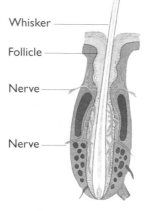

Whisker
Follicle
Nerve
Nerve

Above and right: Whiskers are twice as thick as the outer hairs on a cat's coat. Kittens grow whiskers before their other hair and these are fully functional at birth. Most whiskers are white, but black cats can have black whiskers and Burmese cats, brown.

If a whisker moves only five nanometres (a distance 2,000 times smaller than the width of a human hair) the nerve at its base is activated. With such sensitive 'antennae', the cat can feel its way around in the dark, in narrow spaces, or in the

Below: The thick skin on a cat's paw pads allows the cat to have a sure but silent tread. On the underside of a forepaw are five toe pads and two further pads.

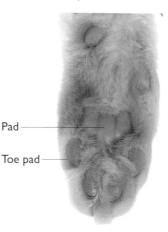

Pad
Toe pad

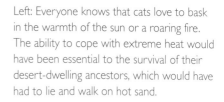

Left: Everyone knows that cats love to bask in the warmth of the sun or a roaring fire. The ability to cope with extreme heat would have been essential to the survival of their desert-dwelling ancestors, which would have had to lie and walk on hot sand.

undergrowth, where it may need to close its vulnerable eyes to protect them from injury.

The whiskers are so sensitive that they may be able to feel the changes in air eddies around objects, allowing the cat to avoid any obstacles in its path almost automatically. It is said that blind cats function well by feeling their way with their whiskers but are lost if their whiskers are cut off.

Whiskers are highly mobile and can be flexed backwards and forwards. When the cat is eating, they can be held back against the face, out of the way. When it is hunting, they are thrown completely forwards to maximize their sensitivity.

In most cats, the whiskers extend to about double the width of the face (about the same width as the body) and further vibrissae are sited above the eyes and on the cheeks and chin. This provides a forcefield of sensitivity surrounding the cat's head. Similar hairs are also found on the back of the the front legs and may provide a cat with information when it is using its claws to climb or grasp prey.

SENSORY PADS

The pads on the underside of the cat's paws are also highly sensitive, particularly the front ones. Not only do they cushion the cat as it walks, but they are also finely tuned sense organs. The cat is said to be able to 'hear' with its feet because the pads are so sensitive to vibration. Special pressure receptors may detect vibrations in the ground caused by rodents moving around. They also give information on the texture and temperature of the surface the cat is walking on.

HEAT SENSITIVITY

Although they are great heat seekers, cats do not seem to be as sensitive to temperature as we are. Humans cannot tolerate anything over 44°C (111°F), but cats do not mind a skin temperature of up to 52°C (126°F). Domestic cats often sit too close to the fire or walk over the cooker hob while it is still warm and seem not to notice. This could be an adaptation retained from their desert-living ancestors.

Above: Cats usually have 24 whiskers above the lips, 12 on each side in four horizontal rows. Each row can function independently. The cat can feel the prey it is carrying in its mouth using the lower sets of whiskers, while still sensing any obstacles in the environment with the top layers.

Right: A cat feels its way through a narrow opening with the help of its sensitive whiskers. They help it to judge whether its body will fit through the space.

The other areas of the cat's skin that are known to be particularly sensitive to touch and temperature are the nose and upper lip. When they are newborn kittens, cats find their mother by following their heat-sensitive noses to the warmest place. This is under her belly, where a meal just happens to be available too.

Hearing

It is a beautiful summer afternoon and you are dozing in the garden with your cat on your lap. Life seems perfectly peaceful and yet your cat's ears are twitching and swivelling around, reacting to a wide variety of sounds that are passing you by.

Indeed, even if your hearing were relatively as acute as that of your cat, you might not be able to hear the sounds because they may well be pitched about an octave higher than the human ear can register. Your cat is monitoring all the sounds produced by its prey – small rodents that communicate through ultrasonic squeaks. The hunter in the cat pinpoints the source of the sounds accurately, even if it cannot be bothered to get up and look for the prey.

CHANNELLING SOUNDS

Cats hunt by sound as well as sight. Their ears are highly developed to enable them to use every clue to find their prey. More than 12 muscles in the pinna, or ear flap, allow the ears to turn towards sounds, channelling and amplifying them into the middle ear.

The sound waves collected by the pinna pass down towards the ear drum, which vibrates. These vibrations are transferred into the inner ear via tiny bones called ossicles. The organ of hearing, called the cochlea, is snail-shaped. It is filled with fluid and lined with nerve cells that are tuned to particular notes or pitches. These translate the signals into electrical impulses that travel, via the auditory nerve, to the brain. Here, all the information is deciphered to give the cat information as to the precise source of the sound. Also within the ear is the vestibular system, which informs the cat of its body position and exact orientation (see page 34).

JUDGING DIRECTION

The difference between the sounds that come to each ear helps the cat ascertain the position of the sound source. This can be a complex procedure, depending on the frequency and direction of the sound.

The cat is believed to be able to distinguish between sound sources that are 8 centimetres (3 inches) apart from a distance of 2 metres (6½ feet), or those 40 centimetres (16 inches) apart from a distance of 20 metres (66 feet) – sufficient information to allow the cat to pounce with great accuracy. The ears can move independently or together and are also used in communication (see page 43).

Kittens often tilt their heads to the side and, as well as making them look

Right: The ability to hear is present early in life and is well developed by the time a kitten is one month old. A kitten will respond to sound at only five days old and can orientate itself towards sounds at about two weeks old. By the time it is four weeks, it is able to pinpoint sounds with the accuracy of an adult cat.

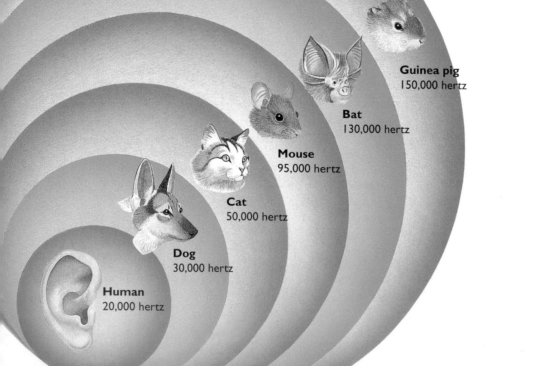

Left: The top range of hearing of different species. The pitch of a sound depends on its vibration rate and loudness, measured in cycles per second or hertz. The cat's ears are sensitive to sounds between 30 hertz and 50,000 hertz. It can hear sounds at almost as low a pitch as humans can and also at frequencies beyond human sensitivity.

Guinea pig
150,000 hertz

Bat
130,000 hertz

Mouse
95,000 hertz

Cat
50,000 hertz

Dog
30,000 hertz

Human
20,000 hertz

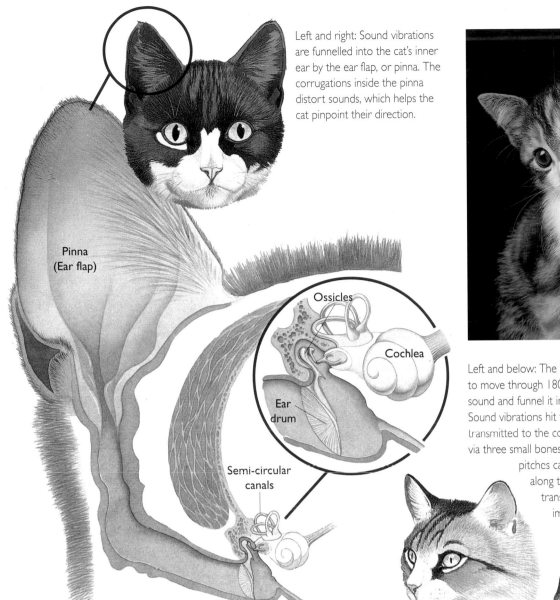

Left and right: Sound vibrations are funnelled into the cat's inner ear by the ear flap, or pinna. The corrugations inside the pinna distort sounds, which helps the cat pinpoint their direction.

Pinna (Ear flap)

Ossicles

Cochlea

Ear drum

Semi-circular canals

Left and below: The cat's outer ear is able to move through 180 degrees to capture a sound and funnel it into the inner ear. Sound vibrations hit the eardrum and are transmitted to the cochlea in the inner ear via three small bones called ossicles. Different pitches cause varying vibrations along the cochlea, which are translated into nerve impulses to the brain.

Below: Successful hunting depends on a cat's being able to pick up the slightest sound made by its prey animals. It needs to assess where that sound is coming from so that it can judge its final pounce correctly. Cats are even more sensitive than dogs to high-pitched sounds.

very appealing, this helps them to locate the source of a sound and test the direction it comes from. It has been found that three-week-old kittens hear twice as well as adult cats. And while a mother is suckling her kittens, her hearing is also enhanced so that she can hear the ultrasonic sounds made by her young.

RANGE OF SOUNDS

Cats are able to hear a wide range of frequencies – the only animals with a larger range are the horse and the porpoise. The cat can hear almost everything we can hear and much more. Its range spans ten and a half octaves – an octave more than humans – and it can hear ultrasound.

More than 40,000 nerve fibres are present in the auditory nerve, compared with the human total of 30,000.

The cat may have trouble hearing sounds at the lower end of the human range. Perhaps this is the reason people often talk to cats in a higher voice than usual or call them with a high-pitched sound. Perhaps the cat's ability to pick up vibrations with the pads on its feet (see page 27) allows it to detect the sounds at the lower end of its airborne range.

Sight

Huge in proportion to the size of its head, a cat's eyes are beautiful and appealing. Feline eyes may be a variety of colours, but more importantly, they are perfectly adapted for crepuscular (dawn and dusk) hunting.

Like humans, the cat has binocular vision – its eyes are located at the front of its skull and allow it to focus on an object and judge distance. It has a wider field of vision than we do, which allows it to combine the types of vision available to both the hunter and the hunted. A prey animal such as a rabbit has eyes on the sides of its skull, allowing it to watch all around for predators as it eats.

NIGHT VISION

The cat's eyes have several specialized characteristics that enable it to see extremely well in low light, the time when most of its prey animals are moving around. The cat's pupil – the aperture that lets light through on to the light-sensitive retina at the back of the eye – can open about three times as wide as the pupil of a human eye. Large numbers of rods – the receptors that are highly sensitive to light – pack the retina. These, combined with the provision of a special reflective layer at the back of the eye, give the cat very effective night vision – about 40 to 50 per cent better than that of human beings

This reflective layer, called the tapetum lucidum, is made up of highly reflective zinc and certain proteins, which throw back rays of light not absorbed by the retina when they first enter the eye. This gives the eye a second chance to use them. The tapetum shows up as a fluorescent greenish gold when the cat's eye is illuminated at night by artificial light, such as car headlights or the light from a camera flash.

Light striking the retina excites nerve cells, and messages are passed via the optic nerve to the brain. Here, all the information is deciphered to let the cat know what it is seeing.

The cat's oval eye consists of a transparent cornea, iris and lens, which direct light on to the sensitive retina. Cells in the retina give the brain information about colour and movement via the optic nerve.

Cats see best when the object they are focusing on is 2 to 6m (6½ to 20ft) away. Their close vision is less good. When a cat is about to pounce, it wiggles its hindquarters, shifting from one foot to the other and getting ready to leap. It is thought that this happens because the cat is not good at estimating distances. Wiggling its rear moves its head from side to side and helps it get more information about distance before pouncing.

DAY VISION

Because the cat has such sensitive eyes it has to ensure that its visual system is not swamped with glare on a bright sunny day. Therefore, it has the ability to narrow its pupils to fine vertical slits, as well as to lower its eyelids. The

The third eyelid is a layer of skin which helps to keep the cat's eye moist. Usually tucked away at the corner of the eye, it can rapidly cover the eye to protect it. It sometimes covers part of the eye when the cat is unwell.

horizontal and vertical damping allows only a small amount of light to enter the eye.

The cat probably sees only fuzzy images at these times. Photographers know that a film that is very sensitive to light and allows photographs to be taken even when the levels of light are low, gives results with a much grainier quality than a film that is made to function in bright light. The same principle is probably true for the cat's eyes – light sensitivity takes precedence over the sharpness and clarity of the image.

Cats probably do not see colour in the same way as humans. They have only about one-sixth of the number of cones (colour-sensitive cells) on the retina. Scientists suggest that cats can see some blue and green, but that they are not sensitive to light in the

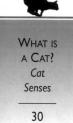

Pupil in dim light

Pupil in normal light

Pupil in bright light

Left: In dim light, the pupil in the cat's eye is large and round, admitting as much light as possible to the retina. In normal daylight it narrows to an oval shape, and in the brightest sunlight the pupil becomes a mere slit so that the cat is not dazzled.

Left: A cat's eyes glow eerily if caught in car headlights because of the tapetum lucidum, a special layer of cells at the back of the eye that reflects light back to the retina. This helps the cat make use of what light is available. Cats can see in dim light but, contrary to popular belief, they cannot see in complete darkness.

Below: The colour of a cat's eyes can be one of its most striking features. Colours range from orange and yellow to hazel and green. Siamese and some white cats have bright blue eyes.

red wavelength and see reds and oranges as shades of grey. They may see a somewhat washed-out colour picture (much like what we see in the twilight period, just before it gets dark in the evening).

The ability to see colour may differ among the cat species. Cats can perceive as much colour as they need to survive in their own environment. Daytime hunters or cats that seek out highly coloured prey may see life in a wider range of colours.

A cat's eyes are also supersensitive to movement. If the cat's brain is triggered by a movement of the right type travelling away from it, it instinctively begins predatory behaviour.

Taste and smell

The cat eats only meat. But has it discarded the ability to discern other tastes because they are of little importance to its survival? Can it tell the difference between a mouse of one species and a mouse of another? Does the flesh of a blue tit taste different from that of a pigeon?

TASTE BUDS

How other animals perceive 'taste' – what they actually experience when the receptors associated with certain chemicals are activated – is almost impossible to tell. Like humans, the cat has a tongue covered with small lumps called papillae. Each is a cluster of taste buds that are excited by different components of the cat's diet. As the cat eats, the saliva in its mouth dissolves some of the food and the chemical components activate cells in the cat's taste buds.

Taste buds on certain areas of the tongue are sensitive to particular chemicals, and the combination of signals from all of the areas will help the cat to recognize a taste.

Results from tests that aim to see whether cats can distinguish between water, water and sugar, and water and salt or some other substance, suggest that cats are sensitive to tastes that we would categorize as sour, bitter and salty. However, they do not seem to be sensitive to sweet tastes.

However, many owners report that their cats seem to like the taste of certain sweet foods such as ice cream or cake. It could be that the cat is attracted by the fat content of these foods, or by their creaminess and texture, not the sweetness. The cat's tongue is sensitive to different amino acids (these are the building blocks of protein, which makes up a large proportion of the cat's diet). It is possible, perhaps, that certain amino acids or groups of amino acids give the cat that same pleasurable sensation that we associate with 'sweet'.

Given the choice, cats will usually choose food that has a high meat and

A NATURAL HIGH

Catnip, or catmint, is a plant that has an extraordinary effect on many cats. They appear to become very excited by the smell of the plant, and sniff and roll in it, often showing the flehmen reaction (see opposite) as they do so. Not all cats are affected by catnip, however, and young kittens show no reaction to it at all. The active chemical in the plant is called nepetalactone and has been extracted for use in cat toys. Its effect is harmless and short lived.

Catnip (*Nepeta cataria*)

fat content, a strong smell, a mixture of soft and crispy textures, served at a temperature of about 35°C (95°F). They enjoy variety in their diet and will often try a new food or flavour in preference to one they are more used to.

A SENSE OF SMELL

The cat's nose is small and neat, yet hidden behind it is a maze of bones and cavities that warm and moisten air. Lining the nose is a special area of 200 million cells called the olfactory mucosa. If these were laid flat, they would cover an area of 20–40 square centimetres (3–6 square inches). This is twice the size of the similar structure in human beings but not quite as large as that in dogs. These cells recognize certain airborne

chemicals and relay the signals to the olfactory bulb in the brain, which links the type of stimulation with a particular smell.

The senses of taste and smell are closely linked. Just consider how bland food tastes if you have a cold and have lost your sense of smell. Cats, too, lose their appetite when they have a respiratory infection which affects their sense of smell. But cats are equipped with an exceptionally useful extra piece of smell/taste equipment that adds another dimension to their ability to decipher smells and tastes. This is the so-called Jacobson's organ, or vomeronasal organ, which is situated just behind and above the front teeth and allows cats to sample scent molecules.

Jacobson's organ links the cat's senses of taste and smell. It is a tiny, cigar-shaped sac connected to the roof of the mouth via a narrow passage just behind the front teeth. The organ is lined with olfactory cells, which stimulate the parts of the brain associated with appetite and reproduction.

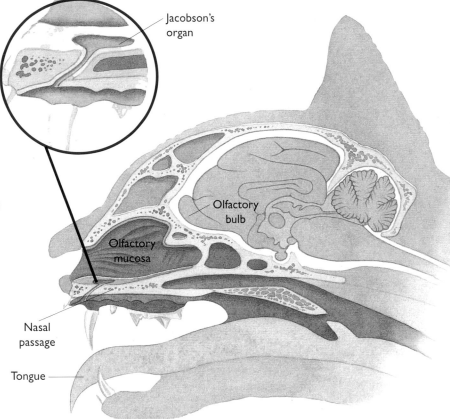

Jacobson's organ

Olfactory bulb

Olfactory mucosa

Nasal passage

Tongue

Tongue covered with papillae

Above: This highly magnified photograph shows the rough edge of the cat's tongue – essential for scraping meat from the bones of prey and for grooming fur.

Right: When a cat encounters an 'interesting' smell (such as a female in season), it presses its tongue against the roof of its mouth, forcing the air through the Jacobson's organ. This concentrates the molecules it wishes to sample in order to smell-taste them and gives it a great deal more information than just smelling. The particular expression the cat makes when it is smell-tasting in this way is known as the flehmen reaction.

Movement & Balance

Agility and speed ◆ *Reflex actions* ◆
Organ of balance ◆ *Falling on its feet* ◆
Climbing, walking, and running

As it measures the jump,
the cat crouches slightly.

The cat's skeleton and muscles are designed to give it great flexibility, agility and speed of movement. Its supple joints and 'floating' collar bone, or clavicle, (see page 20) enable it to bend and turn with fluid grace.

One reason for its efficiency is that the cerebellum, which is the part of the cat's brain that coordinates its balance and movement, is proportionally larger than in other mammals. It brings together all the information supplied by all the cat's exceptional senses and, via lightning-fast nerve messages, coordinates the body's movements to provide the superb control essential for a top predator.

When it jumps, for example, the cat seems to defy gravity and can leap up to five times its height or six times its length, seemingly without exertion. A cat preparing to jump up high will measure the distance by eye, crouch and then leap, landing far enough forward to allow its back legs to land on the object, and correcting its balance with its tail and the rest of its body.

Cats have an excellent sense of balance, although they are not infallible. They navigate narrow fences like seasoned tightrope walkers – but do occasionally fall off.

Left: Seemingly without effort, a cat steps daintily along the narrow top of a fence, placing each foot neatly in front of another. The flexible shoulderblades and collar bone allow the cat to keep its front legs close together, making it easier to negotiate small spaces.

REFLEX ACTIONS

Many of the cat's essential reactions are 'reflex' actions. The information from the organ of balance is relayed directly to the muscles that set into motion pre-programmed movements.

Right: As a kitten plays and leaps excitedly on a fly or a flower, it is practising the vital coordination skills it will need as a hunter.

Powerful back legs thrust the cat up and forward.

The cat lands with enough room to bring its hind legs up behind the front ones and spread the load.

Vestibular apparatus

Left: The vestibular apparatus is part of the inner ear. These fluid-filled canals, lined with millions of tiny hairs, help control the cat's balance and tell it which way up its body is.

The animal then reacts and moves instantly, without any loss of valuable time for 'thinking'.

The organ of balance is called the vestibular apparatus and is part of the inner ear. It consists of three fluid-filled, semicircular canals, lined with millions of tiny hairs. When the cat's head moves, the fluid in these canals moves around too, touching the hairs and sending signals to the brain to tell the cat about the direction and speed of any movement. Tiny crystals in the larger chambers at the base of these canals press on the hairs and give the cat information about the precise orientation of its body.

The information from the organ of balance is added to that coming from the eyes and the muscles, and the cat reacts quickly, often automatically, as information is processed.

FINELY TUNED BALANCE

A good balance system is common to most mammals, but the cat's is particularly finely tuned. In the cat the positions of the canals are precisely aligned to detect movement and to alert the cat to the slightest change in the normal head position. (Birds of prey have a similarly well-developed system that allows them to control their head position accurately.)

In this way, the cat's actions are controlled with great finesse, giving it the ability to regain its balance immediately, probably even before it realizes that it is off-balance. Our sense of balance is less finely tuned and much slower to register. By the time we realize we are tilting over, it is too late to fight gravity and we fall.

Below: Continuous minute corrections in balance are made automatically as a cat moves around. This means that stepping accurately from one narrow ledge to another is easy for a cat.

Movement & Balance

FALLING ON ITS FEET

The cat is famed for its remarkable ability to save itself in a fall by turning around in midair. It generally lands safely, as long as it does not fall from too great a height.

Within 70 milliseconds of a cat beginning to fall, information from its eyes and vestibular system cue an automatic sequence of events aimed at making a safe landing on its feet. First, the cat turns so that its head is horizontal and upright. This is done by flicking the front half of its body around through 180 degrees to face the ground. Nerves in the spine then automatically move the front legs, held close to its face during the first manoeuvre, down. The back legs stretch out sideways and the back end of the body turns around. The tail stops the body from rotating too much. Arching its back to allow it some 'give' in its body as it lands, the cat usually lands on all fours!

Kittens have to learn to control their movement and balance. As soon as their eyes are fully open, they start to coordinate the information coming from all their senses. It is a couple of weeks before they are approaching anything like the sophistication of balance shown by the adult cat. Games of jumping, running and climbing all help kittens to practise their coordination skills while they are still young and extremely light, thus minimizing the risk of any serious injury.

CLIMBING

Despite the cat's athletic skills, it is not infallible when climbing. Cats are adept at climbing up but not so good when it comes to getting down again. The beautifully designed claws are excellent crampons, allowing the cat to hang on to a tree and pull itself up, rapidly gaining great height. When it turns downward, however, the cat's claws provide no assistance; the sudden lack of traction from its feet can be somewhat daunting.

Cats do learn to climb down (sometimes after a couple of rescues by worried owners), but their usual grace abandons them and they look as worried and ungainly about it as the rest of us. When the cat reaches a certain distance from the ground, it usually hangs on with its back feet, walks down the tree as far as possible with the front ones to get them closer to the ground, and then leaps off. But nature has not let the cat family down

---

BALANCING TAIL

◆

The cat uses its tail as a tightrope walker would use a long pole – as a counterweight to aid balance. Although the tail is exceptionally useful for this and in communication (see page 44), cats born without tails, such as the Manx, or cats that have their tails amputated because of accidents, do manage. Their other methods of balance compensate well, allowing them to lead a normal, active life.

Below: When a cat is running fast, or galloping, its spine alternately bows and stretches, increasing its stride length. It pushes off with both back feet, then lands on one front foot and transfers its weight to the other one. The back feet land together and then push off again.

Above: This Burmese cat is finding that climbing down a tree is much harder than going up. It will clamber down as far as it can and then jump to the ground.

extra length of limb that this gives allows them to lengthen their stride, touch the ground briefly with their toes and move on again.

When walking, the cat places its feet neatly in front of each other – its footprints in the snow make an almost straight line. The cat's fluid movement is achieved by the synchronization of the front and back legs. The cat is propelled forward mainly by its back legs. Its front legs are less important for propulsion but balance the front of the body.

The cat can break into a trot for more rapid motion and, when it wants to run fast, it gallops. The back legs hit the ground together and push off again, the body stretches and the spine bows as the hind limbs reach forward; it straightens again as they extend. This increases the stride length and allows the cat considerable speed. However, cats tire easily and only sprint over short distances.

altogether. There is a tree-living wild cat with unique double-jointed feet that can swivel around to point backward for the downward climb.

WALKING AND RUNNING

The cat's body is adapted to allow it to use its front legs to catch prey, balance and groom. The back limbs are specialized for power. Cats walk on their toes; the pads on their feet are equivalent to our toes plus the part of the foot in front of the ball. They tiptoe along, light and fleet of foot. The

GRATEFUL CAT

◆

An old legend provides one explanation as to why cats always fall on their feet. One day the prophet Mohammed was sitting with his cat Muezza sleeping on the sleeve of his robe. Mohammed was called to prayer and, instead of disturbing the animal, he cut off the sleeve of his robe. On his return, the cat bowed gracefully to thank him for his consideration. As a reward, Mohammed gave cats the knack of always falling on their feet.

Above: Thanks to the cat's righting reflex, a series of automatic reactions turn and align the body as it falls so that the cat lands on its feet. But the cat does not always manage to land safely. Falls from heights of several storeys of a building can be fatal.

Top Predator

Hunting strategies ✦ Learning to hunt ✦ Playing with prey

The cat's agility and speed help to make it a highly successful hunter. This much-loved pet is also an expert predator.

The special adaptations the cat is blessed with enable it to take advantage of the twilight times of dawn and dusk for hunting. However, cats can and do hunt at any time of day, depending on the routines of their prey. Most birds are active only in daytime and some mammals may be out and about when the temperature as well as the light conditions suit them.

HUNTING STRATEGIES

Mice and other small mammals are the cat's normal choice of prey, accounting for about 75 per cent of catches. Most cats employ a 'sit and wait' strategy for hunting rodents. Their sense of smell may be used to detect a regular route used by prey, but it is the senses of hearing and sight that are highly attuned and on alert as the cat silently waits. When the mouse appears, the cat pounces.

A more active 'stalk-and-spring' type of approach is usually employed for birds. They are harder to catch and comprise only about 10 per cent of catches. The cat approaches in alternate bursts of movement and low-slung creeping, freezing when the bird looks around or seems to be aware that something may be amiss. The cat's paws have tufts of hair between the cushioning pads to muffle sound, and claws are sheathed to avoid making any noise.

The cat's whole body is focused toward its prey, eyes fixed and ears pricked forward. It creeps forward until it is about two metres (six or

Above: For kittens, play is a serious business. Playing with a ball or other toy is the first step in the process of learning to hunt. Once a kitten has left its mother, it is essential to provide it with toys to chase and catch.

seven feet) from the victim. A final brief sprint and spring then brings the cat on to the bird.

As it nears a bird or mouse, the long-sighted cat cannot focus very well. To compensate, its whiskers point forward and 'feel' the prey like an extra hand, telling the cat where its prey is. When the sensitive skin and hairs around the mouth come into contact with the prey, they set off a sequence of automatic movements. These turn the cat's head and position it to make the killing bite.

Left and below: A cat crouches low, waiting for the moment to pounce. Every sense is alert for the slightest movement of the prey animal. When the moment is right, it makes its final pounce.

Another set of receptors along the lips make the jaws open; more receptors in the mouth trigger the bite itself. In a successful nape bite, the canine tooth slips between the neck bones and severs the prey's spinal cord. Death is instantaneous. The canine teeth and claws are also sense organs in that they can tell the cat how much resistance, or pressure, they are meeting. Hunting requires rapid reactions, so such automatic signals mean that no time is lost. Split seconds could mean the difference between feasting and starving.

HUNTING SUCCESS

Cats hunt whether they are hungry or not. The areas of the brain that control hunger and hunting are different and have separate triggers. Lack of food causes the cat to feel hungry; movement or sound triggers the hunting response. Thus a well-fed cat will still chase a moving object, even if it does not actually eat the catch.

According to researchers, cats catch prey in about 10 per cent of pounces, unless need drives them to be more successful. Female cats with kittens can increase their performance fourfold, catching prey every three or four pounces – about once every one and a half hours. Kittens instinctively stalk and capture prey but are taught to kill by their mother. She will bring home injured prey when the kittens are about four weeks old so that they can practise this skill. Good hunters usually have mothers that are hunting experts.

BRINGING PREY HOME

Cats may bring in their prey to keep it safe in a den, just as a leopard takes a carcass up a tree to eat later – except that pet cats, with a bowl of cat food

The rat was being besieged in its little dwelling by the weasel, which with continual vigilance was awaiting its destruction, and through a tiny chink was considering its great danger. Meanwhile the cat came and suddenly seized hold of the weasel and forthwith devoured it. Whereupon the rat, profoundly grateful to its deity, having offered up some of its hazel-nuts in sacrifice to Jove, came out of its hole in order to repossess itself of the the lately lost liberty, and was instantly deprived of this and of life by the cruel claws and teeth of the cat.

LEONARDO DA VINCI (1452–1519), NOTEBOOKS

ready and waiting, do not need to eat their prey. Perhaps they are bringing it in as a present, in the way a mother cat brings prey for her kittens to practise their hunting techniques. But since a cat's role with humans is often referred to as that of perpetual kitten, it is owners who should be giving cats prey, not the other way around. Perhaps cats like the reaction that bringing prey in elicits in their owners – nobody really knows.

PLAYING WITH PREY

Humans do not like to see their cats playing with their prey. If the animal is already dead, we may not worry, but live 'torture' is not appealing. Why do cats do it? Some researchers have suggested that cats 'play' more with relatively dangerous animals, such as rats, in an effort to deal with the prey, while keeping out of the way of retaliation from it. Or it may be that the cat has not managed to inflict a fatal bite. Movement is necessary to maintain the cat's interest in killing the prey and throwing it around causes movement. It could, of course, simply be that the cat enjoys the hunting game.

A Cat's View of the World

High vantage points ✦
A sensory machine ✦ *Smell profile*

To imagine the world as the cat experiences it we need to think past our own limited sensual abilities. Humans rely on their senses of sight and hearing when entering a room. We look around at eye level and take note of things that may affect us physically. Unless the room has an overwhelming odour, we do not take much notice of what our sense of smell is telling us and do not rely on it for additional information.

A cat may have much the same visual view of the world as a human toddler. People are extensions on top of legs and feet. Items on tables and other furniture are out of sight.

The differences between the cat and the toddler lie first of all in the information that the cat gathers through its other senses, and then in its confidence in its own ability to move from one plane to another with the minimum of effort. A cat does not have to stay on the floor like a young child or a dog; it can leap up to get a better view, to reach items it is interested in, or to escape from any ground-level dangers.

A SENSORY MACHINE

Look at the cat as a sensory machine. The front of its body, including the head and front legs, collects vast

Above: No part of the house is sacred to a cat. Cats love to leap up on to furniture and shelves to give themselves a better view. If the room is full of strangers, being up high will help the cat feel more secure.

amounts of information about its surroundings. The cat probably sees in muted tones of blue and green with grey, but it notices the tiniest movement; dark corners or evening light pose no handicap, since the cat's night vision is at least six times better than that of humans.

But this is just the beginning of the clues the cat can pick up when entering a room. A forcefield of hairs and whiskers allows it to sense the slightest air movements. Sensors on its pads even tell it about the texture of the floor it is walking on and pick up vibrations of other movements going on around it.

SMELL PROFILE

The additional weapon in the cat's arsenal of detection is its sense of smell. The cat recognizes its owners not only by sight and sound but also by their scent – the group smell of the household, which is familiar and reassuring and with which the cat feels comfortable. Just as humans see in

Left: This picture gives you an idea of the cat's view of your home. Most things are happening well above its eye level, which increases the cat's feeling of vulnerability and makes its perceptions of its surroundings very different from those of its owners.

From the Laws of Cats.
This is my Man. I am not afraid of
him. He is very strong for he eats a
great deal; he is an Eater of All
Things. What are you eating?
Give me some!
He is not beautiful, for he
has no fur. Not having enough
saliva, he has to wash himself
with water. He miaows in a
harsh voice and a great deal more
than he need. Sometimes in
his sleep he purrs.

KAREL CAPEK,
INTIMATE THINGS, *1935*

colour and recognize a place by its visual layout, the cat builds up a smell profile of its home. It recognizes certain smells associated with people, dogs or other cats, not only those present but also those who have visited the room recently, as well as the scent signals it has left itself. Visitors may be sniffed, either obviously or surreptitiously, as the cat tries to find out more. Even your shoes may bring in a host of unfamiliar scents of things you have walked through or even accidentally stepped in.

If the visitor is another cat that has left scent signals on the furniture from rubbing, scratching or spraying (see page 48), the cat may be able to tell which cat made the signals, how long ago, the sexual status of the scent leaver and perhaps even the mood it was in.

Scent signals are an essential part of the the cat's world. Despite our poor ability to detect them ourselves, we must be aware of their power in feline terms (see page 46).

Right and top right: Cats like high places –
vantage points, which allow them to watch
the world below in safety and be entertained
by the movements beneath. They can watch
for prey, see what neighbouring cats are up
to and keep an eye on humans.

Communication

Solitary cats ✦ Warning messages ✦
Staring battles ✦ Using ears, whiskers and tail ✦
Body positions

The need to communicate varies throughout the animal kingdom and the complexity and methods of the communication depend on how the animals live. Some exist in groups, which need to cooperate over hunting or other activities. Others survive on their own, coming together only for mating or the raising of offspring.

Cats – except for lions – are solitary animals. They usually live and hunt alone, seeking each other out only in the mating season. The females then raise the resulting young by themselves. But some domestic cats also live wild in groups. Feral cats, for example, gather at a source of plentiful food and shelter, such as a holiday resort or hotel.

Cats do mix with other cats for more sociable interactions, especially in the safety of our homes. They have a complex body language, which they use, together with scent messages and a few vocal signals, to interact with each other. Although they usually like to keep other cats at a distance, they can be sociable if they wish.

Compare this to the pack-living dog and its ancestor, the wolf. In order to function successfully as a group, individuals must be able to cooperate for hunting and to resolve disagreements without injury. An injured animal weakens the pack; an animal that is ostracized from the pack finds survival alone difficult. Dogs need methods of communication that allow them to show domination or submission so that they fit into the social hierarchy necessary to maintain a cohesive pack.

Cats, on the other hand, have no need to fit into a set pattern. They need to be able to communicate with other cats in the vicinity so that each keeps to its own 'patch'. They must let other cats know when it is time to mate, and solve disputes that arise over resources or mates, preferably without injury. They do much of their communicating at a distance, leaving scent messages for each other that can be interpreted and acted on without meeting face to face. Any vocal communication outside mating time is usually restricted to insults.

BODY LANGUAGE

Most feline communication is used to convey 'keep your distance' messages. These are passed via a system that eludes humans – scent signals. The body language of cats does not include the elements of compromise

Above and top: When a domestic cat encounters an unfamiliar visitor on its territory, a confrontation may ensue. Generally, the cats do not fight, but convey their displeasure through their body language. The owner of the territory is in a stronger position and will stare aggressively at the intruder to show its displeasure. The other cat may crouch down, flattening its ears and lashing its tail back and forth. If the aggressor advances, the intruder usually backs off, avoiding the risk of direct conflict.

seen in dogs, such as rolling over to submit. Cats do not need to compromise with each other in the same way; if there is a dispute, the loser will run away. There is no group to be weakened by the loss of its presence and a lone cat does not feel vulnerable, as a dog would outside its pack.

Scientists have noted at least 25 visual signals used by domestic cats

1   2   3   4

Above: Watch a cat's ears for clues about how it is feeling. A happy, relaxed cat (1) holds its ears facing forward as it listens quietly, but an angry cat (2) swivels its ears round to face backward. A cat concentrating on its prey (3) holds its ears pricked and pointing slightly forward. A worried or defensive cat (4) flattens its ears down on to its head, partly as a way of protecting them should there be a fight.

Left: This tabby female is in season for the first time and is reacting nervously to the approach of a strange cat. Her ears are swivelled round and slightly flattened, but she remains crouched down in the hope of avoiding conflict.

Below left: This Burmese has gone a stage further. Its tail is fluffed out in attempt to make itself look larger and more fearsome.

and there are probably a great many more subtle exchanges. The cat uses its whole body to communicate how it feels, but when we try to interpret these messages it is useful to look at several different parts of the body. When taken in combination, the different actions go some way to telling us what the cat is trying to say. We need to look at the way the head is held, the pupils, the attitude of the ears and whiskers; the tail and its size; and the body position. These postures and movements can be accentuated by the erection of the hair along the cat's back, over its entire body and/or along its tail, in an attempt to make itself look bigger.

Ears can tell us a great deal about how a cat is feeling. They are very flexible and can be moved to improve hearing as well as to signal mood. They swivel through 180 degrees and can be flattened on the head, independently of each other if necessary. Ear positions can convey quite subtle messages. A happy, relaxed cat usually sits with its ears facing forward but tilted slightly back. Slightly pricked, forward-pointing ears show that the cat is interested and concentrating. If they start to twitch, it is usually a sign that the cat is a little worried and is trying to work out what is going on or to pick up on sounds that are causing some concern.

If the cat feels threatened, its ears may begin to flatten on its head as part of an attempt to protect them, as well as to make itself look smaller and less noticeable. It may also lower its head and body slightly, keeping its senses on alert to flee if necessary. If the threat continues, the ears may flatten right down on the head and the cat opens its mouth to hiss in an effort to scare off the threat.

A cat that is feeling aggressive does not flatten its ears but swivels them around to face backward. This, combined with dilating pupils and other body postures, gives us clues as to whether the cat is being assertive rather than defensive.

Body Language

Above: This young kitten is bravely adopting a defensive pose against a strange dog it has encountered. Its back is arched and the fur raised in an attempt to make itself look as large as possible. For the moment, the kitten is standing its ground, but it will edge away if it can.

Above: In a conflict with another cat, this male silver tabby holds his ears back. As he keeps his opponent at bay, he also steps slowly sideways in an attempt to get away.

While eye contact between humans may be a sign of interest or friendship, prolonged eye contact, or staring, between cats is assertive behaviour. It is often seen in tussles between toms, when one tries to out-will the other before a fight ensues.

Sometimes cats 'stare into space', seeming to be day dreaming. They are probably taking in information from their peripheral vision, rather than focusing on anything in particular, and so seem to be in the 'land of dreams'. As it relaxes, the cat may half close its eyes and blink slowly. Blinking is a reassuring signal between cats. It breaks any stare that could otherwise be understood as being unfriendly or challenging.

The pupil – the central black part of the eye – reacts to light levels, but its size can also be a good indicator of mood. In daylight, the pupil would normally be constricted. If it is dilated in daylight it is because it is influenced by an internal hormone, such as adrenaline, which makes the pupil widen, despite the fact that the light level is telling it to close up.

Fear or excitement can cause the pupil to dilate in this way. But an angry cat asserting itself may have pupils that are constricted to a slit. It all depends on the cat's internal chemical environment, which is affected by mood and stress. Thus it is necessary to look for additional clues as to how the cat is feeling.

WHISKERS
Whiskers can indicate mood. Like the ears, they are held 'pricked' or slightly forward when the cat is interested. If the cat feels threatened and is trying

Above: A kitten holds its fluffed-out tail at an angle known as an 'inverted L' position, which indicates conflict. The kitten is engaging in a mock battle with its siblings.

to make itself seem smaller and avoid conflict, the whiskers are drawn back on to the face.

TAIL MESSAGES
The tail is used for balance and also for communication and can be held in a variety of positions, from straight up in the usual 'greeting' position, to sweeping from side to side when the cat is confronted by an adversary on its patch. Fear or excitement may cause the hair on the tail to become erect and look twice its normal size.

The cat has a more mobile tail than the dog. It incorporates more bones and therefore has more flexibility.

The cat also has a muscle in the rump region, which the dog does not have. It uses this muscle when it lashes its tail from side to side.

BODY POSTURES

By using different body postures and erecting its fur, the cat can considerably change its perceived size. In dealing with a threat, a cat can either try to make itself as small and unthreatening as possible in the hope that it will be passed by, or try to bluff by looking larger and so rather too dangerous for an opponent to take on. To decrease its profile, the cat may crouch low, pulling down its ears and whiskers – shrinking into the background if possible. Alternatively, it

Above: This cat is feeling threatened and is vocalizing an attempt to scare off an approaching rival.

Right: Not all body language is a warning. This ten-week-old kitten is demonstrating its enthusiastic greeting for an approaching cat or person. Its tail is held up straight, its whiskers are pointing forward and its ears are pricked.

may try to frighten the threat away by erecting its fur, arching its back, and fluffing up its tail to make itself seem larger. The cat may attempt to escape

but will walk slowly in a crab-like sideways manner. This allows it to put distance between itself and the threat while still keeping an eye on it. If it gets an opportunity, the cat will dash away to safety.

Kittens at play enact almost the entire repertoire of feline body postures, including strange inverted tail positions that are not often seen in adults. In their investigations, they often leap off the ground with all four feet, fur erect along their backs and 'bottle brush' tail – the classic frightened witch's cat.

Threatened cat

Inquisitive cat

Left: Whiskers show a cat's mood. Normally they stand out on either side of the face, but a threatened cat holds its whiskers drawn back. An inquisitive cat's whiskers are held pricked or pointing slightly forward in an attempt to feel what is immediately ahead.

Scent language

Smell is the most powerful of all the cat's senses and an integral part of every moment of its life. To the cat, smell is probably as vivid, rich and informative as the sense of sight is to humans, and as important in comprehending what is going on around it.

Smell is used primarily as a method of communication. Although it can and does communicate with cats from the same household and sometimes with other cats in the vicinity, the cat usually wants to keep others at a distance. It does this by leaving scent messages so it does not necessarily need to meet and confront other cats.

But when a female cat is in season – ready for mating – she needs to find a mate and must let toms in the area know that they are welcome. The most direct method is to make a lot of noise to attract attention. Queens do this when they 'call'. But they also need to be able to leave messages for other cats that tell them to come closer or to keep out of the way.

These messages are relayed by means of scents which the cat produces. They contain information about its sex, sexual status, health, strength, when it last passed by and probably much more. The cat has the capacity to leave scent markers in several different ways, depending on the message and the strength with which it wants to get it across.

SCENT SOURCES

As it moves through its daily life, the cat lays these scent messages all around its home and its outdoor territory. If you watch carefully, you will get a clue as to where the scents are produced on the cat's body and the typical sites for posting the messages.

Certain areas of skin on the cat's chin, lips, temples, neck and shoulders, and at the base of its tail, have special sebaceous glands that produce an oily secretion. As the cat grooms, it not only keeps its coat in tip-top condition but also spreads the secretions from these glands all over its coat.

When the cat rubs itself against objects around the home, other cats, the dog, the garden fence and even its owners, it smears them with some of this diluted scent. Also, by rubbing its chin and mouth along objects, raising its lip as if sneering, it anoints them with secretions directly from the glands around the mouth. This is known as bunting.

When the cat stops to strop its claws on a fence post – or on the furniture – it is not only sharpening its

Above: As it grooms itself, a cat not only licks itself clean but also spreads secretions from its scent glands over its own body. When it then rubs against you or sits on your lap, some of this scent is transferred to you.

claws by pulling the blunt layer of the old nail off to reveal a new pointed claw, it is also leaving a scent mark. Glands between the pads on the underside of the paws secrete a type of sweat, which keeps the pads oiled, supple and sensitive. The scent also

Left: As they sharpen their claws – hopefully on a log or scratching post and not inside the house – cats leave scent signals. Glands in the feet leave secretions, letting other cats know who has been there.

larger distances, are those that involve the use of faeces or urine. Nobody can walk into a room in which an unneutered tom cat has urinated and not notice the smell. It is strong, unmistakable and lasts a long time. Leaving faeces in the open as a calling card is known as middening and is a ploy used by many animals.

The cat uses both urine and faeces to mark its territory, but it has a special way of ensuring that urine messages are broadcast. Urine passed on the ground may seep away and be covered over by other smells from the earth. It is also too low to be picked up and carried on air currents. The cat overcomes this by spraying its urine. Male and female, neutered and unneutered animals can and do spray, usually outside in the garden. Animals looking for a mate or trying to beat other rivals to a mate frequently use this method of scent laying.

Above: This cat is marking its territory by rubbing its head against a fallen branch. By doing this, it spreads secretions from a gland by its mouth that leave a message for other cats saying, 'This is my patch'.

lets other cats know that it has been there. Confident cats may scratch in front of others as a sign of strength, leaving behind a scent marker as well as a visual sign of scratched bark.

The strongest messages of all, which can be picked up over much

Below: In certain places on the cat's body there are special sebaceous glands that produce the secretions used to leave scent messages. These glands are clustered around the cat's face, on its neck and shoulders, near its tail and on the underside of its paws.

Areas containing sebaceous glands

Scent language

When a cat sprays, it usually takes up a characteristic position, with its tail held high. A quivering action follows, accompanied by a paddling or treading motion with the back feet. A fine spray of about 1 millilitre (0.035 fluid ounces) of urine is squirted backward, usually on to a vertical surface and at nose height for other cats.

The unneutered male mixes urine with other pungent chemicals from his anal glands, giving his mark that unmistakable odour of 'tom cat'. It is thought that on a still day tom-cat urine can be detected by another cat from more than 12 metres (40 feet) away. The scent lasts a long time (up to two weeks, depending on the weather) and over this time the chemicals degrade at a fixed rate. Cats can tell just when the mark was made and when that particular cat passed by.

Cats not only use their scent as a marker for other cats but also gain a

Above: When your cat rubs itself lovingly against your legs, it is not just being friendly. It is also spreading scents from its body to yours – and picking up some of your smell on its fur. This creates the group smell that the cat associates with home and safety.

Left: The strongest form of scent marking is by spraying urine (1). In tom cats, this is mixed with secretions from the anal glands. Rubbing the body or head against objects (2 and 3) leaves a slightly milder scent. Scratching (4) marks and leaves secretions from glands on the paws.

sense of wellbeing or confidence from familiar smells around them. If a strange cat comes into your home and sprays, you will notice how upsetting it is for your own cats. Their safe indoor den has been violated by an outsider. This can set a more timid resident cat into spraying indoors itself – probably in an attempt to restore the status quo and make it feel safe with smells that are familiar.

The more a cat feels threatened or uneasy, the more likely it is to try to

Above: All cats can mark their territories by spraying out a jet of urine. Humans may not notice the scent signals of female and neutered cats, but the smell of the tom is unmistakable. The spray is directed at bushes, posts or other landmarks, and the action is clearly different from the cat's usual way of passing urine.

Above: This cat is rolling over playfully on the grass, but at the same time it is spreading its scent from glands on its body and marking its territory. The scent leaves a message about itself for other cats. The next cat to pass that way will pick up the scent and be able to analyse the information it carries.

use a variety of scent-laying methods to increase its feeling of security. This is like us surrounding ourselves with familiar belongings and people, in order to make ourselves feel safe and relaxed in our homes.

A GROUP SMELL

'Home' to the cat means not only the house itself but also its inhabitants. By rubbing and 'chinning' the resident people or dogs and grooming any other cats, our pet cats anoint us with their scents as well as taking on some of ours. These, combined with household smells, make a unique group smell. The cat need only sniff you to know if you are 'part of the family'.

Lions in a pride rub each other's heads and bodies in order to create and maintain this group smell. Any new member joining the pride gradually incorporates his or her own smell and takes on the smells of the resident pride members – thus changing the smell profile of the whole group – before being fully accepted.

Although we may not be able to recognize any but the ultra-strong tom-cat spray, understanding the importance of smells used by cats in their everyday lives can give us a

much better insight into the behaviour of our pets. A new carpet, for example, smells strong, even to us. Imagine the enormous effect it must have on our cats. Not only has the old carpet with its familiar smells been removed, but an overpowering new scent has come into the house. No wonder some cats immediately start spraying or scratching the new carpet to try to regain some security by adding their familiar smells.

Above: Cats that live together and have a close bond will often groom each other, attending to parts of the body they find it hard to reach for themelves. As they do so, they exchange smells, spreading scent secretions over each other's fur, which reinforces their bond. Cats in the same household develop a group smell.

Vocal communication

Cats also use a number of forms of vocal communication. Feral cats in a colony, or cats living together, may purr to each other as they groom. Cats also use the higher end of their vocal spectrum either for 'calling' (the noise female cats use to let the males know they are in season) or yowling or hissing if another cat comes too close. Tom cats are also extremely vocal in their battles over territory or mates. A mother, too, needs to be able to call her kittens if they wander off, to warn them of danger and to be able to communicate a great deal of information in the short period between birth and weaning.

But cats often have a more vocal relationship with their human companions than with other cats. They do not usually miaow to each other as they do to us. As a rule, this form of communication is restricted to kittenhood, when the kittens miaow and make sounds of distress, hunger or fear. Cats use these kitten communications with us, and indeed their mews and miaows are usually pleas for attention or food, just like those kittens make to their mother. When they live with us, cats learn that communicating vocally with humans can be rewarding. They teach us to respond to their demands – to feed them or let them in or out if they speak.

Cats do not make sounds in the same way as we do. They can vocalize and breathe in and out at the same time and do not use their tongue in the same way to form sounds. The sounds are made farther back in the throat by pushing air at different speeds over the vocal cords stretched across the voice box. By changing the tension in the throat, they alter the phonetic quality of the noises.

Most vocal communication is for short distances. Exceptions are calling and caterwauling sounds made by courting cats or the angry, warning cries of rival toms used for night-time communication, when visual signs are not of much use.

CAT TALK

Researchers have noted some 16 vocal patterns in cats, although individual cats may also have their own personal sounds that they use with their owners. Most of the sounds cats make fall into three groups: murmurs, strained intensity sounds and vowels.

Murmurs include that most famous of all cat noises, the purr, and

Left: A hungry cat is not slow to voice its demands. This tortoiseshell-and-white cat is making sure its owner is aware that breakfast is long overdue. An attentive owner soon gets to know the many different tones of miaow which a cat uses to signal its needs.

Below: This cat is angry and is yowling ferociously at its attacker in an unusual display of vocal intensity. It may also spit and hiss. Such sounds should have a powerful effect on the other animal.

the little chirp cats make when they greet us. The cat makes these murmur sounds with its mouth closed and they are generally sounds of contentment. Purring, the most rewarding of all feline sounds for owners, is still something of a mystery to scientists, who have not yet worked out how cats do it. Cats not only purr when snuggled on a warm lap, but also when sitting on a sunny windowsill, anticipating a treat, or grooming.

Cats may also purr when in pain, perhaps in an effort to make themselves feel reassured and less fearful. A queen uses her purr to communicate with her nursing kittens, and by the time the kittens are two weeks old, they will purr back to let her know that all is well.

Strained intensity sounds are made by holding the mouth open and tense, usually when the cat is in an emotionally charged state. The sounds include growling, snarling, hissing or spitting, sounds of pain and the wails of females in season. These are the sounds that adult cats use to communicate with each other. They may also make ultrasonic sounds beyond our range of hearing.

'Miaows' are in the vowel category. The sound can be manipulated in different ways by individual cats to get our attention. Listen carefully and note the variety of 'pleas' your cat makes in a variety of nearly always amicable encounters. The cat makes these sounds by opening its mouth

and gradually closing it as its voiced breath passes through, at the same time altering its throat tension.

The amount of vocal communication the cat uses in its everyday relationship with its owners depends on the individual cat, the owner's response and the breed (some breeds such as the Siamese are notoriously chatty). The cat can produce a variety of miaows, which allow it to let its owner know that it wants something. This includes the 'silent miaow', when the cat mouths a plaintive 'miaow' but no sound comes out – perhaps the most compelling plea of all.

Dr Turton says, 'The cat has a more voluminous and expressive vocabulary than any other brute; the short twitter of complacency and affection, the purr of tranquillity and pleasure, the mew of distress, the growl of anger, and the horrible wailing of pain.'

CHARLES H. ROSS, THE BOOK OF CATS: A CHIT-CHAT CHRONICLE, *1868*

Above: Contented kittens purr as they snuggle up to their mother. They can purr at the same time as suckling and it is thought that the sound may even stimulate the flow of milk from the mother.

Left: A little ginger kitten, spitting at a sibling who has been playing too roughly, has already learnt an effective way of expressing its displeasure.

Territory & Socializing

Feral cats ✦ *Territories* ✦
Secret signals ✦ *Time sharing*

Cats are 'territorial'. They become upset if a strange cat is in the area and will chase other cats out of our homes. Humans are generally blissfully unaware of the undercurrents of emotion moving between cats and probably miss many of the interactions and power games that go on, often over territory.

Wild or feral cats must be able to 'make a living' for themselves. They protect a certain area of land in which they have a resting place or den, and an area where they can hunt. They do not want other cats coming in and taking advantage of scarce resources.

Feral toms have an area about three and a half times that of females, although they will not be able to patrol all of it all the time, especially if they are busy courting. Females defend a smaller territory; the presence of kittens may make them more fiercely defensive and also less willing to share any prey in the area.

The dynamics of the feline social system are dramatically altered if the availability of food increases. People who have travelled in Mediterranean countries will have noticed the large numbers of stray and feral cats that congregate around hotels, where there is a bountiful supply of food.

The availability of food means that the cats do not have to defend a territory big enough to provide them with enough wildlife to survive. Such flexibility in the cat's social repertoire means that it can live near to and have friendly interactions with other cats if it needs or wants to.

Above: A nine-week-old kitten approaches its father for the first time. Most kittens have little or nothing to do with their fathers, but this tom looks disposed to be friendly.

Below: A feral mother and her kittens lie by the hollow log she has chosen as a safe den for her litter. She will defend this territory vigorously.

Right: This chart shows examples of territory sizes, and demonstrates the dramatic difference between the needs of the urban pet and the wild cat.

Average territory sizes of different types of cat

— Urban neutered pet (male), about 80 square metres (95 square yards)

■ Urban stray (male), about 800 square metres (950 square yards)

Feral cat (male), about 150 acres (60 hectares)

Scottish wild cat (male), about 70 hectares (175 acres)

While an unneutered, feral tom may have a huge range of many hectares (acres), most urban pet cats have a core territory within their owner's house, which extends into the garden and may perhaps include the neighbours' gardens. The cats have regular pathways, places where they like to sit and view daily life, and favourite sunbathing spots.

TERRITORY SIZE

In most urban and suburban areas, the density of cats is so great that there is not the space for huge territories that exclude other cats. Because most pet cats are neutered, have a regular food supply and warm, secure sleeping places provided by loving owners, they have much less need for a large area of territory that has to be defended. The size of the territory also depends on the personality, age and sex of the individual cat, how many, and what type of, other cats live nearby, and whether there are fierce dogs in the vicinity.

FELINE TIME SHARING

Cat owners know little about the outdoor part of cats' lives – the battles, compromises and friendships that go on outside the door. There may be all sorts of intricate pathways and boundaries around our homes and gardens, which are marked with secret signs – scent marks that provide cats with complex information about the other cats in the area.

These marks do not necessarily say 'No trespassing'. They are more likely to say 'Tiddles is in the garden now' or, 'Ginger uses this run at dusk'. Cats in an neighbourhood often seem to have a kind of time or territory share, whereby certain cats are able to use the space during certain times. The strongest individual probably has access to the best hunting area at the time when prey is most likely to be out and about. The least confident or territorial will have to fit in at times when nobody else wants to be around. Scent marks mean that these things can usually be sorted out without conflict. Cats do meet and have staring matches to try to outwill each other, and may even have the odd fight or two, but owners would probably be surprised how 'civilized' it all is.

Below: Groups of feral cats are a common sight in areas where there is plenty of food to scavenge. These Cretan cats no doubt get rich pickings from nearby restaurants, so there is no need for rivalry.

Scale

= 1 hectare
(2.5 acres)

People & Cats

The bond between cats and humans ✦ *Levels of understanding* ✦ *A maternal relationship*

Above: The bond between cats and humans can be extremely close. It varies greatly depending on the needs of cat and owner.

Below: Do human owners bring out the kitten in their cat? Cats living in the comfort and safety of our homes, and under our loving care, do retain many kitten characteristics. Whether they actually view us as mother substitutes is not certain.

Some cats and people seem far happier with each other than with individuals of their own species. This says a great deal about the strength of the bond between cats and humans and our ability to live together in a mutually rewarding relationship. On the human side, the relationship works well, perhaps because it relieves us of the need to worry about the normal social rules and taboos. It is free from criticism or judgement and allows us to display affection without fear of rejection.

For the cat, the relationship may mean food and attention without competition, the security of a safe home, a common liking of warmth and comfort, and the enjoyment of the sensation of touch provided by stroking. The secret of success in the bond between cats and humans lies in simple, consistent actions, patience and observation, and generosity of spirit from both sides – a good recipe for any relationship.

HOW OUR CATS VIEW US

We will never really know how cats view humans. Our only clues lie in studying the relationship and the behaviours our cats exhibit with us and comparing this with how they interact with other cats.

Cats are actually more vocal with us than they are with other cats; they miaow to convey what they want, and we usually comply. We build up a one-to-one relationship with a particular cat based on a vocabulary of sounds, behaviours and responses. This may reach a reasonably high level of understanding – albeit only on simple matters, such as feeding, coming in

> *The cat is the only non-gregarious domestic animal. It is retained by its extraordinary adhesion to the comforts of the house in which it is reared.*
>
> FRANCIS GALTON,
> INQUIRIES INTO HUMAN FACULTY, 1883

and out, or having a cuddle. Because most cats live into their teens, owners have time to create a range of communications that become almost second nature between cat and person.

The relationship between cats and humans has been described as a maternal one – the cat seeing us as a surrogate mother (see reasons listed on page 55). Other researchers suggest

Above: Provided that children are gentle, cats will happily accept them as part of the family group. This cat is obviously very relaxed with his young carer. Young cat owners should be encouraged to move quietly and slowly at first while the cat gets used to them.

Above: A tail held straight up conveys welcome, friendship and trust between cats, and a cat may also greet its approaching owner in this way. The tail-up signal is often accompanied by miaowing in response to, or to elicit, the owner's closer attention.

that cats treat owners as if they were superior members of their social group. This is partly based on the observation that cats initiate rubbing behaviours with us. In the cat world, it is usually cats of 'lower rank' that initiate rubbing – kittens rub their mothers and female cats rub males.

Perhaps it is just that cats use behaviours with us that they usually display only with other cats that do not pose any threat to them. For kittens, this would be their mother at a time when they are dependent on her for nourishment and protection. For adult cats, it may be other cats with whom they are relaxed.

Our cats may feel that they can also exhibit these behaviours in our presence and retain their juvenile characteristics. This shows that they trust us enough to drop their defences around us and allow themselves to become vulnerable.

A MATERNAL RELATIONSHIP

◆

Why the human bond with cats may be seen as maternal:

✦ Kittens communicate vocally while they are young and this vocal communication persists with us.

✦ Cats also purr to humans – another communication that kittens and their mothers use as a method of letting each other know that all is well.

✦ Cats sit on our laps and knead with their feet. This is a kitten behaviour, used to stimulate milk flow when they were sucking from their mother.

✦ Cats greet us and other cats they know by raising their tails. This is also a kitten behaviour – raising the tail allows the queen to clean and investigate the ano-genital area under the tail.

✦ Cats rub around our legs as kittens rub around their mother.

✦ Owners strengthen the relationship by providing food, safety and shelter as a mother cat does.

The Cat's Life Cycle

Life spans ✦ Rhythms of life ✦ Reproduction and mating ✦ Pregnancy and birth

Our home-loving pet cats have somewhat different life cycles from wild or feral cats, principally because most pets are neutered. This means that their lives do not have to revolve around finding a mate and raising kittens.

Ideally, the pet cat – pedigree or non-pedigree – is homed with caring human owners at about 8 to 12 weeks. It receives its vaccinations to combat many of the infectious feline diseases, is treated for worms and fleas, and is well fed. When they are around six months old, both male and female kittens are likely to be neutered. They reach physical maturity at about one year old and, barring accident or serious illness that cannot be overcome by good veterinary care, most will live about 14 years.

Pedigree cats used for breeding are kept warm and well protected and usually have a special diet supplied by loving owners to ensure that both

mother and kittens remain as healthy as possible. They are probably allowed to breed only once a year.

FERAL LIFESTYLE

Compare these comfortable lifestyles with that of the feral cat. It is usually born into a colony, where it will stay

Above: This beautiful red tabby, indulging in a luxurious stretch, is likely to have a longer, more comfortable life than its feral cousins. All its needs are provided for by its owners.

with its mother for a couple of months, during which time it must learn how to look after itself. It may then have to move away to find its own territory. It becomes sexually mature at around six months old, when females are likely to become pregnant for the first time. Females may have two or even three litters per year, which drains their strength and exposes them to the dangers linked with pregnancy and birth and the rigours of bringing up kittens.

Young male feral cats have to fend for themselves from the time that they are a few months old. Although they may not mate until they have their own territory the following year,

Left: These playful ten-week-old kittens will soon be going to new homes. Feral kittens of this age need to start being self-sufficient and finding food for themselves.

they will have to learn to deal with the tough life of being an unneutered, or entire, male in a competitive world.

Feral cats also have to cope with the hazards associated with traffic, other predators, bad weather, disease and the daily need to find food. Most are unlikely to reach double figures. Entire males will be lucky to reach five years old, their lifestyles leaving them vulnerable to accident and starvation and to infection from fight wounds or disease.

THE CAT'S LIFESPAN

In general in the animal world, the smaller the creature the shorter its lifespan. The cat has a relatively long life for its size; it outlives most dogs, except the tenacious terriers and hard-working collies, which can also live into their teens. Factors that promote longevity are neutering (removing all the dangers associated with reproduction), a well-balanced diet, good preventive health care (vaccination, worming and parasite control), lifestyle (indoor cats are less likely to suffer accidents) and prompt veterinary care for illness.

The cat matures quickly. This is particularly important for feral cats, since they need to be self-sufficient from an early age. Humans take 12 years to reach sexual maturity – a kitten has reached the equivalent stage by about six months old. In fact, the cat packs birth, weaning, re-homing, sexual maturity (even a first litter if an unneutered female) and physical maturity all into its first year.

	CAT	HUMAN
Birth Weaning	3 months	9–12 months
Adult communication	4 months	3–4 years
Sexual maturity	6 months	12 years
	1 year	15 years
	2 years	24 years
	3 years	28 years
	4 years	32 years
	5 years	36 years
	6 years	40 years
	7 years	44 years
	8 years	48 years
	9 years	52 years
	10 years	56 years
	11 years	60 years
	12 years	64 years
	13 years	68 years
	14 years	72 years
	15 years	76 years
	16 years	80 years
	17 years	83 years
	18 years	86 years

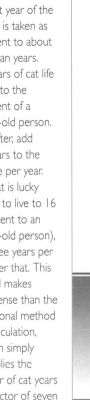

Cat years
The table sets out some comparisons in the ages of cats and humans to give an idea of the cat's age in human terms. The first year of the cat's life is taken as equivalent to about 15 human years. Two years of cat life bring it to the equivalent of a 24-year-old person. Thereafter, add four years to the cat's age per year. If the cat is lucky enough to live to 16 (equivalent to an 80-year-old person), add three years per year after that. This method makes more sense than the traditional method of calculation, which simply multiplies the number of cat years by a factor of seven to reach the human equivalent.

Below left: Two feral kittens peep out of their den in a wall. They have been fed and cared for by their mother but will soon have to go off and find their own territories.

Below right: This elderly cat takes a nap in its basket, secure in its comfortable home. Few feral cats live to old age. Their lives are too uncertain and dangerous.

Rhythms of Life

All animals must align their lives with the elements in order to survive and produce offspring at a time when food is plentiful so that they have the best chance of survival. The cat is no exception and is affected by the natural rhythms around it. Its internal clocks are in tune with day and night, and with the changing seasons, daylengths and temperatures. And although our pet cats do not have to feel the cold and pinch of hunger during the hard winter months, they still follow seasonal rhythms.

FOLLOWING RHYTHMS

Humans, too, are in tune with certain circadian rhythms (those influenced by light) in that we have a wake-and-sleep pattern over 24 hours. The cat follows a more fragmented rhythm. Instead of one period of sleep and one of wakefulness, it drifts in and out of sleeping and waking cycles throughout the day and night. Just when a cat is awake may depend on its lifestyle, its owner's lifestyle, its need to hunt (the period when prey is active) and where it lives.

The cat is also affected by circannual, or seasonal, rhythms. These, too, are governed by light and affect hair growth and mating patterns. When days start to shorten in the autumn, cats begin to grow longer hair in readiness for the winter. The change

Above: Although pet cats live in centrally heated homes, they still grow longer, thicker fur in the winter months to protect them from the cold.

in daylength also affects the female cat's reproductive cycle. In the northern hemisphere, unspayed female cats are not receptive to males during the months of October to December. They come into season, known as oestrus, during which time they are able to reproduce, between the months of January and September.

Increasing daylength switches on the sequence of mating behaviour in the cat. Light falling on the retina in the eye is relayed to the part of the brain called the hypothalamus, travelling via a different nervous pathway from that of sight. The hypothalamus regulates the cat's eating, sleeping and sexual activities – it sets the clock that controls daily body rhythms.

For the cat, this time of oestrus is not one long period but many short ones, which begin when daylength increases and stop when it begins to decrease. The increase in daylight hours in spring affects the pituitary gland in the brain, which produces a particular hormone called follicle-stimulating hormone (FSH). FSH stimulates the cat's ovaries to produce eggs and another female hormone called oestrogen. This hormone influences the female cat's behaviour in preparation for reproduction.

FINDING A MATE

The female, sometimes called a queen, must now let other cats, principally males, know that she is in this reproductive state. She does this in several ways. Oestrogen is excreted in

Below: Cats nap during the day, whether they are old or young. Their cycles of waking and sleeping are more fragmented than ours.

Left: As the male mounts the female for mating, he grabs the scruff of her neck in his jaws. If she is receptive, she flattens her body and lifts her rump.

Brain

Pituitary

Right: As in all mammals, hormones control most of the cat's bodily functions. Increasing daylength triggers a cascade of chemical messages from the hypothalamus and pituitary glands and the reproductive organs.

her urine and she urinates and sprays urine much more frequently than usual, leaving scent markers for male cats to find. She also 'calls' – a vocal encouragement to males in the area to come and find her. People who have not owned an entire female in season before sometimes think that their cat is in pain and worry that her strange behaviour of rolling on the ground, stretching, and raising her hindquarters is a sign of illness. Such behaviour is perfectly normal in a female cat in search of a mate.

When suitors do arrive, the queen mates only when she is ready. She will then allow the tom to mount her and grasp her by the scruff of the neck. The mating is brief and usually ends with the female 'screaming' and trying to attack the male. Scientists do not really understand this behaviour, but it may be to do with the fact that the penis of the tom is covered in backward-facing barbs. Whether the barbs cause pain on withdrawal is not known, but the action does stimulate the female cat to ovulate. Eggs are released from the ovaries and travel down the fallopian tubes and into the two horns of the uterus, where fertilization occurs.

It can take several matings before ovulation is stimulated and the female may mate with more than one tom at this time. It takes about two days for the eggs to reach the uterus and the sperm remains viable for several days, as it moves up the vagina and into the uterus to meet the eggs. This is why it is possible for queens to have litters which contain kittens from different fathers. When fertilized, the eggs implant in the female's uterus. The foetuses are positioned in rows in each of the two horns of the uterus, where they develop for nine weeks.

If mating and fertilization do not occur, the cat becomes non-receptive again. This period lasts from two days to two weeks. The whole process then begins again until she becomes pregnant or day-length decreases. For this reason, the cat is referred to as polyoestrus – having many periods of oestrus, throughout the breeding season.

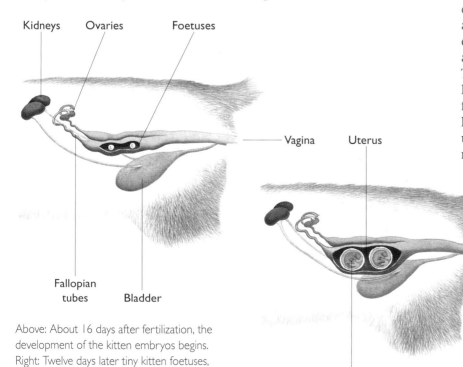

Kidneys   Ovaries   Foetuses

Vagina   Uterus

Fallopian tubes   Bladder

Foetuses

Above: About 16 days after fertilization, the development of the kitten embryos begins.
Right: Twelve days later tiny kitten foetuses, with their organs intact, have developed.

Pregnancy and Birth

Pregnancy in cats lasts about 63 days (nine weeks). During this period the body of the queen changes. By about three weeks into the pregnancy, the hormone progesterone causes her mammary glands to swell and her nipples, or teats, to become pink and more visible. She also starts to put on a little weight. As the pregnancy progresses, she becomes heavier and more rounded, depending on the number of kittens she is carrying. As the day of the birth approaches, her milk glands begin to fill.

PREPARATION FOR BIRTH

A couple of weeks before the birth, the queen may become restless and start trying to find a suitable nest. In the wild, this site is vital to the survival of the kittens, and pet cats instinctively try to find somewhere safe, too. Although many queens happily take to a cardboard box or a specially built kittening box provided by their owner, others are only content with somewhere of their own choice, such as the owner's bed or the top of the wardrobe. The queen may prepare more than one nest, following her instinct to provide several safe options should danger threaten any one of them.

For several hours before the birth the queen licks herself, concentrating on cleaning around the birth passage

and the teats. Scientists think that in doing this she lays a trail of saliva that helps to lead the kittens to a teat after they are born.

During the first stage of labour the queen breathes faster (sometimes through her mouth) and she may also purr. This can last for several hours. In the second stage of labour, contractions of her uterus get stronger and she starts to push to expel the kittens. Each kitten is born in its own sac of amniotic fluid, which the mother

Above: The swollen belly of this queen shows that she is well into her pregnancy. She will soon begin to select nest sites where she can give birth to her litter of kittens in comfort and safety.

breaks by licking and nibbling it. She also licks around the newborn kitten's face with her rough tongue, clearing away any membranes and fluid and stimulating it to breathe, and bites through the umbilical cord. Soon after the kitten is born, its

A developing embryo

Yolk sac

Embryo

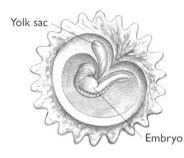

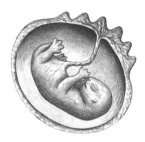

For the first 18 days the yolk sac provides the embryo with all the nutrients that it needs.

The yolk sac then shrinks and the embryo receives nutrients from its mother via the placenta.

By about four weeks the embryo is about 2.5 cm (1 in) long and has many of its internal organs.

The embryo is now called a foetus. Between four and nine weeks it doubles in size and its bones form.

Above and above right: As each kitten is born, the mother cat carefully cleans its face and bites away the umbilical cord. (The remains eventually dry and drop off.) She licks the kitten all over to clean its fur and rests until the next kitten is born.

Below: These day-old kittens are completely helpless. They cannot see or walk and are totally reliant on their mother to feed them and keep them warm and safe. They cannot even urinate unless she stimulates them by licking.

Above: The mother replaces valuable nutrients by eating the placenta of each kitten as it appears.

individual placenta follows and is eaten by the queen. For wild cats, eating the placenta replenishes some of the vital nutrients the mother needs. She will not leave the kittens much in the first few days of their lives and her energy resources are rapidly drained. Also, if it were left lying in the nest, the placenta would provide an ideal breeding ground for infections, and could attract predators.

As more kittens arrive, the queen deals with them as she can. Some queens have kittens every 15 minutes or so; others produce them at longer intervals of several hours. There is no set pattern. When the last kitten has been born, the queen lies on her side, encircling her babies and encouraging them to suck by nudging and licking their bodies. The newborn kittens are guided by smell and warmth to her teats, where they find colostrum, the mother's first milk, which is rich in antibodies.

The average litter size is four or five kittens, but some breeds tend to have more. Siamese and Burmese cats, for example, may have eight kittens and occasionally as many as 11 or 12.

Initially the queen must do everything for her litter of kittens. She keeps them safe, warm and comfortable and provides all their nutrient requirements. She also removes all their waste material to make sure that the nest stays clean and healthy. In fact, the kittens cannot urinate or defecate unless the queen licks the ano-genital area under the tail, swallowing the waste or depositing it outside the nest.

The Growing Kitten

Below: Newborn kittens feed little and often, taking less than a teaspoonful of their mother's milk at each meal. This quantity doubles by the time the kittens are about two weeks old.

Soon after birth, the kittens make their way to their mother's teats. They follow an increasing temperature gradient and the scent she left when she groomed and licked her belly. Several automatic behaviours help the kittens to do this. A 'rooting reflex' makes them nuzzle and nudge at the teats in order to find them and clamp on. This stimulates the milk flow and a 'sucking reflex' then takes over. Treading movements soon follow and these, too, stimulate the flow of milk. Many cats still make these movements on our laps, even when they are adults. Purring follows a little later.

The kittens do nothing but eat and sleep. They may suck for eight hours a day and so grow at a rapid rate. Initially weighing between 100 and 120 grams (3½–4 ounces), kittens may double their weight in the first week.

Above: A week-old kitten can manage to pull itself along the ground with its forelegs if it becomes separated from its mother.

They are still totally dependent on their mother for food and on her licking them to stimulate bladder and bowel movements to get rid of waste.

The kittens cannot regulate their own body temperature and although they can make rather crude paddling movements to try to pull themselves along, they cannot move easily. Hence they are extremely vulnerable if separated from their mother. Because their eyes are shut and their ears are covered by folds of skin, kittens must rely on their senses of touch (particularly their sensitivity to temperature) and smell to keep them close to their mother and to reach the teats. The queen recognizes her kittens by their

Wanton Kitlins [kittens] may
make sober old cats.
THOMAS FULLER,
GNOMONOLOGIA, 1732

Left: This Burmese mother is licking under its kitten's tail to stimulate urination. Without this, the kitten would not be able to urinate or defecate and would soon die. She continues to do this until the kitten is about four weeks old. If a kitten is hand-reared by humans, the rearer must stimulate the ano-genital area with damp cotton wool to try to imitate the actions of the mother.

Below: By about four weeks old, the kittens start to engage in rough-and-tumble play. They run and jump, leap on each other's back and roll over. These are mock battles only and nobody gets hurt. Play helps them practise their hunting moves and gain control of their exceptional senses.

cry and their scent and hardly leaves the nest at all for the first day or two after giving birth.

The kitten's eyes start to open between days five to ten and usually take about three days to open fully. Siamese and Burmese cats may open their eyes earlier. Sight may not be fully developed until the kitten is about four weeks old, when it can judge distance and depth accurately. This visual development continues until the kitten is about four months old. Kittens have blue eyes at first. They start to change colour when a kitten is around six weeks old, but do not take on their adult colour until it is about three months old.

STARTING TO MOVE

By ten days old the kittens are able to crawl, and by about day 15 they begin to try to stand. Their milk, or infant, teeth also start to come through and their ears begin to function normally, although hearing is not fully developed until they are about four weeks. The queen still spends about 70 per cent of her time with the kittens and they have constant access to her milk.

At about three weeks the queen may initiate the beginning of weaning. This is a huge change for the kittens, which are used to having food constantly available. The mother spends longer and longer away from them or sits or lies in positions where

The Growing Kitten

Above: This five-week-old kitten is getting used to human handling. Research suggests that a kitten needs to meet different people and have lots of new experiences during the vital socialization period between two and eight weeks if it is to make a good pet.

Below: Pouncing on objects such as a fluffy toy mouse stimulates a kitten's natural hunting instincts and is important practice for its future life as a predator.

it is difficult for the kittens to get to her teats. At the same time, she starts to turn her kittens' attention to prey or food provided by the owner and they may spend up to half an hour a day experimenting with solid food. The frustration the kittens experience at not being able to suck can be redirected to learning about this new source of nutrition, weaning them off the queen and allowing her to save some of her energy.

STARTING TO PLAY

At around this time, the kittens start to take an interest in objects as well as each other. Scientists suggest that this is practice for hunting and developing the predatory skills that will be required in the future. Although chasing and catching prey seems to be instinctive, the techniques of the final killing bite are learned from the mother. A successful hunter teaches her kittens how it is done.

At three to four weeks old, kittens also gain control over urination and defecation and leave the nest to

relieve themselves. Kittens learn by watching their mother and will imitate the actions she performs in the litter tray; they automatically scratch at substrates that have a soil, sand or litter consistency.

By four weeks, the kitten is able to run and balance fairly well. This development continues rapidly until it reaches something near adult performance at about 11 or 12 weeks old. Grooming is well developed from five weeks and kittens can start looking after their own coats. The righting reflex (see pages 36–7) is present from about six weeks.

Not only are kittens facing up to the frustrations of weaning from about three weeks onward, but they are also having to deal with the many new experiences life throws at them. From about 3 weeks to between 9 and 13 weeks of age, the kittens are in what is known as the socialization period – a time in which they form relationships with their own species and practise different methods of communication (see pages 42–51).

Kittens first learn how to react and respond to their siblings. Their play is punctuated with leaping games, mock battles and stand-offs, which allow them to learn to moderate the strength of 'attacks' and to avoid contact in 'fights'. At about 14 weeks, object play – the chasing and pouncing actions used in hunting – largely replaces social play and becomes the kittens' primary activity.

MEETING PEOPLE

The period from two weeks to seven or eight weeks of age is a sensitive period for socialization to humans and other animals. During this time, the kitten needs to experience plenty of handling by people so that it will be relaxed in a human home and make a good pet. If kittens fail to meet other species during this time, it is unlikely that they will ever be fully relaxed with them. An example is the feral kitten that does not meet humans

Above: By about six months, a young cat is able to fend for itself in the wild and to come and go independently if kept as a pet. All its senses are fully developed and it has excellent control of its movements.

Left: As well as getting used to humans, kittens need to meet other cats and even other types of animals. This young cat is sniffing inquisitively at the first rabbit it has ever encountered.

during this period. It seldom, if ever, makes a good pet, since it does not lose its fear of humans.

By about three to four months old, the kitten has good coordination and balance and has learned to control its exceptional muscles and senses to a great extent. It can live entirely on solids provided by the owner or, if necessary, can hunt for its own food. Most pet kittens will have gone to a new home by this time, but in a wild environment, this is the age when the kittens may have to disperse to find their own territories. Their mother may actually be pregnant with the next litter and eager to push these now self-sufficient offspring out into their own worlds.

CARRYING KITTENS

◆

A queen often moves her kittens a couple of days after birth, perhaps to a safer position or a larger space. She may also need to remove them from the birth site because it has become damp and soiled from the birth itself, making it a suitable site for microbes to grow and infections to start. The queen picks up the kittens by the scruff of the neck – the kitten relaxes, its forelegs go limp, and its tail and hindlegs curl inward. Because kittens automatically adopt this posture and remain still and quiet, they can be safely carried between sites.

Daily Life

The daily cycle ✦ *Sleeping and dreaming* ✦ *Grooming*

In the wild, the cat's pattern of activity is organized to be in tune with the activity of its prey. Cats that have to hunt to support themselves nutritionally are generally active at dawn and dusk, when most small mammals are out and about, or they must adapt to the habits of the particular prey that is available.

They dream and take the noble attitudes of Sphinxes lazing in deep solitudes, Which seem to slumber in an endless dream...
CHARLES BAUDELAIRE
THE CATS, *1847*

The well-fed pet cat does not have to do this. It can afford to stay asleep or have an early night without fear of starvation. If the cat has eaten well, or if there is no prey available and it wants to conserve energy, it will sleep. In fact, as most owners know, the cat is one of the best sleepers in the animal kingdom. And when it is not hunting or sleeping you will probably find your cat grooming its fur.

THE SLEEPING CAT

Typically, cats rest for about half the day in a mixture of cat naps and deeper sleeps, refreshing their minds and bodies. The pampered pet may have a nap in a warm linen cupboard in the morning, a long rest on a sunny windowsill after lunch, a session on various laps in the evening,

and then perhaps retire to bed with its owners for a well-earned sleep under the duvet.

The place where a cat chooses to sleep may depend on its character. Confident cats can stretch out in the middle of a roomful of children and other pets and sleep quite happily amid the chaos. A more nervous cat

may need to be on top of a cupboard in the spare room of a quiet house before it feels secure enough to go 'off duty' for a sleep.

Do twitching paws and whiskers mean that cats dream? Scientists think it probably does. Cats experience slow wave or quiet sleep and active or rapid eye movement (REM) sleep as we do – their bodies are relaxed but minds are active. We can only guess what cats dream about – catching mice is probably the most likely supposition we can make.

Newborn kittens spend 60 to 70 per cent of their time asleep. This starts to decrease when they are about three weeks old to levels of about 40 to 50 per cent of the day as adults, depending on how much 'work' the cat has to do to survive. In a survey of older cats, owners reported that their pets slept at least 50 to 75 per cent of the time and this proportion grew with increasing age. The real geriatrics (those in their late teens) were awake for less than a quarter of the day, returning to the levels of sleep required by kittens. An old cat, however, sleeps more lightly and wakes more easily than a kitten.

GROOMING

Most cats have their own grooming routine and some spend up to a third of their waking time pursuing a head-to-toe clean-up; others hardly bother. Friendly cats make good use of each other to get to those 'inaccessible' places at the back of the neck and under the chin.

Cats living together use mutual grooming as part of their social bonding by way of creating a group smell. But grooming is not simply about

Above: Mutual grooming helps friendly adult cats to reinforce the social bond between them. It also allows them to anoint each other with secretions from their scent glands, producing a reassuring group smell.

hygiene and social bonding. It is also an important way of relieving tension. Watch your cat if something startles it – it leaps away and then stops to look around. If the danger is not imminent, the cat often grooms in a effort to calm itself.

Left: During a light sleep, the cat's eyes may be only half closed and its head balanced on its chest like a sphynx. A deeper sleep requires more muscle relaxation, and the cat lies down. In deep sleep, the cat is so relaxed it must lie stretched out flat or curled up in a doughnut shape. Several hundred times the stimulation is needed to wake the cat during this type of sleep. Cats often choose strange places to take their naps: the cat (left, top) is cosily curled up on a plate.

Left: Grooming may take up a third of your cat's waking hours. An important activity, grooming cleans the fur and helps to keep it smooth and waterproof.

Right: A cat usually grooms symmetrically and systematically. It begins by using its forepaws to clean the face and behind the ears, covering each foreleg with saliva before wiping the 'dirty' area several times in a circular motion from back to front. It then licks its front legs clean, moving on to the back legs and tail. If it encounters a parasite, the cat stops to bite at the insect as it licks. The supple cat can reach almost all parts of its body by twisting and leaning.

PART 2

CARING FOR CATS

The first chapter of this book looked at the natural cat – how it sees the world, what motivates it to behave as it does, and how it develops. The next chapter is a guide to caring for this unique creature as a pet, from choosing a kitten to the special care of an older cat. Keeping a contented cat means not only correct feeding and grooming but also thinking about such matters as the way in which we treat our pet when we first get it, and how we introduce it to the rest of the household to give it the best start in life.

Coping with changes, such as a new baby in the family, moving home, or just deciding to introduce another cat into the house, can cause stress to both cat and owner, which can be minimized with a little fore-thought. Understanding the natural behaviour of the cat provides a basis for dealing with the behavioural problems that our cats may suffer from.

Why a Cat?

A symbiotic relationship ✦
A chance to nurture

Left: If a cat gets accustomed to children while young, it also makes an ideal family pet. Cat owners also appreciate the fact that their pets are independent and able to come and go while the family is out.

Right: Although independent, most cats stay close to home and are there waiting to greet you with a loving purr when you return.

How is it that this small desert carnivore from Egypt has become an integral part of the lives of millions of families across the world? What is it about the feline/human relationship that has made the cat so successful as a pet?

A SYMBIOTIC RELATIONSHIP

Cat haters sometimes refer to cats as parasites – taking what they can from us and not even having the grace to do as they are told in return. But to cat lovers the relationship is more symbiotic, with both cat and human benefiting from each other's presence, albeit in different ways. Ask anyone why they love their cat and you will get a wide variety of answers.

> *If man could be crossed with the cat it would improve man, but it would deteriorate the cat.*
> MARK TWAIN, NOTEBOOK, 1894

Among them are likely to be references to its beauty, companionship, cleanliness, independence and character. Dog owners asked the same question would probably add loyalty and obedience to the list – qualities not sought by most cat owners. This may be another reason for the success of the relationship – that we do not expect cats to do as we ask and so do not get upset if they ignore us. This type of unconditional human love is usually reserved for young children and is completely different to the give-and-take type of affection necessary for successful adult relationships. Our cats reward our loving care with attention and companionship and we are grateful.

A CHANCE TO NURTURE

We all need to care for something. In this age of work pressure and limited time for families, a pet can provide an outlet, allowing us to combine our own busy lives with a chance to care. A dog would have been the pet of choice for many families until recently, but it is becoming increasingly difficult to keep one. This is primarily because in most households, both adult members now have to go out to work to earn enough to pay the bills. Dogs cannot be left all day without being able to get out or without some form of companionship.

Moreover, if you happen to have a dog with a behaviour problem it is likely to affect your life quite considerably, usually because it is destructive in the home or because it is aggressive to other dogs or people.

Thus many people now prefer a feline, rather than a canine, friend, and pet cats outnumber dogs all over Europe. An additional benefit of cat ownership is that it is much less guilt-ridden than dog ownership. Owners know their cats do not usually pine for them while they are out at work. Most cats can come and go as they wish or have a litter tray available, and they do not have to wait for their owners to return to walk them. The only feline behaviour likely to affect anyone other than the owner is a cat digging up the neighbour's garden to use as a latrine; aggression is not a worry, nor usually is noise nuisance.

Some people suggest the cat may be a child substitute. While this may be true, in that many women are waiting longer to have children and enjoy caring for cats until this happens, the real reason is probably that cats let us enjoy our need to nurture, whether we are male or female, old or young, have six children or none. When you come home at the end of the day, perhaps feeling tired and tense, the cat runs to greet you. It miaows a welcome, rubs against you with its soft body and waits to spend the evening purring on your lap.

Choosing a Cat

Pedigree or moggie ✦ *Cat or kitten* ✦
Long- or short-haired ✦ *How many cats?*

W hether you are choosing your first cat or you already own a cat and would like another, you first need to make some decisions. Think about whether you want an ordinary cat or a pedigree breed, a kitten or an adult, and how many, as well as where you will go to get your cat. The animal that you choose may be with you for 14 years or more, so think carefully.

PEDIGREE OR NON-PEDIGREE?

Most pet cats are non-pedigrees, or 'moggies' – their lineage is mixed and quite often unknown on the male side. Unlike dog owners, who may become very 'fixed' on a particular breed in preference to all others, cat owners often have both pedigree and non-pedigree cats and enjoy them both for their feline attributes.

Above left: A kitten is great fun to watch and probably adapts more easily to life with energetic young children than an older cat.

Above: Elderly people or families who are out all day may prefer not to have the responsibility of a lively kitten. There are always plenty of adult cats which need re-homing through no fault of their own and they make excellent pets once settled.

Look through the breeds section of this book and you will be amazed at the range of different types of cat that are available, although, unlike dogs, they vary little in size or proportion. Different breeds may have particular characteristics, such as the talkativeness of the Siamese, but researchers have noted that the difference in character between individual cats, be they moggie or pedigree, are greater than

the differences between breeds. Every cat has its own unique personality.

However, Siamese and Burmese cats do tend to demand more attention in terms of time and interaction than many other cats. If you want a quiet life, you may want to choose one of the more self-reliant breeds or a non-pedigree. If you want to see the different breeds 'in the flesh', you may like to visit a cat show and talk to the exhibitors and breeders there. They will give you an idea of the foibles of their particular breed and you can see the size, shape and coat make-up of each for yourself.

CAT OR KITTEN?

Many people prefer to start at the beginning as cat owners, with a kitten. Not only do they have the chance to enjoy all those ultra-cute kitten

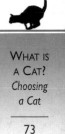

WHAT IS
A CAT?
*Choosing
a Cat*

73

**ADVANTAGES OF
A KITTEN**

✦

✦ A kitten's behavioural and
medical history is known.
✦ You can form a bond while the
animal is still young.
✦ You can enjoy watching a kitten
grow up and develop.
✦ It will probably fit in with
another cat more easily.
✦ Age and life expectancy are known.
✦ You can look forward to a long
life together.

**ADVANTAGES OF
AN ADULT CAT**

✦

✦ An adult cat is usually more
sedate and less destructive.
✦ Adult cats are usually litter
trained and neutered already.
✦ It is less likely to get into trouble
indoors or out.
✦ It can be left on its own during
the day without worry.
✦ It does not need as much
human attention.

Top: Non-pedigree cats are inexpensive to
acquire and make beautiful, friendly pets.

Above: The Siamese is popular and much
admired for its elegance. Most Siamese cats
are intelligent and friendly and even willing to
take walks on a lead. However, they are also
very voluble and like plenty of attention.

behaviours, but they can also get to
know their cat from the start of its
life. Others feel that they really do not
have the energy to go through the
baby months of curtain climbing, litter training and worrying what the
curious little creature will be up to
next. They may opt for an adult cat
that will be rather more mature in its
outlook and better able to look after
itself without getting into mischief.
There are pros and cons to both (see
the tables on this page).

Below: Decide how much work you are
willing to put into your cat. Long-haired
breeds, such as these appealing Persians,
must be groomed daily, or their beautiful fur
quickly becomes a tangled mess. It is best to
accustom your long-haired cat to grooming
as a kitten. It will then accept the procedure
more easily and cause less fuss later on.

LONG- OR SHORT-HAIRED?

Many people are attracted by the long,
luxurious coat of the Persian, or
Longhair, cat but are unaware of the
great deal of work required to keep it
free from knots and looking good.
This dense coat requires human as
well as feline attention daily. Unlike
the semi-longhair breeds, such as the
Maine Coon, Persian cats cannot look
after their coats on their own.

Of course, even a short-haired cat
enjoys a little help in grooming, with
a gentle brush or grooming glove.
You, the owner, must decide whether
you want to do a full groom on a vast
amount of hair as a daily routine, or
just want to enjoy doing it when you
have the time or inclination. If it is
the latter, then go for a short-haired
cat and leave the responsibility for
coat care to the feline expert.

Choosing a Cat

ONE OR TWO KITTENS?

◆

ADVANTAGES OF TWO KITTENS
◆ They need less close attention.
◆ They play and exhibit a wide range of behavioural repertoires that are delightful to watch.
◆ They provide companionship for each other, particularly during the first weeks of settling in.
◆ Removes the problem of introducing a new cat later.
◆ Lessens the 'guilt' of leaving one kitten alone at home.
◆ May protect an older resident cat by providing a young playmate.

DISADVANTAGES OF TWO KITTENS
◆ Twice the cost of buying, neutering and vaccinations.
◆ They may interact more with each other and less with humans, although they are usually happy to do both.
◆ Two long-haired cats would need a lot of grooming.
◆ Twice the destruction wrought by kittenish acrobatics.

HOW MANY CATS?

There are no hard and fast rules about how many cats are happy to live together. It depends on the individuals involved, their previous history and their particular preferences. But do bear in mind that the cat is a solitary hunter and does not necessarily need the company of other cats.

If you do want to have more than one cat, it is worth doing this from the beginning and obtaining a pair of kittens at a time when they are still able to form a bond with each other. Neither gets first claim on the territory and they grow up together. Most other combinations can cause some upset, permanent or temporary. The extent of this disruption depends on the sex of the cat you choose, their age, whether the cats are neutered, the space you have and how you make the all-important initial introductions (see pages 84–7).

As a general rule, if you want two cats, start with two kittens. If you already have one cat, do not assume it wants a friend – it is probably you who wants another. Most adult cats are less 'offended' by a new kitten on their territory than by an adult cat, and by choosing the opposite sex you may escape some of the competition between same-sex cats. Neutering also helps to remove tensions.

Above: Some cats prefer to live alone; others are happy to share their space and food. It is easier to start with several kittens than to introduce another cat later on.

If you like the idea of having one of the more interactive breeds, but worry that you cannot give it enough company, you may prefer to choose two kittens so that they can amuse each other while you are out. Having a pair also makes absences from home or late nights less guilt-ridden, since you know the kittens can provide each other with plenty of company and entertainment.

Another reason for starting with two kittens is if you have decided that

where you live is just too dangerous for cats outdoors and you intend to keep your cat indoors permanently. Introducing a second cat into an indoor cat's territory at a later date can be extremely difficult.

WHICH SEX?

If you do not have any resident cats the choice of sex of your new cat does not really matter, as long as you are going to neuter it. There is little difference between the sexes in terms of behaviour once they are neutered. When buying two kittens, some people prefer to get one of each sex to minimize any sexual competition. You must then make sure that you neuter them before they reach sexual

Left: Most breeds of cats are happy to be the only pet in the household. A semi-longhair, such as this Maine Coon, does not need as much grooming as a long-haired cat.

Left: Young kittens may be shy and nervous when they first leave their mother. Going to a new home with a litter mate may help them to feel more secure.

Below: The Abyssinian is a beautiful pedigree cat and since it has short hair it does not need much grooming attention.

maturity. Cats are not influenced by human taboos such as incest. If you already have a resident cat, it is worth trying to introduce either a kitten or an adult cat of the opposite sex to reduce possible tension.

WHEN TO BUY

If you want to take on an adult cat from another home or one from a rescue centre, there are plenty of lovely cats available all year round. Most cats have their kittens in the spring or summer, so young kittens are plentiful during the warmer months. Some pedigree cats breed throughout the year or are kept in artificial light conditions that maintain queens in a breeding state. It is best to check with individual breeders as to when kittens will be available.

Whether you take on a kitten or an adult cat, try to devote some time to your new family member, helping it to settle in. This is especially important if you are bringing home a new kitten that has not been away from its mother or home before. Some gentle reassurance and company will help the kitten to feel more relaxed. Be prepared to spend at least a weekend with your new kitten, learning about its needs and character and helping it with litter training if this has not already been done.

Avoid getting a kitten just before Christmas or before you go on holiday, or at other times when there may be a great deal of disruption in the house. It is also unwise to take on a new cat or kitten just before a baby is due, since there is unlikely to be enough time to help the cat settle in. Let the baby grow up a little and then introduce a cat into the family.

Where to Find a Cat or Kitten

Accidental litters ◆ *Pet shops* ◆ *Adult cats* ◆ *Rescue cats* ◆ *Pedigree kittens*

*I*n spring and summer, there are innumerable non-pedigree kittens advertised as 'free to good homes'. These usually come from owners who have not realized that their little female 'kitten' has reached sexual maturity. The local tom has been only too well aware of the fact, however, and about nine weeks later a litter of kittens arrives.

Kittens from private homes like these usually make excellent pets. They are born into a loving family environment and become used to children, dogs, noise and all the usual household activities. Nothing in a new home can cause them much anxiety after this baptism of fire and they grow into well-adjusted cats, able to deal with novelty and a wide range of people and other pets.

PET-SHOP KITTENS
In general, it is best to avoid buying a kitten through a pet shop, since it is often impossible to ascertain its age, health or vaccination status. A pet-shop kitten may also be housed with other individuals from different sources, which may be carrying disease. And the stressful conditions make pet-shop kittens much more vulnerable to infections.

Right: Always try to see a kitten with its mother. This gives you an opportunity to check the mother's health – a fit mother is more likely to produce healthy kittens. Do not be tempted to choose the runt of the litter – it may cause you problems.

FINDING AN ADULT CAT
For people who would prefer to take on an adult cat, there are many sources to investigate. Veterinary surgery noticeboards or local papers often carry advertisements for cats needing new homes. The reasons their present owners are not able to keep them vary widely – they may be moving house, have difficulties with other pets, or a family member who may have developed an allergy to cats.

While some cats are moved out because of behavioural problems, most are normal animals that simply do not fit into the current circumstances of the family and they will make good pets in a new home. The advantage of taking a cat straight from its old home is that you can find

Above: A adult cat that is unwanted in its present home can make a loving and well-adjusted pet for its new owners.

out about its history, age and likes and dislikes from the owner, who may even keep in contact to see how the cat is getting on in its new home.

RESCUE CENTRES
Rescue centres or cat sanctuaries range from large national organizations to dedicated individuals who take unwanted cats into their homes. They vary greatly in their standards of accommodation and management.

No, I will not have any Persian cat; it is undertaking too much responsibility. I must have a cat whom I find homeless, wandering about the court, and to whom, therefore, I am under no obligation.

SAMUEL BUTLER, LETTER TO HIS SISTER, 1885

If the rescue is based in someone's home, make sure that there are just a few cats kept in a group. Most responsible and knowledgeable rescuers take on only a litter or two at a time, or find homes for kittens and cats individually. They maintain strict rules for hygiene and manage the cats' environment very carefully.

The proprietor of the rescue may ask you questions about your home and your ability to look after the cat or kitten, and may even want to visit you at home. If you have chosen a kitten, the rescue centre will probably ask you to neuter it when it is older to prevent more unwanted litters.

BUYING FROM A BREEDER

If you decide that you want a pedigree cat or kitten, contact breed clubs or individual breeders. Most breed clubs run a welfare group that re-homes adult cats of the breed in which they specialize, and these may be a good source for an adult pedigree cat. If you want a kitten, contact suitable

Above: In good rescues, each cat has its own 'chalet' and individual run.

breeders to find out when kittens will be available. Most insist that kittens reach a certain age (usually 12 weeks) before they go to their new homes and that they have received all the necessary vaccinations against infectious diseases before they go.

Tell the breeder whether you plan to breed from your kitten or simply keep it as a pet. Breeders sometimes have kittens that have minor 'faults', such as small markings in the wrong place, which make them unsuitable for showing. These are sold at a lower price than breeding-quality kittens. Owners who are not intending to show or breed from their cat are usually unconcerned about such faults and happy to get a kitten of the breed they like. Make an appointment to visit the breeder and see the kittens with their mother.

As a rule, the more cats that are kept together the greater the chance that any disease present will spread through the whole group. Therefore any rescue centre must be run with meticulous care to minimize this possibility. Before you choose your cat, choose your rescue centre carefully – see the advice in the box above.

Left: The cats and kittens in this rescue centre are being kept in family groups and have their own individual food bowls and litter trays. Too many cats sharing such facilities increases the risk of potentially serious diseases being transmitted.

The Right Choice

Early experience ♦ Healthy kittens ♦ What to look for

Consider what personality you would like your cat to have. Most people want a cat that is friendly, confident and joins in with the family and other pets. If this is the type of cat you want, then you must choose carefully. All too often owners select cats on the pattern of their fur or the colour of their eyes, without looking any further. They risk ending up with an animal that is beautiful but too nervous to come out from hiding when anyone except close family is around. Although you can never guarantee exactly how a cat or kitten will turn out, you can try to avoid some of the pitfalls.

Several factors influence a cat's character. These include its genetic make-up, its mother's behaviour and its own experiences. Researchers have found that there do seem to be different types of cat in terms of their friendliness or willingness to interact. Some cats enjoy being sociable; others do not want human attention, nor do they happily accept living with other cats. The sociability of the mother also influences how her kittens view people. A queen that is relaxed with her owners and happy to let them touch her kittens is passing on the message that humans pose no threat. Kittens learn a great deal by watching and copying their mother, including their attitudes to humans.

THE FIRST WEEKS
Perhaps the greatest influence on the kitten's ability to become a happy, interactive pet is its early experience.

Above: Some kittens are so appealing that they are hard to resist! But try to make sure that the animal is healthy and has an outgoing personality before you give in.

There is only a very short period in a kitten's early life (up to about eight weeks of age) when it can meet other species and accept them as friendly and part of normal life. This is also a time when it can learn about everyday objects, noises and happenings without fear. If it has a varied and interesting environment during these weeks, a kitten learns quickly and

will be inquisitive and confident in dealing with novelties that arise thereafter. This is the making of a calm, outgoing cat.

If a kitten misses out on these early experiences, it is likely to be fearful and nervous for the rest of its life. There is not a great deal that can be done to help it once this narrow window of opportunity has passed. Anyone who has taken on a feral kitten (one born to a cat living in the wild) of more than eight weeks old will testify to its wild personality. Although optimistic owners may

Below: Getting two kittens together gives the owner twice as much fun. Being with a sibling can also make going to a new home a much less frightening experience.

Right: Three Siamese kittens will keep their owner extremely busy and they are likely to get up to all sorts of tricks. Siamese are usually lively, sociable cats, but be prepared to give them plenty of attention.

expend a great deal of love and effort on trying to 'tame' such kittens, they rarely have much success.

The average 'accidental' kitten, born into a household that did not get around to neutering its own kitten before it reached sexual maturity, is likely to have to deal with lots of new experiences in its first few weeks and usually makes an excellent pet. It may be able to go to its new home when it is six to eight weeks old and so the new owners will have some opportunity to influence it during its vital socialization period. Kittens from a rescue centre may not get as much early experience, so choose where you go for your kitten carefully and find out about its early life.

Breeders of pedigree cats usually do not sell kittens until they are about 12 weeks old, so it is up to the breeder to ensure that they are well socialized. Successful breeding requires a combination of attention to health and hygiene and a knowledge of the social development of cats. Kittens kept in immaculate, but boring or quiet, conditions may be healthy, but they may not cope too well with life's ups and downs.

Above: Choosing one or two from a litter of appealing kittens is a difficult task. Try to assess their personalities and do not be tempted by the quiet, sorrowful kitten.

Below: A contented, relaxed mother is likely to produce well-adjusted kittens. She will give her kittens a good start in life and they are likely to make friendly, confident pets.

Think about what you want the cat to cope with. Are there children and dogs in your family and lots of visitors, or do you live alone and lead a quiet life? A good rule of thumb is to choose a kitten from a home that has a similar profile to your own. While a kitten from a quiet, single-person household is likely to be fine in a similar new home, it may be shocked

The Right Choice

by the activities of a lively family with young children and other pets. A kitten born into this type of home is likely to be able to adapt to anything.

CHOOSING A KITTEN

If you can, see the kittens with their mother. Her personality and attitude to people will have influenced the kitten you choose. Look for one that is interested and lively and interacts with its litter mates and with you. See how it deals with noises or surprises and assess the confidence of its approach to everything around it. Does it enjoy being stroked or does it object to being picked up? Unless you are happy to take on a quiet or nervous kitten, knowing that it is likely to stay this way, do not be overcome by sentiment or feel sorry for the kitten that is hiding in the corner looking miserable. It may simply be fearful or it may be ill.

It is easier to judge the personality and approach of an adult cat than a kitten, but bear in mind that the environment the cat is in has an effect. If you are taking over a cat from a friend or another family, go along and meet it in its own home. If choosing from a rescue centre, be aware that the stresses of the situation may put great pressures on a cat and you may not see it at its best. If the rescue is

Above: This silver tabby kitten looks healthy and confident – an ideal pet. Its ears are clean, its eyes are bright and alert, and its fur is smooth and glossy.

overcrowded, with too many cats packed together, not only will they be more likely to exchange diseases but they may also repress each other. Cats are solitary hunters and do not necessarily want to be in close proximity with other cats. In a crowded rescue centre, each cat will try to find some space to to call its own and sit there quietly.

Left: If you buy an adult cat or a kitten from a breeder, you can be reasonably certain about the sex of the cat you choose. However, it can be difficult for inexperienced owners to tell the difference between young kittens and you may want to double check the sex yourself. The following guidelines may help:

In the male kitten, the top opening is the anus and the scrotal sac is situated below this. About 1 cm (⅓ in) below the anus is the opening for the penis.

In the female kitten, there is a vertical slit below the anus, which is almost joined to the anus; together they look like the letter 'i'.

A good rescue with animals in small groups or individual pens allows cats to relax in their own space and to interact with potential owners in a more natural way. You should be able to judge how friendly and confident the cat is in this situation. Ask about its previous history. Is there a behavioural problem in its past? Why is it being re-homed? Of course, there may be no answers to these questions, but any good rescue centre will offer to have the cat back if it does not fit into its new home.

HEALTH CHECK

Whether you are taking on a kitten or an adult cat, you need to check its health for yourself, as well as gather information on its previous health record. Find out about vaccinations and worming so that you can start or complete any courses.

Taking on a sick cat or kitten can cause great heartache and may also cost a great deal of money. Just because you have travelled a long distance to see a specific litter, or you are desperate to take home a kitten that day, do not be tempted to rush into a decision. Remember that once you get the kitten home and everyone falls in love with it, any illness or loss is going to be traumatic.

Follow your instincts. Does the cat or kitten look bright? Is its coat shiny and are its eyes clear? If you feel something is not quite right, make more enquiries. Ask your vet to come with you if you are unsure or inexperienced and pay for his or her advice, or take your kitten for a full veterinary check-up once you have collected it. If problems are noticed, decide quickly whether you want to have the animal treated or take it back before you become too attached to it. If you are taking on a cat that has been badly treated and you want to coax it back to health, you may need a vet's advice on the best care.

Below: If you want a pedigree cat, such as this beautiful Abyssinian, find a reputable breeder and ask them to let you know when a litter of kittens will be available.

Above: If possible, have a look inside the cat's mouth. The gums should be pink and the breath should not smell. Older cats can get a build-up of tartar on their teeth and may need to be taken to the vet for thorough cleaning and scaling.

WHAT TO LOOK FOR

Look at the eyes, ears, mouth and nose – there should be no discharge or obvious injuries. The eyes should be bright and the third eyelid (which looks like a white membrane at the corner of the eye) should not cover the eye. The cat's coat should be glossy, with no bare patches or flaky skin. Ears should be clean. Deposits

of wax may mean that the cat is suffering from ear mites.

Check inside the mouth. The gums should be pink and healthy and a kitten's teeth should be white and its breath should not smell. If you are taking on an older cat, it is possible that its teeth may need some care, such as de-scaling. Have a look or ask your veterinary surgeon to check its mouth to ensure there are no serious problems. The cat or kitten should not be snuffling or sneezing and its breathing should be quiet, not noisy or wheezy. Look under the cat's tail – there should be no signs of diarrhoea, such as soiled fur or reddening of the skin. The cat or kitten should walk without stumbling or limping and it should look comfortable in all its movements.

If you are happy with your choice of kitten or cat in terms of personality and health, prepare to take it home. If you are choosing from a pedigree breeder, you may have to leave a deposit and return for the kitten once it is old enough to be re-homed.

Below: If you would like to take on an adult pedigree cat, such as this tabby-point Siamese, contact the breed club to find out if there is a welfare officer to give you advice.

Preparing for Your New Cat

Collecting and equipment ◆ Identification

Collect your new cat or kitten in a secure carrier lined with newspaper (in case of accidents) and some washable bedding. If possible, bring a piece of bedding from the animal's previous home. The scent of something it recognizes will provide some security for the cat or kitten in its new home, where it will be surrounded by strange sights and smells. There are many types of carrier available, ranging from temporary cardboard to wicker, solid plastic and plastic-coated wire mesh. The one you choose needs to be secure and easy to clean. The simplest type to use, clean and get the cat in and out of is a plastic-coated mesh basket that opens at the top.

Cats do not need many accessories, but you should have food, bowls and grooming equipment, if necessary (see pages 98–9), ready for your new pet. Feeding bowls should be sturdy with non-slip bases. Keep a separate one for providing water throughout the day. Whether you have a cat or kitten, you need to keep it indoors until it has had its vaccinations or has settled in and will therefore need a litter tray (see pages 88–9).

Your new cat or kitten will need its own bed, in which it will feel secure and warm. The bed can be simply a cut-down cardboard box, with a warm cushion or blanket tucked into it, or a purpose-made cat bed or basket. A

Right: Specially constructed "leisure centres" provide cats with the opportunity to play safely indoors and use up some of their excess energy as well as sharpen their claws.

piece of bedding from its old home may help for the first few days but generally bedding should be washable or disposable. Site the bed in a safe, draught-free position, where the cat can have sanctuary away from children or dogs and have a peaceful sleep. Of course, most cats like to choose their own sleeping places around the house when they feel more settled in, but at first it helps to provide a place they can call their own. Cats enjoy feeling comfortable and settle well if they are given the right conditions. Some cats adore the 'cradle' beds that hang on radiators and provide a good vantage point and warmth at the same time.

Above: A cosy bed gives security and warmth to a new kitten, which may have just left its mother and siblings and be facing its first night alone in a new home. A 'hooded' bed also gives its occupant greater privacy.

If you are bringing home a kitten, you may want to keep it in a kittening pen or indoor crate for the first few weeks. This provides a secure den for the new arrival and houses its bed, litter tray and food. When you are not around to supervise the inquisitive new kitten, you can shut it safely in the pen knowing that it will sleep and not get into trouble while you are out. The pen also makes introductions to other cats or dogs much easier.

IDENTIFYING YOUR CAT
If you would like your cat to wear a collar for identification or to carry a magnet or electronic key to open a cat flap, then get it accustomed to wearing one from kittenhood if possible. Be sure to buy a collar that is elasticated or has a safety catch that will open should the cat be caught up on a

Above: Use a cat carrier to bring your cat home – never transport a cat or kitten loose in the car. Introduce the cat to the carrier before using it. Wait until you are inside your home before letting the cat out of the carrier.

CARING FOR CATS
Preparing for Your New Cat

83

branch or get its foot stuck through the collar. Secure the collar fairly tightly so that it does not slip off, but make sure there is room to put two fingers underneath it. A tag with your name, address and telephone number aids identification if the cat gets lost.

You may wish to have your cat fitted with a microchip for permanent identification. The tiny device, which is about the size of a grain of rice, is implanted under the skin using a special needle, and the cat's identity is logged on to a national computer database. Should the cat become lost and be taken into a rescue facility, its identity can be read by a scanner and the owner contacted.

Claw sharpening is a natural part of the cat's behaviour, so a scratching post is essential for the cat that is kept indoors permanently. It can also

Above: Make sure that the cat's collar is not too tight. The cat may scratch at it at first but should soon get used to it. Add an identification disc with your name and address in case the cat gets lost.

be useful for cats that do go outside but like to scratch indoors, too. There are many types to choose from at pet stores, but most cats like to stretch up high and pull down from a height. Bear in mind that carpet-covered posts may encourage your cat to see all carpets as a scratching facility.

MICROCHIP IDENTIFICATION

◆

A tiny microchip inserted under the skin at the scruff of the cat's neck gives your pet permanent identification that cannot be lost or altered in any way. The chip is usually inserted at a veterinary surgery. Each cat has its own unique number that can only be read by a special electronic scanner.

Settling In

The first night ◆ *Introductions* ◆ *Getting used to the household*

The first night in a new home can be daunting for anyone, and cats, adaptable as they are, are no exception. For a new kitten, this may be the first time it has been away from its home and its mother. For an adult cat, a new home is a new territory, with all the anxieties and threats this brings. A special secure area for the night will help the cat feel less vulnerable – a kittening pen or crate is ideal for a young animal. Your cat or kitten may be keen to explore its new surroundings, but it is better to let it get used to one room first. Talk reassuringly and let the cat look around and investigate new objects and smells.

Do not panic if the cat or kitten disappears under the bed for a short time or climbs up on top of the wardrobe. Stay calm and coax it back with offerings of food and attention. Keep all the windows and doors shut, provide a litter tray and make sure

Below: Children love kittens but they must learn to handle them properly and gently. Adults need to ensure that animals are not viewed or treated as 'toys'.

Above: Even the boldest kitten will find the transition from its mother and litter mates to its new home a little frightening, but it should soon adjust to its surroundings.

that the cat knows where this is as soon as it arrives. A kitten needs to stay inside the house until it has had all its vaccinations and knows where home is. Keep an adult cat inside for about two weeks or until it has had a chance to form bonds with you and its new surroundings.

When you bring home your new cat or kitten there may be quite a few

Right: Let cats dictate their own pace in a new home. Confident cats may interact immediately but others will not want to be touched at first and should not be restrained or held forcibly. Keep other animals and children away until new cats are settled in.

introductions to be made – to the rest of the family as well as to any other cats and dogs. Adopt a fairly structured approach for the benefit of all concerned. Try to keep everyone calm and quiet and ensure that you are in control of the situation before you begin the introductions. A little time spend preparing animals and children for a harmonious life together at the beginning will be well worth the effort in the long run.

Meeting children

Children are usually very excited about meeting a new pet and tend to rush in with great enthusiasm, accompanied by a great deal of noise. This can be somewhat alarming for a new feline resident. Prepare the children by explaining how frightening an experience this could be for the cat and how they can make it feel welcome by being very quiet and gentle and not all trying to get their hands on it at once.

If the cat or kitten has come from a household with children it will probably take everything in its stride, but if it has not, take things slowly and avoid any sudden movements or loud noises. Sit the children on the floor and let the cat or kitten approach them. Show the children how to stroke the cat on its back, where it is likely to enjoy being touched, and discourage them from picking it up or squeezing it so that it feels hemmed in and threatened.

Allow the kitten to investigate its surroundings and the children and do not let the children follow or chase it. Use food to encourage the cat to interact. After a few days the initial

Right: A kittening pen or crate gives your new cat or kitten some security and makes introductions easier. Pens are expensive to buy but you may be able to rent something suitable from a cat breeder.

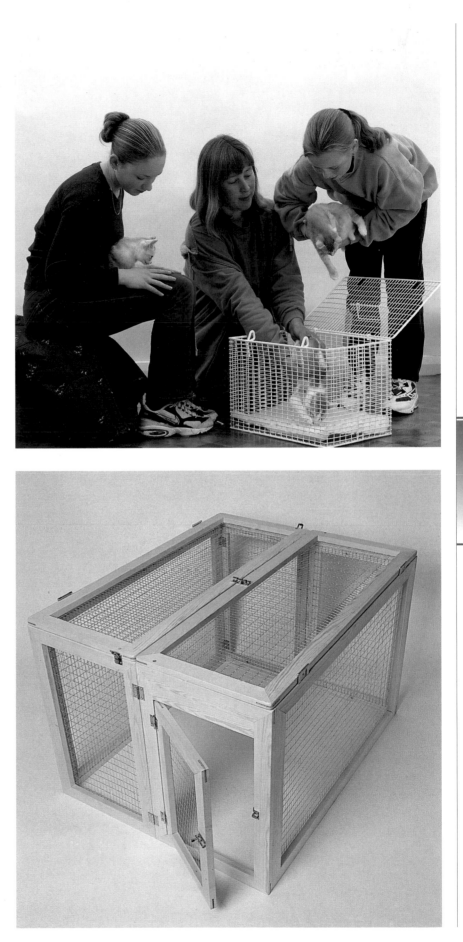

Settling in

excitement usually calms down; the cat is no longer the focus of attention and can continue settling in quietly.

INTRODUCING A NEW CAT TO A RESIDENT CAT

Your resident cat may not be quite so pleased about the addition to your family as you are. Unlike the pack-oriented dog, the cat functions quite happily on its own without a social structure around it and does not need to be part of a group.

There is no need for a resident cat to accept a new arrival as part of its group and no benefit to it in doing so. However, if there is no competition for food or safe sleeping places, cats can and do accept each other and even seem to form close bonds. Whether this happens depends very much on the personality of the cats involved and the way you help them to become acquainted.

The resident cat's territory is of great importance to it. Most owners are pleased when their cat chases away another cat that has intruded through the cat flap, but we then expect it to welcome a new cat of our choosing into its home. Cats do not know our intentions for happy families. They need time, space and the observation of social rules to discover that the new cat is not a threat.

USING A KITTENING PEN

It is up to you to make both the new cat and the resident feel as secure as possible, and to prevent the new-comer from being threatened or chased. The best way to do this is to use a kittening pen, indoor crate or a cat basket for initial introductions. This allows the resident cat to investigate the new one without threat to its territory and protects the new individual against attack. The bars allow the cats to get close together but provide a feeling of distance at the same time.

Even before you let the cats meet, stroke first one and then the other and repeat this several times over a

couple of hours. It may help to mingle the scents of the cats. The new animal will seem a little less alien if it smells slightly of the house and of the resident cat. Place the new cat in the pen or carrier and put it above ground level so the cats are not forced to make direct eye contact with each other. Let the resident cat into the room and give it attention and calm reassurance. Allow it to investigate the new arrival and praise it for not

Above: Energetic young cats enjoy lots of love and attention, and older children, who know how to handle animals properly, make ideal minders for them.

being aggressive. If the cat decides to run away without investigating the new cat, do not force it to come back but accept that things may take time.

If the cats show signs of aggression, distract them with a noise. Praise them for any quiet encounters. Feed

Above: Cats and dogs can become the best of friends. Close relationships like this are more likely to develop between animals that have grown up together.

Below: If carefully introduced to the newcomer, an older cat can learn to accept a younger one and in time they may even become good friends.

resident cat in the cage. When you decide the time is right to let them meet without the pen, use a favourite food to distract them and feed them some distance apart. Make sure that there is somewhere for the new cat to run to and hide if it wants to and be ready to interrupt if the situation gets nasty. If all goes well, graduate to supervised meetings in other rooms.

INTRODUCING THE DOG

Once again, the use of a carrier or pen is ideal for introductions between cats and dogs. Keep the situation calm and let the dog sniff the cat through the cage. If both animals are used to the other species, you will probably have no problems. If they are not, continue the introductions while keeping some control over the dog.

Bear in mind the age and type of dog you have. Young pups may get excited and try to 'play' with the newcomer, who is unlikely to want to join in. If you have an excitable hunting breed, such as a terrier, you may need to work hard to keep things calm and take care that a sudden movement from the cat does not induce a chase. Praise the dog for calm interactions and progress to using a lead for introductions outside the pen when you feel the time is right. Usually the cat soon decides that it is boss and the relationship blossoms.

both cats in the same room with a special treat and gradually move the resident cat's bowl nearer to the cage containing the new cat so that they are sharing space as they eat. Place the crate on the floor and feed again. Throughout the process there may be some hissing and spitting, but this should calm down to curiosity. There is no set time for all these procedures. It may take only a day or two for the cats to get used to each other or it

may take several weeks. Watch closely and judge for yourself how well things are going.

Keep these meetings short and sweet. Continue mixing the cats' scents and allow the newcomer to visit all the rooms of the house so that smells mingle and both house and cats start to take on the new group smell. Before you let the cats meet face to face, try swapping them around and let the new cat sniff the

Litter Training

Trays and litter ◆ Getting started

A new kitten should not go outside until at least a week after it has had all its vaccinations. A re-homed adult cat needs to be kept in the house for a couple of weeks until it has had a chance to bond with its new surroundings. During this time, or if you intend to keep your kitten or cat indoors permanently, you will need to provide a litter tray for your pet. There is a range of trays and types of litter – choose whatever best suits you and your cat. Initially, it is best to keep to the type of litter that the cat or kitten has been using previously so that it has something familiar in its new home. Change over to another type gradually if you wish.

EQUIPMENT

Litter trays vary from a simple open tray made of plastic to a covered tray with a charcoal filter in the hood to absorb smells. Cats like to scratch in litter that is at least 2.5 cm (1 in) deep, so the tray should have reasonably high sides to prevent the contents from ending up on the floor. Your choice may depend on how long you intend your cat to use the tray. If it is only a temporary arrangement, then the simplest and cheapest type is fine. If it is to be a permanent fixture for an indoor cat, consider the more sturdy, covered type, which gives the cat some privacy and security. A covered tray also keeps smells from escaping into the room and looks much less unsightly than an open tray.

There are different types of litter on the market. The most common are clay-based, wood-based, and fine-grain litter. Some have added air fresheners or scents to mask the smell of soiled litter in the tray, but if these smell strong to us they are probably even more overpowering to cats. If smells

Above: A closed tray gives an indoor cat greater privacy, and litter is less likely to be scraped on to the floor. A carbon-filter in the hood also absorbs smells and makes life more pleasant for the owner.

Left: Urine drains through to the bottom section of this tray for emptying, leaving the non-absorbent litter in the top constantly dry. Solid waste is scooped out of the top.

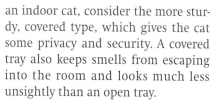

Right: A simple plastic tray is perfectly adequate for most cats.

are a problem, it is better just to clean out the tray a little more frequently. Some people use newspaper to line the litter tray, but there are drawbacks to this. Ink may come off the paper on to the cat's feet and be walked around the house and may be toxic if licked off. The cat may also come to regard all newspaper as acceptable for toileting purposes.

Place the tray somewhere quiet so that the cat is not disturbed at a time when it is rather vulnerable. Keep the tray away from the cat's bed and food bowls and make sure that dogs and toddlers cannot get into it. If you have a number of cats, provide a tray for every two cats. Initially at least, try to keep a new kitten to its own tray to minimize any disease risks.

At first, clean out the tray only every two to three days, removing the solids with a plastic scoop. This gives the cat a chance to learn to associate the smell of the litter with its toileting area. However, if you have several cats, you will need to empty and clean the tray more often, since the cats will not want to use it if it is too soiled; a dirty tray is also a potential source of infection.

Wash the tray with hot water and disinfect it weekly. Be careful in your choice of disinfectants. Cats are sensitive to certain chemicals found in disinfectants, particularly phenols. In general, it is best to avoid those that turn cloudy white when they are put in water. Dilute the disinfectant as directed on the manufacturer's instructions. Do not be tempted to use a higher-strength solution, since this could increase toxicity.

Right: Cat litter absorbs moisture and some of the smell of cat's urine and faeces. Solid waste and clumps of damp litter can be removed with a plastic scoop so the whole tray does not need to refilled every day. Many brands of the main types are available.

TRAINING YOUR KITTEN

Owners often pride themselves on 'training' kittens to use a litter tray. In fact, the mother cat has usually done most of the work. By watching her and by following their natural instincts to rake soil-type substrates, kittens learn to associate toileting behaviour with the litter tray. When you bring your kitten home, place it on the tray and move its paws through the litter. It will soon get the idea. Put it on the tray regularly, especially after it has eaten or woken up. If it should have an 'accident' then clean up with a tissue or cloth and place this in the tray as a scent reminder to help the kitten make the association you want. Never punish a kitten for making a mistake; simply place it on the tray and praise it when it gets it right.

If you want your cat or kitten to start going outdoors instead of using a tray, gradually mix some soil with the litter and move the tray closer to the cat flap or to a door to the garden. (Make sure your kitten has completed its vaccination course first.) When it is safe for the kitten to go outside, dig up a piece of ground so that it is soft and easy to use. Tip some used litter on to this so the cat associates the soil with a litter site. Cover children's sand pits or these will be seen as ideal large litter trays.

Wood-based litter

Clay-based litter

Fine-grain litter

Right: Cats are clean by nature and need little encouragement to use a litter tray. The tray must be big enough for the cat to sit in comfortably and should be cleaned regularly or the cat will not want to use it. Kittens usually learn by watching their mother and following her example.

Feeding

Types of food ✦ Feeding kittens ✦ Milk and water

Above: Cats like to feel relaxed while eating. Try to provide your cat with a quiet spot in which to eat, where it will not be constantly disturbed or trodden on.

The cat must have meat to eat and cannot survive on a vegetarian diet. It needs very specific forms of nutrients, such as vitamin A, niacin and taurine, which are found only in animal tissue. It must also have high levels of dietary protein, with the correct balance of amino acids to build body tissue, carry out repairs and implement biological reactions. The cat uses protein in the same way as humans use carbohydrate, as a source of daily calories, hence the importance of the type, quality and proportion of protein in its diet. It must also have certain animal fats, which are contained in milk, meat or fish.

Most cats are naturally 'snackers', and will eat 10 to 20 small meals a day. If you feed your cat dry food on an ad lib basis, you will notice it return to the bowl many times a day for a snack, rather than eating large amounts at once. Cats fed on moist food do tend to eat larger meals. Canned food is more likely to go off if left uneaten and perhaps cats eat more when the tin is freshly opened and the flavour, taste and smell are at their most potent.

A KITTEN'S DIET

A kitten needs to eat little and often in order to be able to ingest and digest enough nutrients to grow rapidly. It gains about 10 grams (a third of an ounce) of bodyweight per day from birth to five to six months of age. A kitten's diet must be able to provide all that it needs nutritionally, as well as give it the energy to cope with the stresses of adjusting to a new home and to combat infections that may be

Above: Dry food is good for a cat's teeth and is perfectly safe as a complete diet, as long as the cat has access to water. It is also more hygienic to leave out than moist food.

lurking in the big wide world. Its food must also contain all the necessary vitamins and minerals.

It can be difficult to get the right balance of nutrients and energy content in a diet of a fresh foods that you put together yourself. Most of the major food manufacturers make a kitten food, which you can provide for the first six months or so of life.

Left: An automatic feeder can be useful if you work long hours. The food is put into the tray and the lid set to open at a any time up to 24 hours later.

Right: Most cats live on commercial brands of moist or dry food. These are specially formulated to provide all the nutrients the cat needs. Fresh foods, such as chicken or fish, make a welcome change. Special biscuit treats can be used as an extra or as a reward.

Moist canned food

Choose a good-quality brand that suits your pet – one that your little cat enjoys eating and looks well on, and that does not cause stomach upsets. Changing diet, particularly at times of stress, such as moving to a new home, can cause digestive problems. If possible, it is best to continue with the food the new kitten or cat has been used to in its previous home for a week or so, until it has settled in.

Kittens need more frequent meals than adult cats. When you first get your kitten at 8 to 12 weeks old, it will need about five meals day. If you are out all day, one way to get around this is to provide dry food, which does not go stale as quickly as canned food and can be left out so that the kitten can help itself. You could also try using an automatic feeder – a dish that remains covered until a time you set, when the lid will open and allow the kitten access to the food. Always feed your kitten in a quiet spot where there is no competition from other cats or dogs or interruptions from young children.

When your kitten is six months old and about three-quarters grown, reduce its meals to two a day. If you are feeding dry food on an ad lib basis, then your cat or kitten will decide for itself how many meals it wishes to have every day. When your cat is fully grown – around one year old – start to monitor its weight. Most young cats are very active and excess weight is not a problem. If your cat does start to put on weight, adjust the calorie content of the food you give.

1

2

3

Above and left: There is a wide range of feeding dishes for cats. These sturdy plastic dishes (1 and 2) have non-slip bases so they do not move when the cat eats. The stainless steel dish (3) is hard-wearing and hygienic.

Right: Your cat may seem to drink very little of the water you leave out for it. Like its desert dwelling ancestors, the cat is able to obtain most of the moisture that it requires from its food and so does not need to drink a great deal of extra liquid. It is, however, important that fresh, clean water is always readily available for your cat.

Weight gain can be more of a concern with indoor cats, or with older or inactive cats. If you are worried about feeding, ask your veterinary surgeon for advice.

DRINKING MILK

Cats and kittens do not need cow's milk as part of their diet. It should certainly not be used a substitute for

clean water, which should always be available. Soon after kittens are weaned, they lose the ability to digest lactose, a sugar that is found in milk. This is why some cats cannot tolerate cow's milk and may suffer from stomach upsets if they are allowed to drink it. However, there are now specially formulated milks available for cats, which some pets enjoy.

Complete dry food

Fresh cooked chicken

Biscuit treats

Hazards

Avoiding outdoor and indoor dangers ◆ Poisonous plants

Lily of the valley

Prevention is always better than cure and the potential dangers for cats in your home and garden can be avoided with a little care. Pay particular attention to kittens. Confident and curious, they can get themselves into all sorts of trouble, and will squeeze into the smallest spaces, get into any box or bag that is lying around, or climb up to the top of furniture. Like human toddlers, they have little sense of danger and are driven by curiosity. Check the list opposite for dangers in your home.

POISONOUS HOUSEPLANTS

◆

Cats enjoy nibbling grass and may try your houseplants. Most are harmless, but some to avoid are philodendron, crotons, ivy, poinsettia, polka-dot plant, chrysanthemum, cyclamen, castor oil plant, cherry laurel, azaleas, dieffenbachia. Some cut flowers, such as lily of the valley, are also poisonous.

Poinsettia

Left: If you live in a high-rise apartment, remember that, despite their righting reflex, cats are not infallible. Watch out for open windows and consider putting up a wire mesh screen on a balcony.

Below: A cat intent on play, or chasing a fly, may inadvertently break precious possessions if it leaps up on to furniture.

♦ Keep electrical flexes out of the way if your kitten or cat tends to chew such things.

♦ Guard open fires – cats often sit too close and singe their fur.

♦ Do not leave needles, pins, sewing thread, rubber bands or other small items lying around to be played with or swallowed.

♦ Keep delicate ornaments in cabinets with the door shut.

♦ Keep the toilet seat down so that kittens cannot fall into the toilet.

♦ Keep medicines and chemicals locked in cupboards.

♦ Shut the doors of the microwave, washing machine, tumble drier and cooker in case a curious cat crawls inside. Check before you use appliances.

♦ Leave cooker rings covered with pans of water until they cool down and discourage cats from walking on the hob.

♦ Keep rubbish bins closed.

♦ Take care to use disinfectants that are not harmful to cats. They can absorb chemicals through their feet or lick them off their fur. In general, avoid those that turn milky in water. Dilute disinfectants to the correct concentration, rinse well and let the area dry.

♦ Ventilate the kitchen if you are frying with oil. Fumes from burning oil can be toxic to cats.

OUTDOORS

Cats often get shut into sheds or garages, having gone in for a quiet sleep or simply out of curiosity. There can also be dangers from stored garden chemicals or paint. When grooming, cats ingest any substance that has stuck to their fur, so be sure to clean up spillages carefully and keep lids on containers. Creosote, for example, is toxic to cats, so if you are painting a fence, keep the cat in until it is dry and do not let it brush against or walk in creosote. Take similar precautions with oil, diesel, petrol and antifreeze.

Choose any weedkillers and other garden chemicals such as slug pellets carefully, selecting the 'pet friendly' types. Store rat and mouse poison

safely and be careful when laying poison. Cats do not usually eat the poison itself, but can suffer if they eat a rodent that has taken the bait.

Cats that are allowed to roam freely outside do not often ingest poisonous plants in their own or neighbouring gardens. But cats that are confined in runs or fenced in may be more likely to chew plants out of boredom. Avoid garden plants such as monkshood, honeysuckle, clematis, box, holly, yew or ivy. Check with your garden centre when you buy a new plant to ensure that it is not poisonous. If you want to grow greenery

Above: Cats like to explore their surroundings and a curious cat can easily get itself shut into all sorts of dangerous places

specially for your cat to enjoy, try planting catnip, thyme or ornamental grass in containers.

HIGH-RISE CATS

Ensure that windows are kept shut or covered in mesh if your indoor cat inhabits a flat several storeys up. Cats do generally right themselves in a fall (see page 37), but can suffer serious injuries such as broken limbs or a broken jaw if they fall a great distance.

Lifestyles

Minimizing risks ✦ *Cat flaps* ✦
An indoor life

Above and left: A cat that is allowed outside may roam freely and its owner has little control over its movements. If your cat wears a collar with some identification you can be contacted should it stray or meet with an accident on a road or elsewhere.

side and then from the other. Let the kitten get used to the flap. Then prop the flap half open so that the kitten has to push the door a little each time and let it get accustomed to that sensation. As the kitten gets the idea, gradually shut the flap down until finally it has to push it open from a fully shut position.

Make sure that during the learning process there is nothing outside likely to pounce on the kitten as it goes through – this could put it off for life.

Some owners like to keep their cat indoors at night, or during rush-hours, when they feel it is more dangerous outside. When outside, the cat can wear a collar, which carries details of how to contact you if it gets

Until fairly recently, all cats spent some part of the day outside, hunting, patrolling territory or relieving themselves. It was not until cat litter became widely available in the 1950s that cat owners had a real choice about whether or not to let their cats out. For most people, letting a cat out is the normal thing to do and it allows the cat to lead an active and stimulating life.

USING A CAT FLAP

Once a kitten or cat is ready to go outside, most owners install a cat flap for both their own and the cat's convenience. If you live in an area with a high density of cats and you want to

make sure that only your own cat comes in through the flap, it is worth buying a flap that has a either a magnet or electronic key that is worn on the collar and unlocks the flap once the cat is close enough to it.

However, to begin with you may have to train your kitten to use the flap. If you have other cats, a kitten will probably learn by watching and imitating. If not, then it is best to educate the kitten step by step.

First of all, prop the flap open with a pencil, or stick it up with a piece of tape, so the kitten can just walk through from one side to the other. By using toys, food and praise, encourage the cat to climb through from one

---

DANGERS FOR OUTDOOR CATS

────── ✦ ──────

✦ Traffic on the road.
✦ Risk of injury by dog, human or other cats.
✦ Risk of infection with feline diseases.
✦ Risk of catching disease from infected prey.
✦ Risk of getting shut into sheds or garages.
✦ Risk of your cat moving in with someone else.
✦ Risk of poisoning.

lost. If the cat is out after dark, a reflective collar helps it to be seen.

Ensure that your cat is vaccinated against all the infectious diseases it is possible to protect against. Worm and treat your cat for fleas regularly and make sure it is neutered. If male, it will wander and fight less. If female, neutering will remove the risks of pregnancy and giving birth, and a female cat that is neutered early enough is unlikely to suffer from mammary tumours later in life.

INDOOR CATS

Nowadays more and more people decide to keep their cats indoors all the time because of the dangers outside. Some cats take to this lifestyle well, others do not. You must balance the risks and benefits or perhaps find a happy medium by fencing in part of the garden, though this can be an expensive undertaking.

The most obvious reason for keeping cats indoors is that they generally have longer, healthier lives than outdoor cats. But if you do decide to keep your cat indoors, you will need to keep it exercised and stimulated (see pages 96–7). What you have to weigh up is whether the cat is actually more contented. If the thought of dangers outside have convinced you never to let your cat out again, bear in mind that there can be problems associated with keeping your cat indoors:

✦ Risk of behaviour problems. The cat is a natural hunter and needs to use its energies in this pursuit. If it cannot go out, it may become frustrated or bored and develop problems such as indoor spraying and scratching.
✦ Risk of the cat becoming overweight (with all the potential medical problems associated with obesity) because of lack of exercise.
✦ Risk of the cat becoming oversensitive to changes within its small territory (the house) and unable to cope with new people or objects.
✦ Much greater dependence on the owner for stimulation and activity and risk of over-attachment.
✦ Difficulty of introducing another cat into a small confined territory.

Above: A cat that is able to spend at least part of its time outdoors can indulge in natural behaviour such as stalking prey and marking its territory.

✦ Difficulty of keeping doors and windows shut (especially if there are children in the house). Time and expense of putting wire over windows and balconies so that the cat cannot get out.
✦ Risk that a bored cat may get itself into mischief at home – there are many dangers inside the home, too (see page 93).

Below left: Most cats quickly learn to use cat flaps and can come and go as they wish while their owners are out. Many cat doors can be locked at night if the owner wishes.

A HAPPY MEDIUM?

The problem of keeping an active cat in a safe environment, without condemning it to a life indoors, can be partially solved by building the cat an outdoor run or fencing in some or all of the garden. A run can be made of timber and wire and should have a roof to prevent escape. To make the garden cat-proof, build a fence 1.8 metres (6 feet) high with an overhang at the top about 50 centimetres (20 inches) wide and projecting at right angles or at an angle of 45 degrees to the main fence so that the cat cannot climb out. Check with your local authority and neighbours before you start your construction.

Overhanging trees and shrubs need to be trimmed back and large trees fitted with an 'Elizabethan collar', a 50-centimetre (20-inch) wide wooden or plastic ring. This projects from the trunk about 2 metres (6½ feet) above the ground and prevents cats from climbing up the tree.

Some owners train their housebound cats to walk on a lead and harness and take them out for walks, thus giving them access to the outdoors in safety. The success of this type of exercise depends on the temperament of the cat and the effort that owners are willing to make.

Keeping an Indoor Cat Happy

Life indoors ✦
Entertainment ✦
Exercise

The cat is an active, territorial animal – its behavioural repertoire has developed around hunting for survival. In the wild, it needs to eat about ten mouse-sized meals a day, which may require as many as 30 hunting expeditions. It has to spend time and energy finding prey and avoiding danger. Even the neutered pet cat, fed at home but given access to outside, will hunt, follow its curiosity and patrol a territory, although this may only be small. Compare this to the life of the cat that is kept indoors permanently but has the same levels of energy and curiosity. While there is no doubt that cats are adaptable pets, excellent at sleeping and well practised at 'resting', they do need to use up their natural energies. How the cat reacts or copes with indoor life depends to a great extent on its personality. Some cats are quite happy to stay indoors; others may never settle, and start to exhibit behaviour problems caused by boredom or frustration. Nervous cats may feel protected indoors and are happy to avoid the perceived extra dangers outdoors. The confident, outgoing cat may need more stimulation.

If you are aware of the cat's natural behavioural needs (see pages 38–53) and try to provide plenty of exercise, companionship, and a varied and safe territory within your home, you may be able to keep your cat happy with a life indoors. It is up to you to keep a close eye on how both you and the cat are coping.

INDOOR ACTIVITY

Indoor cats need entertainment. They usually arrange their lives around the presence of their owners, waking when they come home and sleeping most of the day when they are out. You have to provide stimulus by creating new toys and games that exercise the cat physically and mentally. Some cats, usually Siamese and Burmese, learn to retrieve (or perhaps we should say they teach their owners to throw) and will play for hours.

Bear in mind that the cat's life changes drastically when you are there and then again in your absence. If your cat is very attached to you and suffers from withdrawal when you are gone, try to make the differences between your presence and absence less glaring. Ignore the cat sometimes when you are there, especially when you are about to leave. This is the advice given to dog owners whose pets suffer from separation-anxiety when they leave the house. The dogs may manifest their distress by destroying furnishings and barking or howling.

Left: Provide some greenery for your indoor cat. Sow seeds of grass, catnip, thyme or parsley every couple of weeks for a continuous supply.

Above: Provide some outdoor exercise by teaching your cat to walk on a lead with a collar or harness. Get the cat used to the lead in the house first before venturing outside. Choose a quiet spot so the cat does not panic and take things slowly so that you both build up confidence.

Cats are not often destructive, but they may deal with the stress in a variety of ways, such as spraying, scratching, or even overgrooming (see page 115). The balance between giving attention and maintaining an independent and self-reliant cat can be difficult. A cat that does not experience many changes in its life may become extra-sensitive when things

do happen – a visitor with a dog, or a new piece of furniture, can throw its life into turmoil. Make sure your cat meets lots of people when young, and has plenty of novelty so that it can cope with changes in its daily life.

Provide a scratching post – a branch or large piece of bark if you have the space, or one of the other vast array of posts that are available. Many cats may also choose their own post – the furniture, stair carpet or wallpaper – and this may be something you have to accept.

Although cats are carnivores, they do chew grass or herbs when outside. This may be to help them bring up any furballs, or possibly for certain nutrients they need. Whatever the reason, you should give your indoor cat the opportunity to chew grass by buying it or growing your own.

Indoor cats usually use up less energy than their outdoor counterparts and you may need to regulate your cat's food intake to prevent it from becoming overweight. Even a cat that has to hunt to survive sleeps between activities to conserve energy and stay out of sight. A well-fed cat that does not have access to hunting activities may sleep more and not be active enough.

Above: Provide plenty of toys and items such as boxes and paper bags to keep the cat active. Remember that toys on their own may not be very exciting – someone needs to join in. Do not leave all the toys out at once – the cat will quickly become bored with them.

TIPS FOR INDOOR CAT OWNERS
◆

◆ Plan to get two kittens instead of one. They will amuse and exercise each other while you are out and you will feel less guilty about leaving them.

◆ Cat-proof your home very carefully. A bored, inquisitive cat or kitten can squeeze through a tiny space, or pull apart netting that has not be fastened properly, to escape outside or on to a balcony or window ledge.

◆ Invest in some good clippers to keep the cat's claws trimmed. Long claws can get caught in upholstery and carpets and are also more likely to cause damage in the home. Ask your vet to show you how to clip the claws.

Grooming

Equipment ♦
Grooming routine ♦
Cleaning teeth

Self-grooming is an essential part of a cat's behavioural repertoire, and most short-haired cats keep their own coats in immaculate condition. However, because most of us live in centrally heated houses and our cats moult all year round as well as in the spring, it is worth helping your cat with grooming. Whatever type of coat it has, grooming removes loose hair and prevents the cat from swallowing it. Ingested hair can sometimes cause furballs – clumps of fur that build up in the digestive system. Most cats enjoy being brushed and this contact can help to build up close bonds between owner and cat.

For long-haired breeds such as Persians, human help with grooming is essential to prevent dense, long fur from becoming matted. Unless the cat enjoys, or at least accepts this handling, life can become very difficult for both cat and owner. If you take on a cat with this volume of hair, start grooming it in kittenhood so that it is part of the cat's normal daily routine and you both learn to relax and enjoy the contact. Trying to pin down a

Above: Most cats enjoy being groomed along the back but may not like you touching more sensitive areas. Work slowly, praising the cat all the time. If the cat becomes irritated, stop for a while, then try again.

semi-grown cat with a completely matted coat while you attempt to pull a brush through it for the first time or cut off bits with scissors, is a recipe for disaster. The cat will associate grooming with fear and pain and will fight you off in the future. Start with short, enjoyable sessions with your

kitten or cat and reward it with praise or even a favourite titbit.

Basic grooming equipment for a long-haired cat includes both a wide-toothed and a narrow-toothed comb and perhaps a brush. As the kitten's hair grows, you will find out which style of grooming and which types of brush or comb suit you both. Everyone has different techniques.

For short-haired breeds and non-pedigrees you may need only a soft brush or a grooming glove to remove dead hair from the coat. Some breeds,

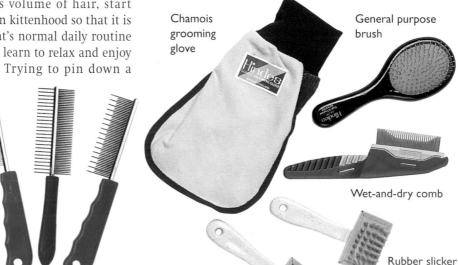

Chamois grooming glove

General purpose brush

Wet-and-dry comb

Rubber slicker brushes for removing moulting hair

Wide- and narrow-toothed combs

Left: A variety of brushes and combs is available. For a long-haired cat, use a wide-toothed brush or comb to work on any tangles and a fine-toothed comb or slicker brush to remove loose hair. A special wet-and-dry comb is ideal for use after bathing. For a short-haired cat, remove loose hairs with a fine comb or a bristle brush. A wipe with a grooming glove gives a shine to the coat.

such as the Cornish or Devon Rex, do not have guard hairs (the main part of the coat in most breeds) but only the soft downy undercoat, which is often wavy. This needs only a soft brush or even just a wipe over with a piece of Chamois leather or velvet. Use a toothbrush to brush gently around the cat's eyes and face.

TACKLING MATS

Patience is essential in tackling a badly matted coat. If you cannot get it under control, you may have to take the cat to the vet so that its coat can be shaved off under anaesthetic. This should be a last resort and it is well worth trying to untangle the coat yourself first. If the cat will accept some grooming, take small pieces at a time, hold the hair at the base and start tackling the mats at the tip. If you need to cut through a large mat in order to try to tease it out – use blunt-tipped scissors that will not stab the cat if it decides to move off half way through the process. Use your fingers or a comb or brush and very gently work down toward the skin.

CLIPPING CLAWS
◆

If your cat goes outside, it should regularly blunt and sharpen its claws during its active lifestyle and you will seldom need to clip them. However, the claws of an older or less active cat may need attention.

Ask your vet to show you how far to clip the nails back. It is important not to trim the nail too far or you may accidentally cut into a blood vessel (known as the quick) that runs down the centre almost to the tip. Special claw clippers are available that will make the job much easier.

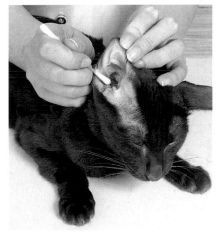

strong irritants such as perfume – to make it easier to comb through a long coat and tackle any stubborn knots. Do this while the conditioner is still on and then rinse it off thoroughly. Dry the cat, using a hair dryer and brush at the same time. An extra pair of hands will be useful throughout the bathing process.

as we do our own. If you have a new kitten, then start immediately. Stroke the side of the cat's mouth so that it gets used to you touching and pressing on its teeth and gums. Slowly and gently introduce a cleaning pad or brush and move it backward and forward and eventually in a circular motion once your cat is used to the

Above: Grooming is an excellent opportunity to check your cat's condition and spot any lumps or bumps, fleas, ticks or lice.

Above: Get a kitten used to having its teeth cleaned when it is young. There are brushes and toothpastes made specially for pets.

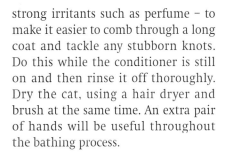

Above: If the external part of the ear looks grubby, wipe it with cotton wool. Never poke anything down into the ear.

People who show their cats may bath them regularly, but most other owners do not want or need to do this. Bathing, if it is necessary, is best begun when the cat is a kitten. Use a shampoo designed for cats, avoid the eyes, and rinse off with clean water. Use a hair conditioner – one without

EYES AND TEETH

Because of the shape of their faces Persians can suffer from watery eyes, which stains the fur around the eyes. A regular gentle wipe with damp cotton wool will keep them clean.

Veterinary dentists now suggest that we should clean our pet's teeth

procedure. Getting an older cat used to having its teeth brushed may be quite difficult and you will need to do one tooth at a time, making it as pleasant as possible. Ask your vet to show you the best technique and for advice on equipment for pets. Do not use human toothpaste on cats.

Neutering Your Cat

When to neuter ♦ *Neutering operations*

Unless you intend to breed from your cat it is best to have it neutered when it is around six months old. Deciding to have a litter of kittens, either with a non-pedigree cat or with a specific breed, is a big step. You will be responsible for the health of the queen and several kittens. This means not only looking after them but also finding new homes so that they do not join the thousands of cats left in rescue centres or put down because there are not enough homes to go around.

Deciding to breed from a pedigree cat is more complex than just letting nature take its course. You need to research the breed, choose a stud cat and have the necessary tests to ensure that your cat is disease free. You must then find out about pregnancy and

Above: This tom cat bears the scars of many battles over territory and mates. He risks catching feline diseases through bites, and the bites themselves can cause abscesses.

kittening, and how to register, vaccinate and sell the kittens. Consult the appropriate breed association for registrations and invest in a good book on cat breeding.

An old wives' tale suggests that it is best to let a cat have one litter before it is neutered. There is no scientific evidence for this (it will not change her character, calm her down or make her less nervous) and the belief is based more on human need than feline considerations. Unless you really want to have a litter and have pre-planned homes for the kittens, have

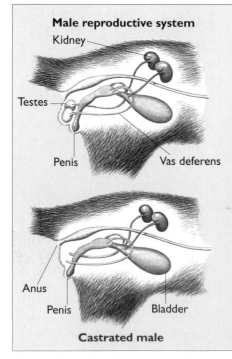

Male reproductive system

Kidney

Testes

Penis

Vas deferens

Anus

Penis

Bladder

Castrated male

WHAT HAPPENS AT NEUTERING?

♦

The castration of male cats involves the surgical removal of the testes and part of the vas deferens under general anaesthetic. The cat does not usually require any stitches and recovers from the operation quickly.

In females, the ovaries, fallopian tubes and uterus are removed under general anaesthetic in an operation called spaying. The wound is stitched and the kitten can generally return home the same day. You will have to take it back to the vet about a week later to have the stitches removed, unless soluble sutures, which are left in and eventually dissolve, are used.

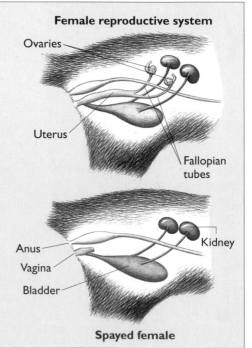

Female reproductive system

Ovaries

Uterus

Fallopian tubes

Anus

Vagina

Bladder

Kidney

Spayed female

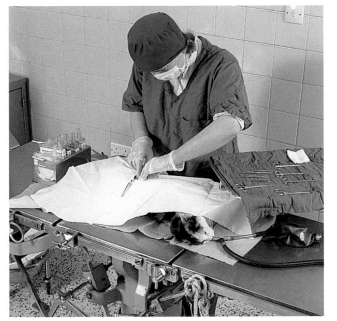

Above: Before performing a spaying operation, the vet will shave away a small area of hair. This will grow back in a month or two.

Above: The neutering of a male cat is a simple operation and the cat rarely suffers any after effects.

your cat neutered. An unneutered female cat will call on and off from spring to autumn if not mated. If you allow her to go outside, it will only be a short time before a tom will find her and she is likely to become pregnant.

Male animals also contribute to the kitten-mountain and responsibilities should be shared. Unneutered toms start to look for females once they reach sexual maturity and will wander great distances establishing territory and looking for mates. During these patrols they are likely to meet other males and some encounters end in fights, which may cause injury. Entire male animals are also likely to mark their territory more, and this may mean they spray indoors as well as out, leaving a pungent reminder of their presence. For these reasons, most people who want pet cats neuter their male animals too.

PUBERTY AND NEUTERING

Some breeds, notably Siamese and Burmese, may reach puberty early – at around five months old – whereas others, such as Persians, may take longer than average. The timing of puberty also depends on when the kitten was born. A kitten born in early spring may reach puberty in the autumn of the same year; a later kitten may not come into season until the following spring. Six months is the common age for neutering, but if your female kitten is showing signs of coming into season and 'calling' (see page 59) and toms are hanging around outside, keep her inside and book an appointment with the vet as soon as possible.

Likewise, most male animals reach sexual maturity when they are about seven months old and are generally neutered at six months. If your kitten came from a rescue centre it may have been neutered at an earlier age – sometimes as young as two to three months old. There is no evidence that early neutering causes the cat any problems later in life.

WILL MY NEUTERED CAT PUT ON WEIGHT?

Neutered animals generally use less energy than entire animals. They do not have to patrol territory, look for a mate or cope with the demands of pregnancy and lactation. They are probably more interested in eating, sleeping and staying around the house and so may put on weight. Owners need to monitor their cat's weight and feed according to activity.

Left: Allowing your female cat to have a litter is not a decision to be taken lightly. It can be great fun, but remember that a loving home will have to be found for each kitten.

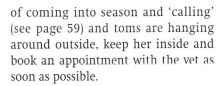

Motherhood & Cats

Cats and pregnancy ✦
Bringing baby home

*I*f there is one time in life when women receive 'advice' from friends, and even strangers, it is during pregnancy. People are always ready with tips on labour, the type of nappies to buy and ... what to do about pets. Many advise getting rid of cats, assuming that they are baby substitutes and no longer needed. Much of this 'advice' is based on old wives' tales and misinformation.

PREGNANCY

Worries about the health of an unborn child weigh heavily on the mind of an expectant mother and there seem to be potential hazards everywhere. People may warn about the dangers of toxoplasmosis and the risk of catching it from cats, as if it is something every expectant mother is in great danger of picking up. There is no need to panic: find out the facts.

Toxoplasmosis is caused by infection from a parasite called *Toxoplasma gondii*. If a woman is infected during pregnancy (especially during the first trimester), it can cause problems for the developing foetus. Cats can carry these parasites if they eat infected

Top: Once the baby is sitting up and moving around, it is more likely to be a danger to the cat than the other way around.

Right: Allow the cat to investigate all the paraphernalia before the baby arrives. Once the baby is home, you may initially want to keep its room as a no-go zone for cats for your peace of mind.

wildlife, but they can only be passed on via faeces and you have to swallow a parasite to become infected. To avoid danger, get someone else to clean the litter tray if you are pregnant or wear rubber gloves. Follow normal hygiene precautions about keeping cats off kitchen surfaces and washing your hands. Wear gloves when gardening.

Cats are not the main source of toxoplasmosis. Humans are much more likely to come across it by eating undercooked meat or vegetables grown in contaminated soil. Precautions are again simple – cook meat thoroughly and wash vegetables. Problems are rare and easily avoided by simple hygiene. If you are worried, ask your doctor for more information. Keep your cat's worming and vaccination routines up to date and there will be no more risk of the cat passing anything on to the baby than you.

Below: Babies and kittens can be great companions but need a watchful eye to make sure they do not get too close.

INTRODUCING BABY AND CAT

Bringing home your first baby can be another fraught time – how will the cat react? Once again, do not panic. Let the cat smell the baby and find out just what this strange-smelling, noisy little creature is. The wonderful thing about cats is that they adapt to almost any situation and go back to their bed next to the radiator, curl up and go to sleep.

A sensitive cat may become stressed and start to urinate in the house, but this can be overcome by increasing its sense of security (see pages 112–113) and maintaining a good hygiene regime.

Every mother has heard the old wives' tale warning that cats may sit on babies and suffocate them. Certainly, all cats love a warm spot and the cot in the nursery is usually cosy, but most cats will wait until the baby is taken out before hopping in. Suffocation is a potential danger only when the baby is very small and cannot turn over or move by itself. A little

Above: Like young children, a kitten needs lots of rest. Lack of sleep is likely to make it nervous and fearful.

care will remove all your anxieties. Make sure that the cat is not in the nursery when you leave the baby to sleep. If you do want to leave the door or window open, place a cat net over the cot (or pram).

SAFETY CHECKLIST
◆

DURING PREGNANCY
✦ Wear gloves to garden or to clean litter trays.
✦ Keep cats off kitchen surfaces.
✦ Always wash your hands after handling the cat.
✦ Worm and vaccinate the cat as usual (see pp.122-127).

CAT AND BABY
✦ Let the cat smell the baby and all its equipment.
✦ Keep the nursery as a cat-free zone initially.
✦ Shut the cat out when the baby is left alone in a cot or pram.
✦ Use a cat net on the cot and pram during the first weeks.
✦ Relax and do not cause stress to baby or cat.

CAT AND TODDLERS
✦ Protect the cat from the baby.

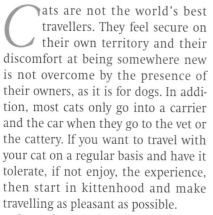

Cats on the Move

Travelling ✦ Moving house ✦ Boarding catteries

Cats are not the world's best travellers. They feel secure on their own territory and their discomfort at being somewhere new is not overcome by the presence of their owners, as it is for dogs. In addition, most cats only go into a carrier and the car when they go to the vet or the cattery. If you want to travel with your cat on a regular basis and have it tolerate, if not enjoy, the experience, then start in kittenhood and make travelling as pleasant as possible.

Invest in a good-quality carrier that is easy to use and that the cat can see out of. Avoid cardboard carriers – these are easily destroyed by a determined cat and, like wicker baskets, cannot be disinfected or cleaned.

Do not use the carrier only when you are going to travel. Get the cat used to being in it – perhaps have it as one of the cat's beds in the house. Travelling in it will then be less traumatic. When you use the carrier for travel, line it with newspaper and put in a piece of the cat's normal bedding or one of your own old jumpers that has not been washed. The cat will be reassured by the smell of owner and home. Some cats feel safer if the carrier is partially covered with a blanket.

Never leave your cat loose in the car. If it panics and gets in the way of the driver, it could cause an accident; when you open the door or window it could escape, and if you brake sharply the cat could be thrown around. Keep the cat in the carrier and place it

Below: Chose a strong, safe carrier (left) for your cat to travel in – you will need it for trips to the vet or cattery or when moving home. You should strap the carrier securely into the car (right) when travelling from place to place.

behind the seat or secure it with a seat belt so that it cannot move.

If you are making a long journey and you have an estate car, consider purchasing or hiring a kittening pen or crate so that you can provide the space for your cat to have a litter tray as well as a bed. You may have to stop and give the cat water and food (depending on what type of traveller the cat is). Never leave your cat in the car on a hot day – the temperature inside can rise extremely quickly and cause heat stroke or even death.

A NEW HOME
Cats are very attached to their own territory (often more than to their owners), so moving house can be traumatic. Comfort and reassure the cat while the packing is going on, during the journey and when you arrive at your new home. You may even choose to put the cat into a good cattery for a couple of days if you are not moving

CATTERY CHECKLIST

✦

✦ Everything should look clean, tidy and well maintained.

✦ The cats should be housed in separate runs, each with its own cabin equipped with heater, litter tray and bed.

✦ Runs should be within a safety corridor – a second skin of wire that prevents escape should a cat side-step the proprietor and get out of its own run.

✦ Each run should be separated from the one next door by a 65 cm (25 in) gap or a solid partition, to stop cats touching or sneezing over one another.

✦ Cats should look contented and the litter trays clean (or only slightly dirty if they were cleaned out earlier in the day).

✦ There should be no smell.

Above: A good cattery will have separate runs for each cat and should be clean and well managed. There should be a safety corridor to ensure cats cannot escape.

Right: Do not let your cat out of its carrier until safely inside its run.

too far and then introduce it to your new home when you have settled everything else in.

Your cat will know that something strange is going on and will probably hide under anything that has not been moved. The disruption may even cause the cat to hide somewhere away from the house and refuse to come when called, especially if your calls are growing more desperate as leaving time approaches. It is best to put the cat in a quiet room before the real move starts and leave it there until you are about to get into the car.

Transport the cat in its carrier in the car, not in the removal van. On arrival put it into a quiet room, with food and water, and leave it alone while you sort out all the furniture. Go in to visit it from time to time, but do not let it out until you are more organized. Then, with doors and windows shut, let it investigate the house one room at time. Keep the cat in for about two weeks so that it bonds to the new house as its territory.

If your cat wears a collar, make sure that your name and address have

been updated, and when you decide to let it out make sure it is hungry. Go out into the garden with the cat and walk around for a while, then let it have the signal you use for feeding time and call it in for a little food. You can do this several times, leaving it to explore a little more each time so that it knows the way back to safety before striking out into the new 'jungle' and all the wildlife there.

CHOOSING A BOARDING CATTERY

Most people need to use a boarding cattery for their cat at some time and making the right choice is vital to your cat's welfare and your own peace of mind while you are away on holiday. Always visit the cattery first and ask to look round. If you are refused, go elsewhere. Your cat will need to have up-to-date vaccinations against cat flu and feline infectious enteritis.

If the cattery proprietor does not ask for this, do not take your cat there. Such precautions are important for the protection of all cats.

Talk to the proprietors about any worries you have. Tell them about your cat's particular foibles regarding diet, handling and any medical problems, and ask if these can be catered for. Remember that the best catteries are booked up well ahead, so do not leave it until the last minute. Some people book their cat into their preferred cattery even before they book their own holiday.

Behaviour Problems

Aggression ✦ *Indoor marking and spraying* ✦ *Nervous cats*

Above: Both cats and owners can relax and enjoy a stroking and cuddling session once the behaviour pattern has been established.

Left: Aggression toward owners is, fortunately, not a common problem in cats, though it can occur in some circumstances.

Most cats live happily with their owners without any behaviour problems. Indoors, they are affectionate and clean; outside they exhibit their natural behaviours without causing harm or upset. However, owners are sometimes faced with behaviour that they find hard to accept in their pets.

What constitutes a 'problem' for one person may not for another. For example, some owners are happy to live with a cat that uses one end of an old settee or a corner of the wallpaper as a scratch post. Others cannot cope with this 'destruction'. On the other hand, few people will tolerate a cat that urinates, defecates or sprays inside the house or is aggressive.

Behaviour problems could be defined as natural behaviours in the wrong place. Most, such as spraying or scratching, are not abnormal; it is just that they should take place out of doors, not in. When behaviour problems occur, owners need to understand what is happening (see pages 38–53 for facts about natural behaviour). Try to find out the cause of the cat's behaviour (or change in behaviour) and attempt to alter it. Tackling any behaviour problem requires understanding and patience and sometimes a little detective work to find the cause.

It helps to remember that the cat is very attached to its territory. If it feels safe and confident in the house, it does not need to mark with faeces or urine and is less likely to scratch excessively. Feeling secure means that other cats do not come in and invade its territory indoors, the cat is not too frightened or intimidated to go outside, and that it is happy with the people or other pets in the household. For most adaptable cats this is no problem. Other less confident felines may be upset by small incidents and need more understanding. Remember, too, that it may not just be 'strange' cats that can cause upsets. Some cats may live with other cats in the same house in a type of truce, which can be stressful to all concerned. Many problems also occur when a new cat is introduced into a house.

'PETTING AND BITING'

The relationship between cats and people has often been referred to as a maternal one because the cat is relaxed enough to engage in kitten behaviours with us – purring, kneading and allowing itself to be groomed. However, some owners find that their cat reacts to grooming or stroking by biting or grabbing their hands, then kicking with its back feet.

When cats relax with us they are dropping their defences; they are not instantly ready to fight or take flight and their safety is in our hands. This vulnerability can be overwhelming for some cats, especially if the owner attempts to touch the stomach. This area is normally kept safe and hidden and can be a target for injury when cats fight seriously. As soon as its stomach is touched, the cat seems to think that it could be in danger and reacts. Most cats react gently; they jump off their owner's lap, take a few steps away and then turn and groom to reassure themselves that there is no real danger. Others react by being aggressive. Some cats can be triggered into this behaviour immediately, while others are more relaxed and are happy to have their tummies tickled in the same way as dogs.

Just why cats react so differently may be down to both nature and nurture. Some cats are naturally reactive; others have probably missed out on human attention at a vital time in their social development (accepting stroking is a learned response rather than a natural adult behaviour). Younger cats may become excited much more easily (like children) but this should improve with time.

Above: Children and young animals can quickly learn how to behave with each other, building bonds of friendship and trust that will last for years.

Owners can try to help their cats feel more secure with physical attention by trying a few simple methods.
✦ Watch your cat and learn to pick up the cues to any change in behaviour. Stop stroking when you notice signs such as twitching ears, dilated pupils or sudden tensing.
✦ Choose a quiet time to stroke the cat, when it can relax without other cats, people or dogs that may put it on edge.
✦ Social grooming between cats usually takes place only for a short time. Keep interactions short and learn to stop before the cat reacts. Stroking little and often, without the cat becoming defensive, will let it learn that it can relax.
✦ Reward the cat with food and praise for behaving in a relaxed way. Never punish the cat – this will only convince it that you represent a danger to be avoided.
✦ Behave in an utterly reliable, calm and reassuring way with the cat, and avoid any erratic behaviour or unpredictable movements.

AGGRESSION PROBLEMS IN HAND-REARED KITTENS

We think of hand-reared animals as being human-orientated and therefore excellent pets, and indeed many are. However, when they are older, some hand-reared animals become aggressive toward their owners if frustrated. It is thought that this is due to the fact that while humans are capable of feeding and weaning the kittens nutritionally, we do not know how to wean them behaviourally.

Just as children must learn to do as they are told so that they can cope when they cannot get their own way and fit in with social rules, queens teach their kittens the equivalent feline behaviour. Much of this learning is to do with dealing with frustration. As her milk dries up and the kittens become upset, the mother diverts their energies and attentions toward prey. In this way, they learn to deal with and redirect the frustration. Many hand-reared kittens do not learn this vital lesson and so react aggressively to frustration when they become adults, biting or attacking their owners if prevented from doing something they want to do.

Below: Some cats resort to biting their owner only if their tummy is being tickled; others may react when stroked normally. For owners of highly reactive cats, stroking can be frustrating and painful.

Indoor marking

Some homes are easily recognizable as cat habitats. There are the obvious signs, such as litter trays and food bowls, catnip mice or radiator hammocks. There may also be the more subtle signs such as a torn chair cover, threadbare stair carpet or patches of shredded wallpaper. Of course, many cats do not cause this type of destruction indoors, so why do others feel the need to behave like this in our homes?

FUNCTIONS OF SCRATCHING

Scratching has several functions, the first being the sharpening of claws so that the cat's hunting weapons are

Above: When you first get a scratching post, gently wipe the cat's paws down the post to show it what to do and to leave some scent.

Left: Do not encourage a cat by giving it attention when it is scratching indoors.

kept in order. But it is also a marking behaviour – secretions of a watery sweat from between the cat's pads leave a scent message on top of the physical marks. Cats usually scratch outside, choosing trees or posts. The wood is just the right texture to allow their claws to be dug in and drawn down, pulling off the old claw sheath to reveal the sharp point of the new. If you look at a regular scratching place, you will find these pieces of sheath embedded in the surface. Why then do cats scratch inside our homes as well as outdoors? There could be several factors at work:

✦ Exercising the claw and sharpening the points. Indoor cats with no access to the outdoors still need to undertake this behaviour as part of their natural repertoire and need a scratching post, such as a large piece of bark or a manmade post.

✦ Boredom or curiosity. A fascination with the wallpaper may occur after a loose piece invites play, or an accidental grab at the wallpaper results in an exciting game of paper removal, with the bonus of chasing

Above: Most cats choose a branch or wooden post to scratch on.

Left: Some cats find that exercising their claws on the furniture can be both satisfying and fun, though not for their owner.

the pieces that fall off. It may have an additional benefit in that owners start to take notice and give the cat attention, albeit often angry attention.

✦ Just what cats are trying to convey when they scratch is not well understood. The fact that some cats will scratch more in the presence of other cats suggests that the display may also contain an element of threat or dominance.

✦ When cats feel vulnerable, they use their ability to produce scents to 'furnish' the room with their own choice of smell (themselves) and this makes them feel secure. While they may not resort to spraying in the house, they may use the scents produced by scratching to do this.

✦ Habit. Some cats seem to enjoy the act of scratching more than others and it may become a reassuring habit.

Indoor marking

HOW TO STOP SCRATCHING

First of all, realize that the cat is not shredding your furniture out of spite or in a deliberate attempt to cause destruction. Part of the art of solving the problem is trying to decide why the cat is scratching. Is it simply that you need to provide an outlet for claw sharpening in the form of a scratch post? Place the post in front of the area that the cat is currently using.

If the damage is caused by curiosity or the satisfaction of scratching off wallpaper and playing with it, then you need to give the cat another outlet for its energies. You may have to change the type of paper you use – cats seem to like wallpaper that has raised textures – or paint the area the cat usually uses.

Where scratching is used as a form of marking behaviour, it is a hint that the cat is feeling insecure and the solution will rely on identifying the cause of this stress or insecurity. Other cats may be coming into the

house. If not, there may be conflict between resident cats or changes within the household. Perhaps the cat does not want to go outside because of nearby threats or because it is nervous and finds any new challenge threatening. Look carefully at the relationships between cats. Restrict your cat's access within the house and concentrate on making it feel secure in

Above: Indoor cats need to be kept active and stimulated as they inevitably lack the experiences of an outdoor life. Involving the cat in your everyday activities and hobbies will help enormously.

Below: An ordinary cat flap allows your cat freedom to come and go, but may also allow other cats to enter your home, leading to feelings of insecurity in your pet.

one or two rooms with a covered litter tray (see pages 88–9) if necessary. Never punish the cat. This makes it feel more insecure. You must be seen as a source of security, not a threat.

SPRAYING INDOORS

While indoor scratching may cause us irritation, indoor spraying – the depositing of small amounts of urine, with its associated smells – can test an owner's patience severely. All cats, male or female, entire or neutered, spray outside. When they start to exhibit this behaviour indoors, we need to find the cause. Spraying is a marking behaviour, bound up with the intricacies of territory, confidence and security. It is performed standing up and involves a small volume of urine being squirted backward on vertical surfaces (see page 48). It is not the same as a breakdown in litter training, when the cat urinates, usually in a squatting position, and deposits a larger volume of urine on the ground or a chair, and its motivations are also different.

A cat is more likely to mark if it is unable to cope with change. This may be because it is nervous and unable to deal with any upsets. A cat kept indoors may be sensitive to changes in its indoor territory – even smells brought in on shoes – because it is not used to dealing with threat.

Indoor spraying is a sign that the cat is under pressure. It is feeling stressed or insecure and attempting to make itself feel more confident in its environment. Causes may be similar to those that induce indoor scratching and include:
✦ New cat in the household.
✦ Strange cat also marking within the house.
✦ Aggression from cats outdoors.
✦ Decoration or building works.
✦ New baby/people in the household.

SOLVING THE PROBLEM

As with scratching, sorting out the problem lies in defining the cause, making the cat feel secure and cleaning up (as for scratching) so that the cat is not drawn to re-mark. Part of the process of passing on messages

using scents is that as they degrade, the cat is attracted back to top-up the mark or mark over another cat's scent. To stop a marking behaviour we need to remove not only the external cause but also the motivation to re-mark the area as the scent fades. This can be done by washing it with a solution of a biological washing powder, then scrubbing with pure alcohol, or even vodka; check a small area first to ensure that the colour does not run. Leave the area until it is dry or dry

Above: An intruding cat may spray if it manages to get inside your home and this will upset resident cats.

Left: Unneutered animals will be much more likely to spray, so neutering is always a first step if this is the case.

with a hairdryer and try to keep the cat away from it for a while. Stopping the cat from re-marking for a couple of days allows the smell to dissipate and helps to break the habit.

When we redecorate our homes or replace the furniture we inadvertently remove all the cat's scents, which have made it feel secure, and replace them with strong-smelling carpets, suites, paints and so on. It may be worth keeping the cat out of a newly decorated room for a little while until the new smells have mingled with the familiar smells of the house.

There is also a product now available from veterinary surgeons that is based on the pheromones cats themselves produce and aims to reduce spraying by making the cat feel secure. This, combined with the other behavioural techniques outlined above, may help you resolve the problem. A consultation with a cat behaviour expert may also help to pinpoint the cause.

Toileting problems

One of the reasons cats make such good pets is that they are usually immaculate in their toilet habits. When a cat does have one 'accident' after another, owners tend to be shocked and upset.

The first thing to do is investigate the cat's health. Has the cat been suffering from an upset stomach and not been able to get outside or to the litter tray in time? Does it have a urinary tract infection, such as cystitis, that might make it need to

Below: The cat is usually such a clean animal that any breakdown in its normal toileting behaviour is a sign that something is upsetting it or that there is a health problem.

✦ An older cat may not want to go outside in bad weather or it may be having problems with the cat flap.
✦ There may be something frightening in the neighbourhood, such as an aggressive cat ready to attack as your cat goes out of the flap or when it is at its most vulnerable, squatting in the garden.
✦ If the cat has not been feeling well and has had an accident, it may now accept that spot as a latrine because of the smell associations.

If you have a cat that has until now used a litter tray but suddenly starts to go elsewhere in the house (usually somewhere where it feels secure, such

the cat on the tray to give it tablets, creating a bad association.
✦ A new or existing cat, dog or child has upset the cat and it feels insecure using the tray.

SOLUTIONS TO THE PROBLEM
✦ Don't punish the cat – this will only make it more fearful and secretive about its toilet behaviour.
✦ If you think that the problem is caused by other cats frightening your cat outdoors or coming into the

urinate frequently? Watch your cat's behaviour and check where it has been. Look out for blood in the urine or signs of diarrhoea. If you have any worries, take the cat to the vet. If all is well, you need to discover why the cat is not behaving as normal.

If your cat is healthy and usually uses the great outdoors, there must be a reason why it has suddenly decided to use the inside of the house as a toilet. Possible causes of sudden problems with toileting include:

as behind the settee or under a table), there may be a fairly obvious reason for the change of behaviour:
✦ There may have been changes to the tray, the litter or the actual positioning of the tray that the cat may not like.
✦ The litter tray may not be cleaned out frequently enough. Cats do not like using dirty litter trays.
✦ The cat may have had an unsettling experience that it connects with the litter tray. Sometimes owners 'catch'

house, try to make your cat feel more secure by shutting the cat flap and letting your pet in and out yourself so that it feels protected. Or change to a more selective cat flap so that intruders cannot come in.
✦ If your cat has refused the litter tray because you have changed the type of litter you use, then return to the old type. If not, try some different types of litter to coax the cat back into using it. Cats usually prefer finer grained and more sand-like litter.

Left: Many cats do not like to be bothered by others when they are using the litter tray. A particularly nervous cat may prefer to have its own tray.

Below left: Providing a covered tray, which gives privacy and helps the cat feel more secure, may solve a toileting problem without the need for further action.

Below: Keeping a problem kitten or cat in a pen for a while, with its bed and a litter tray, may encourage it to become accustomed to using the litter tray again and so stop it from soiling the house.

✦ A cover on the litter tray provides extra security. Even an inverted cardboard box with a hole cut in it may suffice initially.

✦ Clean out the litter tray regularly. If you have several cats, provide one litter tray between two.

✦ Put food near where the cat is soiling to discourage the activity. Cats naturally like their toilet and eating areas to be well away from each other (for this reason, you should never put food next to the litter tray itself).

✦ Prevent the cat from returning to the 'scene of the crime'

If these solutions do not work, it may be worth confining the cat to a kittening crate or pen with its bed and a litter tray. Cats do not usually soil their beds, so they will have little option but to use the litter. What you are trying to do is to bond the cat back to using the litter as a latrine. Let the cat out of the pen when you can oversee it and put it back on the tray if you see it heading for a soiling

point or behaving as if it is looking for somewhere to urinate or defecate. If an accident does happen, clean up and place the tissue in the litter tray so that the cat learns to make the associations you want it to. The cat may get the idea within a few days or it may take a couple of weeks.

When you think the cat is ready, let it out into the rest of the house gradually, a room at a time, so you can still keep an eye on it and prevent accidents from happening.

Nervous cats

A nervous or frightened cat can make a disappointing pet, especially if it lives in a busy, noisy household. During periods of activity in the house or when visitors arrive, the cat will bolt out of the room and dive under the bed or cupboard, remaining there until it feels it is safe to come out. As a solitary species, the cat has no pack to back it up if things go wrong. If threatened, its best chance of survival is to run away and hide, staying quiet until the danger has passed. This is how the nervous cat lives and the behaviour can be difficult, if not impossible, to break.

Your chances of helping your cat become more confident depend on several factors. The first is the cat's kittenhood. Did it have human contact and a chance to learn about noises and novel situations before it was eight weeks old? If not, the cat is essentially feral – the equivalent of a wild animal – and there is very little you can do to help it to enjoy human company. If the nervous behaviour has been caused by some trauma after kittenhood or the cat is of a naturally timid disposition, you may be able, with patience and coaxing, to help the cat relearn about humans and their noises and activities.

To overcome the problem, you have to convince the cat that the rewards you are offering for staying around and being sociable are greater than those it experiences when it runs away. Bear in mind that by bolting off and hiding the cat believes that it has saved itself from a life-threatening situation – the reward is that it is still alive. What you are offering has to be good enough to beat that.

The second thing to realize is that unless the cat finds out that the 'threats' are not going to harm it, it will not change its behaviour.

WHAT CAN YOU DO?

There is no point trying to rush a cure; it takes time and patience. If you go too fast and force the cat into a situation it cannot handle, you may do more harm than good.

It may be useful to obtain an indoor crate or kittening pen for the cat's re-education. Place the pen in a corner of the room and cover it with a blanket so that the cat can see out of the front but the sides are covered. This will help the cat feel protected. Put the cat in the pen during a quiet time at first, so that it can get used to it and relax. Feed favourite treats and provide a litter tray. Let the cat view all the normal household goings-on from its safe haven and gradually add more action to its repertoire.

When the cat seems relaxed, ask a friend to visit. Normally the cat would

Left: Curing a nervous cat is a difficult, sometimes impossible, task. It is best to try to prevent the problem in the first place by encouraging kittens to become familiar with plenty of people and the sights and sounds of a typical household. They will then be able to cope with noise and bustle as adult cats.

run away when the doorbell rings, but now it has to watch and listen, albeit from the safety of its pen. You want the cat to realize that what it thinks are threats are nothing of the kind. If the cat seems to be coping well, ask your guest to feed the cat through the cage with a special titbit and offer lots of praise and soothing talk. You can then graduate to having the cat in the room without the pen and inviting visitors in (again briefed so that they behave quietly). The cat gradually learns that there is no real threat and the rewards of staying around are worth overcoming its fear.

MAD HALF-HOUR

Some cats suddenly tear around the house and then suddenly settle down to sleep again. Why do these moments of extreme activity, often known as a 'mad half-hour', occur? They seem to happen more in cats kept indoors than in those that have access to the outdoors, so it may be the result of pent-up energy.

The timing of the dashes is often dawn and dusk – the cat's natural hunting time, when its biological clock may prime it for action to catch breakfast or supper. The activity is usually stimulated by some type of trigger that sets the already excited cat off, although we may not be able to notice what high-frequency sounds or tiny movements get the cat moving. Cats seem to enjoy the activity. Perhaps it stimulates the release of endorphins and gives the cat a 'high' similar to that experienced by joggers. It may also bring on a feeling of well-being from stretched muscles, like the satisfaction humans feel after a good 'work-out'.

EXCESSIVE GROOMING

Occasionally cats seem to become obsessed with grooming – breaking off the hair and creating bald patches or even damaging the skin. Hair loss can be caused by many things, most commonly flea allergies. However, if the veterinary surgeon has eliminated all physical or medical causes, then it may be down to a behaviour problem. Grooming seems to calm cats – it may induce a feeling of well-being by releasing certain chemicals in the brain, possibly the reason why cats enjoy being stroked. If the cat feels it is in a situation that it cannot escape from or change, it may provide some relief from the anxiety by grooming excessively – a displacement activity that distracts it from the problem and makes it feel better.

As with other behaviour problems, the owner needs to find out the cause and then try to change the cat's behaviour. In Siamese or Burmese cats, which bond strongly with their owners, overgrooming may be due to a type of separation anxiety when they are left alone. In some cases, having another cat or even a dog to keep the cat company can help.

However, these 'self-mutilation' problems can be difficult to solve and you may need the help of an animal behaviour counsellor.

Below: Grooming is a natural activity that takes up a good part of a cat's day. But some cats may groom to excess and even damage their own fur. This could mean that the cat feels insecure or anxious and needs help.

The Best Start

Feeding the queen ✦ *Caring for a litter*

Deciding to breed a litter of kittens is a major undertaking. For the owners of non-pedigree cats, the main responsibilities are the care of the queen and kittens, having the kittens vaccinated and finding good homes for them. If you have decided to breed pedigree kittens, you will have to find a good stud cat, prove that your cat is not carrying certain diseases and find out the rules of the body which governs the breeding and registration of pedigree cats. This is all in addition to the normal care of the cats and the choice of owners for the kittens.

You may learn a great deal by joining a cat club associated with the breed you have chosen. They should give you advice on studs, the particular characteristics of the breed when it comes to kittens and kittening, and lead you through the rules and regulations associated with breeding and registering pedigree kittens.

HEALTH AND WELFARE
A kitten's ability to survive in the big wide world begins before its journey down the birth canal. It goes back to before its existence – the health of the queen both before and during pregnancy will play a large part in her kittens' survival.

Before the queen is mated, she should be in good health, have the best possible protection against disease (which can be helped by giving all the appropriate booster vaccinations) and be free of internal and

Above: When their mother starts to wean them, kittens can be given commercial kitten food to try. Add some water to make it lapable and present it in flat saucers that the kittens can reach easily.

Below: Healthy mothers give their kittens the best start in life. Ensure that the queen's diet is adequate and that she has had all her vaccinations prior to pregnancy.

external parasites. She should be at least 10 to 12 months old, neither under- nor overweight and be fed a good-quality diet.

The amount of food needed by the queen increases gradually during gestation. In advanced pregnancy, she needs about 70 per cent more food than usual to prevent her breaking down her own tissues to produce enough energy for her kittens. Special diets are available – the same energy-rich foods formulated for growing kittens are excellent for queens in the last three to four weeks of pregnancy and throughout lactation. Pregnant queens gain weight constantly and regularly. Extra fat laid down early in gestation is used to produce sufficient milk to support her young and cope with a large litter.

Because the kittens take up more and more space during pregnancy, the queen may not be able to eat large amounts at one time. Food should therefore be highly digestible and be fed freely throughout pregnancy and lactation so that she can snack as often as she needs.

As the time of birth approaches (around nine weeks after mating), prepare a kittening place for the queen. She may ignore you and choose her own spot, but if you can provide a kittening pen with a warm box inside she may accept it. Cut a hole in a cardboard box so that the queen can climb in and out, and line it with layers of newspaper and cotton fabric, which can be removed when soiled. Give her peace and quiet but keep an eye on her at the same time. Most cats give birth with no problem, but you may need to seek veterinary advice if any of the following signs occur:

✦ If the queen seems unwell and unwilling to eat for more than a day.
✦ If you notice a dark-coloured or smelly vaginal discharge.
✦ If she is straining excessively for more than an hour with no results.

THE NEWBORN KITTENS
Like all newborn mammals, kittens should receive adequate amounts of colostrum, an enriched milk that is produced for a short period after

birth and is vital to the kittens' defence against disease. Newborn kittens have very little subcutaneous fat to provide reserves of energy, and if they do not receive adequate nourishment they soon become de-hydrated, weak and debilitated, and may die. The nutritional management of the kittens is handled completely by the queen for the first three weeks of life and her health is vital to their well-being. Talk to your vet if you are unsure of the best diet for your cat at this time or are worried about the health of the queen or kittens.

Above: Non-pedigree kittens can be homed at seven or eight weeks if fully weaned. Breeders of pedigree kittens do not usually let them go until they are 12 weeks old and have received their vaccinations.

As kittens grow, they become more active. A pen may be useful to keep them safe when you cannot oversee them. At four to five weeks the queen will begin to reject their demands for milk and redirect their attention to solid food, be it prey or pet food. They are usually weaned by the time they are six to eight weeks old.

Above: An older cat, happy to sit quietly on a lap for long periods, may suit an older owner better than a younger animal that demands more active attention.

Care of Older Cats

Making life easier ◆ Behaviour changes

Cats are now living an average of 14 years, thanks to better nutrition, good veterinary care and preventive vaccinations. Many remain healthy and active well into their late teens and early twenties. A ten-year-old cat is the equivalent of 56 in human years; at 16 it compares to an 80 year old, and at 22 it is the human equivalent of 100.

Ageing in cats is still as much a mystery as it is in people. It is probably ruled by a genetically controlled clock and, just as some people look old and weary at 60 while others are still fit and active at 80, cats, too, vary in how they age. There is no doubt, however, that cats age a great deal more gracefully than we do. Few show signs of age, such as greying hair or difficulty in getting around, until they are well into their teens. Then they do slow down, their senses become less keen and their reflexes slower. Hearing may be affected and sight and taste dulled.

HELPING THE OLDER CAT

As our cats age we can help to make sure that their lives are as carefree and comfortable as possible. Look afresh at your cat and its environment and reassess some of the simple things. Does it find it difficult to make that leap up to its favourite perch on the windowsill and does the jump down seem to jolt its whole body? If so, provide a chair or stool so that the steps up are smaller and the exit more gentle. Likewise, is that stiff old cat flap proving a struggle to operate or snapping shut on the cat's tail, or is the step on either side too high?

Is it feeling the cold a little more because its coat is not quite so oily and well kept and it is less active? It may be time to provide a litter tray

Left: Take your older cat to the vet for an annual check up. The vet may pick up signs of various health problems, which can be more easily helped if found early.

Above: The ultimate in luxury, a sheepskin hammock provides warmth and comfort for your cat and can be used indoors and out.

inside and shut the cat in at night so that it does not need to go out in bad weather. A bed near the radiator, a heated pad or a hot-water bottle wrapped up in a towel on cold nights may help the cat to settle better.

Some old cats appreciate their eyes being cleaned by wiping with a soft cloth and warm water. Long-haired cats may need extra attention to keep their coat free from mats, especially under the tail, where they can be uncomfortable and itchy. The last thing an old cat needs is a general anaesthetic at the vet to clip its hair short because it has got beyond the stage at which a comb is of any use.

Keep an eye on the cat's claws. As well as becoming overgrown, the more brittle claws of the older cat may not retract as fully as they did when the cat was young, perhaps because the elasticity of the muscles and tendons holding them in place has decreased. The claws tend to remain slightly unsheathed and can easily catch in upholstery or carpets and cause pain and distress. Some gentle claw clipping may be necessary as a cat gets older.

EXTRA ATTENTION

The behaviour of your cat may change as it gets older. While most cats sleep more and generally get on with life

without causing a fuss, some seem to feel vulnerable and demand more attention. Some of the more vocal breeds, such as the Siamese or Burmese, can become even more chatty than usual and will certainly alert you when they need something, be it food or a cuddle, or just to know where you are in the house.

The need for reassurance can often manifest itself in 'night calling'. The cat waits until the house is quiet and then cries desperately. As soon as its anxious owners appear and show concern, the cat yawns deeply and drops off to sleep, reassured that it has not been abandoned. Understand that your cat needs security and perhaps move its bed to your bedroom, provide a radio for company or set up a baby intercom so that you can voice reassurance without getting up. Make the room warm and cosy and try to be patient – it is a small price to pay for years of love and companionship.

Above: Cats love warmth, and elderly cats will appreciate extra comforts during the chill days of winter.

Below: While older cats may still have a need to find interesting roosts, they may not find it easy to climb down afterwards.

PART 3

YOUR CAT'S HEALTH

Your vet should be your main source of advice on the health of your cat from kittenhood to old age. Ask around to find a practice in your area that has a good reputation among cat owners. Consider the following factors:

◆ Expertise – try to find a practice that has a particular interest in feline medicine. Some even specialize in cats or have separate waiting areas for cat owners.

◆ Staff – caring, understanding veterinary and lay staff, who will take time to explain matters to you.

◆ Premises – well equipped and maintained, with a full range of diagnostic, nursing and surgical facilities.

◆ Cost – look for a practice that provides good value for money, but not necessarily the cheapest. Always ask about the cost of any necessary procedures in advance.

◆ Emergency care – find out about the out-of-hours service that the practice provides. If possible, choose one that you can reach fairly easily in an emergency.

General Care

*Signs of ill health ✦ Neutering ✦ Vaccination procedures ✦
Cat illnesses and human health*

Owners become very attuned to the normal behaviour patterns of their pet cats and can often sense that something is amiss before any more obvious signs of illness become apparent. It is always better to seek veterinary advice too soon, rather than to wait until what may start as a relatively minor problem becomes more serious.

Some cats are naturally fussy eaters, and it may not be abnormal for them to go off their food for a day or two. Others are normally voracious and an owner knows there is a problem if they miss even one meal. Generally speaking, if your cat is off its food but otherwise well, you can afford to wait for a couple of days to see if its appetite picks up again.

If the cat is running a temperature, its body may feel hot when held, but it is also likely to seem listless as well as refusing to eat. Look for any puncture wounds on the body that may indicate that your cat has been in a fight and is developing an abscess – one of the most common causes of health problems in domestic cats that are allowed to go outdoors.

Repeated vomiting, significant bleeding, convulsions, severe diarrhoea, extreme weakness or laboured breathing are all examples of more serious signs of disease that require immediate veterinary attention. Constipation can be a relatively minor problem that will respond to treatment with laxatives, but a male cat that strains to pass urine needs urgent attention. This could be a sign of a urinary obstruction, which must be cleared by a veterinarian without delay to prevent any permanent damage to the kidneys or bladder.

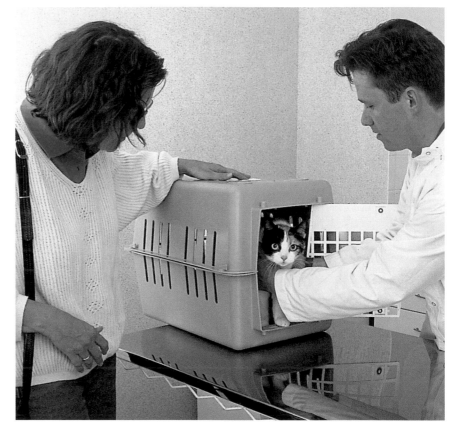

Above: Always take your cat to the vet in a carrier. Modern plastic carriers are safe and easy to clean.

Right: If there are signs of ill-health, the vet may check the cat's temperature. The thermometer is inserted into the cat's rectum – definitely a task for the professional. The normal body temperature for a cat is 38.6°C (101.5°F).

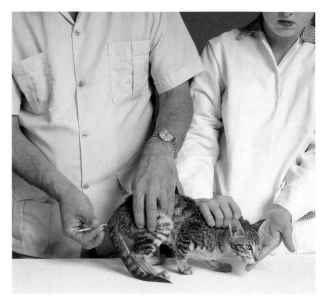

Check your cat regularly for any signs of ill-health

Eyes – should be wide open, bright and free of any discharge

Ears – redness, irritation, or the presence of an abnormal smell or a waxy discharge can all be signs of ear disease

Mouth – check for sore gums, ulcers in the throat or on the tongue, an abnormal smell (halitosis), or pain and discomfort when eating

Nose – a discharge can be a sign of an upper respiratory infection or a problem within the bony chambers of the nose itself

Coat – a matted or 'staring' coat may indicate that the cat is not grooming itself properly. Check for parasites and for dark, gritty flea droppings

Anus – soiling around the anus may indicate that the cat is suffering from diarrhoea. You may also see small white tapeworm segments stuck to the hair in this area

NEUTERING

Neutering of domestic cats is essential to help keep the cat population under control and to reduce the number of unwanted kittens. In the case of males, it also reduces behavioural problems such as roaming far afield, fighting and the spraying of very pungent-smelling urine. Unless you decide to breed from your cat, females are generally neutered at around five months old, since they are unlikely to become pregnant before that time, and males shortly afterwards.

Cats can also be neutered at any time after this, but females should not be in season or feeding young at the time of the operation.

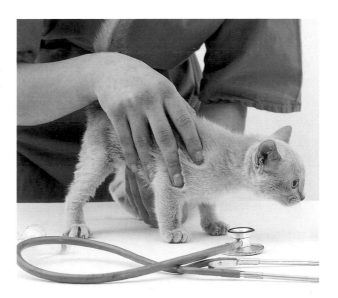

Left: A vet's trained hands and eyes can quickly assess the health of your cat. Sometimes a more detailed examination may be required, using instruments such as a stethoscope, or even ultrasound and X-ray equipment.

General Care

VACCINATIONS

The exact vaccination protocol will vary depending on the disease risks in your particular area, but kittens are usually injected at nine and 12 weeks of age, with a combined vaccine. This protects them against feline enteritis, cat flu, feline leukaemia virus and, in some countries, rabies. Full protection will not be achieved until at least a week after the second injection, and the kitten should be isolated, as far as possible, from any sources of infection until then. The vaccination appointment is also an excellent opportunity to talk to your vet about caring for your new kitten and matters such as feeding, neutering, worming and methods of flea control.

Most veterinarians recommend that cats receive an annual booster vaccination to maintain the protection against disease. This should be preceded by a health examination to ensure that your cat is in a fit state to be vaccinated and is not showing any signs of illness. As your cat gets older, this regular check-up becomes even more important – the sooner any problems that develop are detected, the greater the chance of successful treatment or control.

HANDLE WITH CARE

Although the health risks from a responsibly kept cat are small, there are some cat diseases that can be passed on to humans.

Toxoplasma is a parasite. It rarely causes illness in cats, but is often excreted by them and can cause health problems in humans, particularly in pregnant women or people with a compromised immune system. Those at risk should avoid cleaning out cat litter trays or taking on a cat for the first time, although evidence now suggests that undercooked meat is a far more common source of infection.

Cat scratch fever is another illness that is not relevant to cats themselves but can be transmitted from cats to

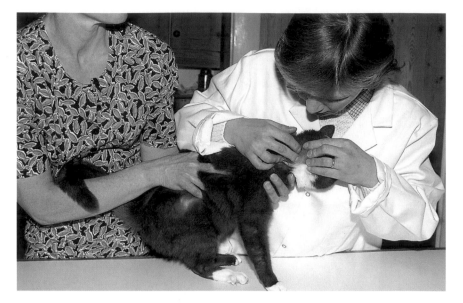

Above and left: It is important that only healthy animals are vaccinated, and the vet will carry out a thorough health check before administering vaccine to your pet.

Right: A single injection can usually be given against all the major diseases, but kittens will require a course of at least two injections, usually three weeks apart. A booster is then given each year.

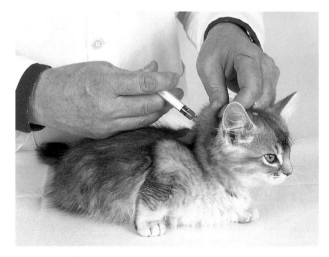

humans. It is thought to be caused by a bacterium called *Bartonella henselae,* and can result in fever and swollen glands in humans who are scratched or bitten by a cat. In rare cases, it can attack the nervous system. Any cat bites and scratches should always be disinfected thoroughly and receive medical attention if they show any signs of becoming infected.

Rabies can pose a serious health threat to humans. Anyone bitten by a

DISEASES THAT CAN BE PREVENTED BY VACCINATION

◆

FELINE PANLEUCOPAENIA
(Infectious enteritis)
Now much less common due to the highly effective vaccine, this viral disease can cause severe vomiting and diarrhoea in young cats and can rapidly prove fatal.

CAT FLU
This upper respiratory disease can be caused by a variety of different agents (see page 133 for more information), but the cat flu vaccine only protects against the two major viral causes: feline viral rhinotracheitis virus and feline calicivirus. Fortunately, the vaccine generally does give a good level of protection against this common disease, and vaccinated cats that do go down with cat flu will usually only get it very mildly.

CHLAMYDIA
Another agent that can be the cause of cat flu, this usually just results in a chronic conjunctivitis. The vaccine is generally only used in cattery situations, where there is a particular problem with this disease.

RABIES (see page 130)
This viral disease is endemic in the wildlife in some parts of Europe, with the fox acting as the main reservoir of infection, particularly in Central Europe. It poses not only a serious threat to animals that may become infected but also to humans, since death inevitably follows once the virus attacks the nervous system. In some countries, feline rabies vaccination is optional, but in areas with a particularly high risk it is compulsory. In the United Kingdom, vaccination is not permitted at present since the disease is kept out by strict quarantine regulations for all dogs and cats entering the country. However, this policy is under review.

FELINE LEUKAEMIA VIRUS (see page 128)
This agent is the commonest cause of cancer in cats. The chances of your cat contracting this disease can be greatly reduced if it is vaccinated against it from kittenhood. Some vets recommend a blood test before vaccination to ensure that the cat is not already a carrier.

FELINE INFECTIOUS PERITONITIS
(see page 129)
A vaccine to prevent this viral disease has been developed in the United States, but it does not offer a good level of protection and is not available in most European countries. It is hoped that a more effective vaccine will become available in the future.

A red fox, the main reservoir of rabies in Europe

Above: Your vet may check your cat's claws but cats do not generally need to have their claws clipped if they can go outdoors or have access to a scratching post. Scratching helps pull off the the old, dead claw to leave a new sharp one underneath.

cat in an area where rabies is known to be a problem should seek medical advice without delay.

Salmonella bacteria are a common cause of severe food poisoning both in humans and many species of animals. Infection may be contracted by eating contaminated food, particularly raw or partially cooked meat, and from other animals or humans in the household. In cats, salmonella causes acute diarrhoea, sometimes with vomiting. The cat is often unwell and running a temperature.

Cats infected with the salmonella organism may pass it on to humans. Strict hygienic precautions should be followed with cats that are suspected of suffering from food poisoning. Clean the litter tray thoroughly with disinfectant; wash hands regularly after handling, and keep cats away from food preparation areas. The animals may remain carriers of the organism for a considerable length of time after infection.

Some skin problems can also be contracted from cats, but most are relatively minor. Flea bites are the commonest problem. Although the fleas cannot live on humans, they can cause a very itchy rash, as can ear mites. Ringworm can also be spread from cats to humans.

Parasites

Flea control ✦ Ticks and mites ✦
Internal parasites

Fleas are the commonest skin parasite of cats in temperate areas such as Western Europe. Wingless insects, they are generally brown in colour with a flattened body. Their powerful legs enable them to jump considerable distances and leap up on to their hosts. Cat fleas thrive in the warm, humid environment found inside most modern homes throughout the year. Fitted carpets have made life easier still for the flea and, since these parasites may cause considerable irritation to owners as well as their cats, a major industry has grown up around controlling the problem.

In order to tackle fleas, you need to know a little about their life cycle. Adult fleas live on the cat, but are

feed upon dead skin cells from their host and the faeces of the adult flea. These contain mainly dried, undigested blood. After about two weeks, each larva forms a pupa in a protective cocoon, and can then lie dormant for months, or even years if left undisturbed. The immature flea can quickly emerge from its cocoon in response to

Pupal cocoon

Adult flea

The adult flea feeds and breeds on the cat. Its eggs drop off into the environment, where they incubate and hatch into larvae. The larva feeds mainly on shed skin cells and flea dirt. It then forms a pupa, which can lie dormant in its cocoon for many months, waiting for a host.

Eggs

Larva

Left: A cat infested with fleas is often seen scratching, but it may over-groom to the point that its hair is worn away and the skin becomes inflamed.

Right: Fleas move fast and can be difficult to spot on your cat. But their droppings, which consist mainly of dry, undigested blood, are easily seen on parted fur.

equally at home on dogs. They suck blood, mate and, during their lifetime of about two weeks, each female lays about 200 eggs. The eggs fall on to the ground, where they mature and hatch out into larvae. These tiny maggot-like creatures crawl downward and away from light, where they

vibrations and carbon dioxide, both of which may indicate that a likely victim is in the area. If not immediately able to jump on to its new host, the flea can wait for up to eight weeks for a meal to walk past.

Environmentally friendly preparations should be used to reduce the

numbers of immature fleas around the living area of the cat. They are not able to act against the pupae, but can kill off the young adults as soon as they hatch out, or stop the flea eggs from developing. Some preparations that are used on the cat itself can help to control fleas in the environment if they are present in the dead skin cells that are shed from the cat and eaten by the larvae. Insect development inhibitors can be given to the cat by mouth once a month, or by six-monthly injection. The inhibitors are taken up by the adult fleas when they feed and affect their young, making them unable to hatch normally. This is because they cannot produce chitin, which makes up the hook on an immature flea's head that it uses to break out of the egg.

Insecticides come in many different formulations and are designed to kill the adult fleas on cats. The older organophosphorus insecticides have been largely replaced by more modern alternatives, and the safest, most effective products are available from your vet. Spot-on formulations, which require a few drops to be placed on the back of the animal's neck once a month, are popular with cat owners for their ease of application.

OTHER CREEPY-CRAWLIES
Ticks are commonly found attached to the skin. Like fleas, they are flight less blood suckers. They feed only once a year, filling up their sac-like bodies with blood and then dropping off to breed on the ground. Cats generally pick up ticks when they brush through long grass, since the immature 'seed' ticks climb up the grass and grab on to any likely meal that walks past. They are, therefore, most common around the head and ears. Ticks should not be just pulled off, since their mouthparts are embedded into the cat's skin and will break off and start a skin reaction. Kill ticks with an insecticidal product, and only pull them off once they are dead.

Skin mites do not often cause a problem in cats, but *Cheyletiella yasguri*, causing chronic skin irritation and scaliness, particularly along the back, is sometimes seen. It is most common in long-haired pedigree cats, and may also cause a rash on owners', skin where they touch the cat.

Ear mites are much more common, and they are often passed on by the mother to her offspring. They live down the ear canal, causing a chronic

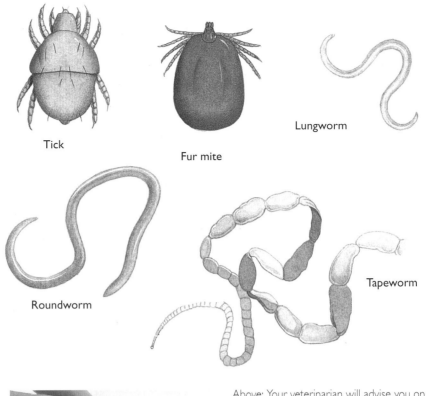

Tick

Fur mite

Lungworm

Roundworm

Tapeworm

Above: Many owners find it difficult to spray their cats with insecticides. New, highly effective products are available that are simply squeezed on to the back of the cat's neck.

irritation and the production of large amounts of black, crumbly wax, upon which they feed. Killing the adult mites is quite easy, with the use of the correct ear drops, but their eggs are more resistant and it is essential to continue the treatment for at least three weeks so that any eggs are killed off as they hatch out. There is an injectable drug for killing off mites in cats that cannot be treated with drops, but the product is not licensed for use in the cat and has to be used at the owner's risk.

WORMS
Roundworms are generally picked up when cats eat wildlife, such as birds or rodents, but they can be passed

Above: Your veterinarian will advise you on the best product to use against worms and ticks. Modern preparations can get rid of the most common types of worm in one dose.

directly from the mother. In kittens, worms can cause severe debilitation and even intestinal obstruction, but they rarely cause problems in adults, although many cats do shed the microscopic eggs and may even pass or vomit up adult worms.

A tapeworm has to pass through an intermediate host, such as a flea, before attaching itself to the wall of the host's intestine with its hooked head. It sheds rice-like segments, which may be seen stuck to the hairs by the anus, that contain large quantities of eggs. Tapeworms cause loss of weight and general body condition in the host and may also result in problems in the digestive system.

Lungworms are commonly found in the lungs of cats, but only rarely cause significant clinical signs of illness, such as coughing. Tiny larvae are coughed up or passed in faeces, and must then pass through an intermediate host before they infect another cat.

Active, outdoor cats should be wormed every three months, or more often if worms are seen.

Cat Viruses

Feline leukaemia virus ✦ *Feline immunodeficiency virus* ✦ *Feline coronovirus*

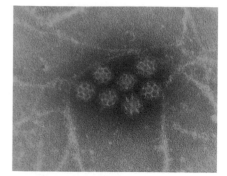

Many of the major infectious diseases of cats are caused by tiny virus particles, usually transmitted via faeces and saliva.

AIDS-LIKE SYNDROME

Feline leukaemia virus (FeLV) can affect the cat's immune system. It causes an AIDS-like syndrome that makes the cat's body less able to defend itself against infection. The virus can also attack the blood cells, causing severe anaemia (a deficiency of red blood cells), infertility and cancers of the white blood cells, often some time after the cat's original exposure to the virus. These include leukaemia, a cancer of the white blood cells circulating in the blood stream, and lymphosarcoma, a cancer of the white blood cells within the lymphatic tissue in the body.

The clinical symptoms of FeLV depend upon where in the body these growths develop, but problems in the lymph nodes of the chest in young cats and in the intestines of older cats are particularly common. The virus is spread by close contact via saliva and faeces and is an important cause of ill-health and even death, particularly in young cats.

The disease is readily diagnosed by means of a blood test, although if a cat proves positive on an initial blood screening, it should be retested after six weeks to see if it has managed to eliminate the virus from its blood. There are no drugs that can kill the virus once a cat is infected, but the problem can be controlled by vaccination (see page 125). Any cats that are introduced into an existing colony should first have a blood test for feline leukaemia virus.

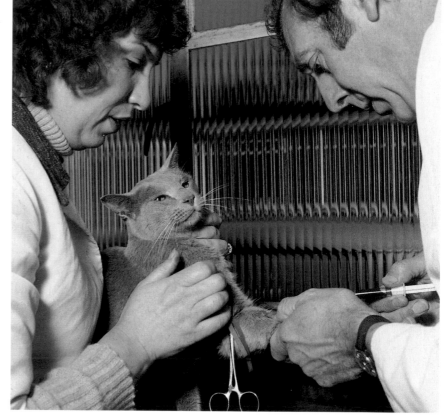

Top: Viruses are the smallest form of life but they can cause severe problems for cats. Antibiotics do not have any effect against viruses, so vaccination is essential.

Above: The signs of illness caused by a viral infection can be non-specific, and a blood test is often needed before the vet can reach a firm diagnosis.

IMMUNODEFICIENCY VIRUS

Feline immunodeficiency virus (FIV) is quite similar to the human immuno-deficiency virus and may also affect the immune system, causing AIDS (acquired immune deficiency syndrome). This can lead to a wide range of clinical signs of illness because the cat is unable to cope with challenges by infectious agents that might otherwise be kept under control. These include wounds that fail to heal, gingivitis or sore gums, chronic respiratory infections, diarrhoea, as well as general malaise, fever and poor appetite.

The virus is spread mainly by saliva to blood contact, so is particularly common in young male cats that fight frequently. Although diagnosis by means of a blood test is relatively straightforward, there is no treatment that can be given to kill off the virus itself and, at the present time, no vaccine that can be given to protect cats against infection.

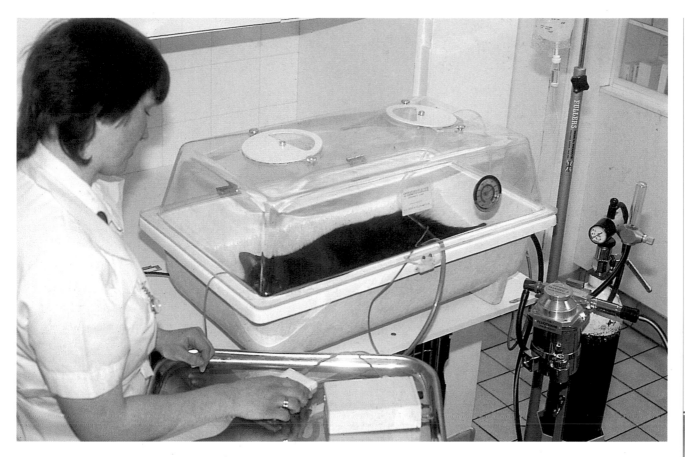

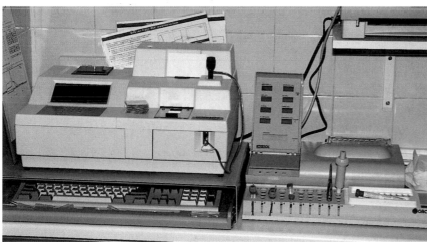

Above. A seriously ill cat may need nursing in an intensive care unit, where all its vital functions can be monitored.

Left: Some simple tests for viruses can be carried out in a practice laboratory, but blood samples may have to be sent to a specialized facility for analysis. Larger veterinary practices are now equipped with blood analysers that provide information about a cat's blood cells and organ function.

OTHER VIRUSES

Feline coronavirus is transmitted via faeces and saliva and is particularly common in households with several cats. It is highly infectious, but only a small proportion of cats that come into contact with the virus actually develop the disease. Therefore a large number of cats may show positive for the virus on a blood test yet not be suffering any ill effects.

The disease infectious peritonitis can take two forms – wet, or dry – and occurs in young and middle-aged cats. The wet form is the most common, and results in an accumulation of a viscous amber fluid in body cavities such as the abdomen and the chest, leading on to breathing difficulties and/or a distension of the abdomen.

In the dry form of the disease, multiple soft tissue swellings develop on the linings of the body cavities, including the area around the brain, resulting in neurological signs such as abnormal behaviour, blindness and even convulsions. This is a difficult disease to diagnose while the cat is still alive, and is one of the more common reasons for a cat being chronically unwell without any easily identifiable cause.

Other viruses that can infect the cat include feline panleucopaenia (see page 125), the cat flu viruses (see page 136) and cowpox, which can cause skin lesions in cats. In rare cases, the cowpox virus can also be transmitted to humans.

Urinary & Digestive Problems

Kidney disease ✦ Excessive thirst ✦ Gastrointestinal problems

Kidney disease is a common problem, especially in elderly cats. The many manifestations of disease include the following:
✦ Infection
✦ Kidney stones
✦ Tumours
✦ Physical injury
✦ Poisoning (with chemicals such as antifreeze)
✦ Auto-immune disease (attack by the body's own immune system)

However, the main cause of kidney disease is simply long-term scarring, known as chronic interstitial nephritis, due to wear and tear over the years. The first sign of kidney problems is an increase in thirst, followed by poor appetite, weight loss and bad breath; these symptoms then lead to vomiting, dehydration and death.

Blood and urine tests will help to detect problems at an early stage, when treatment is most likely to be effective. Cats with kidney problems suffer from a build-up of phosphorus and waste products such as urea, which are produced when protein is broken down within the body and then cause further damage to the kidneys. A special diet that is low in phosphorus and has fairly restricted levels of good-quality protein may do a lot to slow down the progression of the disease.

URINARY TRACT DISEASE
Feline lower urinary tract disease (FLUTD) is a very common condition that causes inflammation in the cat's

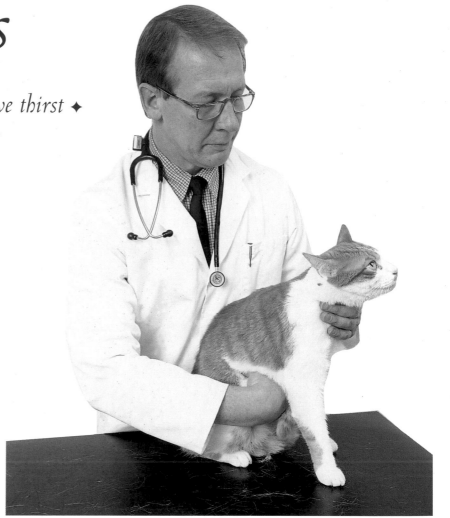

Above: A vet carefully palpates the abdomen of a cat suffering from a gastrointestinal problem. In particular, it may be possible to feel if there is an intestinal obstruction.

urinary tract. If the bladder is inflamed, it will cause signs similar to those of cystitis in humans, but since the problem is often caused by a build-up of crystalline material in the lower urinary tract, it may also cause an obstruction to the outflow of urine from the bladder.

This is especially common in male cats, because the urethra (the tube that carries urine from the bladder to the outside) is much narrower than in the female. An obstruction can cause

irreversible damage to the bladder and kidneys unless quickly cleared. It is vital that urinary straining in a male cat is treated as an emergency and not confused with constipation.

There is no one factor that causes urinary tract disease to develop, but it is most common in overweight, inactive cats that live indoors. Infection may sometimes be present, but is not often a primary cause of the problem, as it is in humans. The acidity of the urine that the cat passes plays a major role in the development of the disease. The commonest form of crystal, called struvite, tends to form if the urine is too alkaline. If the urine is too acidic, a different type of crystal,

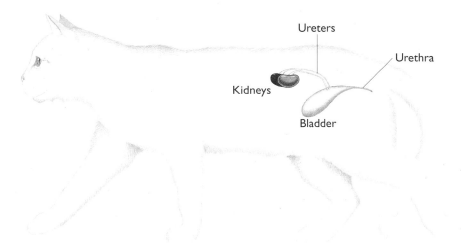

Above: The cat has two kidneys that connect to the bladder via the ureters. The urethra takes urine to the outside, via the vagina in the female and the penis in the male. The male's urethra is narrower than the female's and is more prone to obstruction from debris in the urine.

known as oxalate, may form. Since magnesium forms a major part of struvite crystals, it is also helpful to keep the levels of magnesium in the diet as low as possible in cats that are prone to the condition. Special diets have been developed to dissolve the crystals and to help prevent them from re-forming.

EXCESSIVE THIRST

Polydipsia, or excessive thirst, can be an important sign of disease in the cat, and should not be ignored. It can be difficult to tell when cats are drinking more than normal since they often drink outdoors, but watch out for any changes in drinking patterns. Common causes of an excessive thirst in cats include:
✦ Kidney disease (see above)
✦ Hyperthyroidism caused by a growth in one or both of the thyroid glands in the neck. This causes excessive appetite, thirst and weight loss, eventually leading to heart failure and death. The growths are not usually cancerous and can be surgically removed to cure the condition.
✦ Diabetes mellitus, or sugar diabetes, caused by an inability of the pancreas gland to produce enough insulin, or a resistance of the tissues

in the body to its effect. It causes blood sugar levels to be raised and spill over into the urine. This can be detected by a simple urine test. As the condition becomes more advanced, poisons called ketones build up in the body and eventually cause coma and death. More common in overweight cats, diabetes can sometimes be controlled by diet alone, but more often requires daily insulin injections to keep it under control.
✦ Diarrhoea may cause an increased thirst due to excessive water loss from the body. Owners of cats that have access outdoors do not always realize that their cat has diarrhoea.

Below: Some cats are never seen drinking. If a cat suddenly begins regularly lapping at water or drinking from an unusual source such as a garden pond or a dripping tap, it could be a sign that something is wrong.

✦ Hyperadrenocorticalism, or Cushing's disease, is a hormonal imbalance that can cause polydipsia and results in an overproduction of cortisone by the adrenal glands, situated close to the kidneys. Treatment with corticosteroid drugs, such as prednisolone, can cause similar signs.

GASTROINTESTINAL DISEASE

Although cats are fastidious eaters and are generally much less prone than dogs to digestive upsets from eating unsuitable food, dietary factors are still the major cause of vomiting or diarrhoea in cats. To some extent, vomiting is a natural process designed to rid the body of indigestible matter, such as fur or feathers that may have been swallowed. Perhaps the most common cause of gastroenteritis in cats is inflammatory bowel disease, which is thought to be an allergic reaction to some particular substance in the diet.

Most upset stomachs in the cat respond to conservative treatment. Withhold food for 24 hours if the cat is vomiting, and then start giving a bland, low-fat diet, such as white meat and rice, little and often. If the vomiting is severe and repeated, the diarrhoea contains significant amounts of blood, the cat is otherwise unwell, or the symptoms persist for more than 24 hours, do not hesitate to seek veterinary assistance.

YOUR
CAT'S HEALTH
*Urinary &
Digestive
Problems*

131

Circulatory & Respiratory Problems

Heart disorders ◆ Coughs and colds

YOUR
CAT'S HEALTH
*Circulatory &
Respiratory
Problems*

132

Left: A kitten should have its heart checked for any signs of congenital heart disease.

Some cats have congenital defects of the heart, but such conditions are rare. Heart problems are most commonly seen in older cats, and are often secondary to an underlying condition. These include hyperthyroidism, which causes the heart to beat so quickly that it begins to fail, and a deficiency of the amino acid taurine, which causes a flabbiness of the heart muscle. Heart problems tend to lead to laboured breathing because they often lead to the accumulation of fluid on the chest.

Cats do not have heart attacks due to coronary thrombosis (clogging up of the arteries with fatty deposits) in the same way as humans do, but they may suffer from a condition known as aortic thrombosis. In this condition, a blood clot forms in the main artery to the hind legs, causing sudden hind-limb paralysis. It is usually caused by an underlying heart problem, so the outlook for treatment is not good.

Anaemia is not a disease in itself, but a reduction in the number of circulating red blood cells. This may be caused by blood loss, viral infection, bone marrow disease, dietary deficiencies, or a parasite called *Haemobartonella felis*, which attacks the red blood cells. It causes weakness and rapid breathing, and may eventually prove fatal if the underlying cause is not identified and corrected.

Right: A cat that is suffering from a heart problem may have an enlarged heart, which will be visible on an X-ray. A heart of normal size is pictured in the X-ray on the left, while the X-ray on the right shows an enlarged heart.

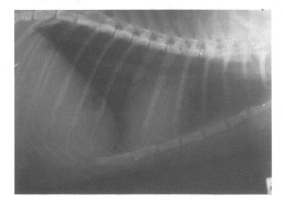

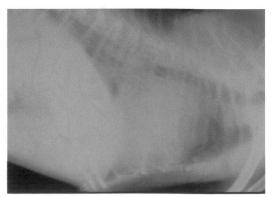

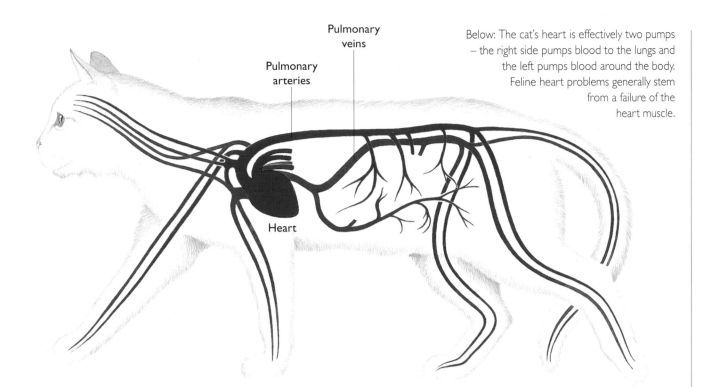

Pulmonary
veins

Pulmonary
arteries

Heart

Below: The cat's heart is effectively two pumps – the right side pumps blood to the lungs and the left pumps blood around the body. Feline heart problems generally stem from a failure of the heart muscle.

RESPIRATORY DISORDERS

A common upper respiratory illness in cats, cat flu may be caused by one or more agents. Commonest and most severe are feline herpesvirus and feline calicivirus, both of which are included in the standard flu vaccinations. Cat flu causes runny nose, sneezing, conjunctivitis, drooling (sometimes due to ulcers in the mouth), general malaise and a loss of appetite. It is spread in aerosol form by sneezing, but cats cannot catch colds or flu from humans.

Antibiotics can be used to control secondary bacterial infection, but there are no drugs that can kill off the flu virus once it has infected the animal. Careful nursing is essential (see page 144).

Trachea

Nasal
passage

Lung

Bronchi

Above: The respiratory system of the cat is similar to that of most mammals. Air passes down the trachea, which splits into two main branching bronchi, one to each lung. In the lungs, oxygen passes into the blood and carbon dioxide passes out.

YOUR
CAT'S HEALTH
*Circulatory &
Respiratory
Problems*

133

CHEST PROBLEMS

Coughing in cats is most commonly caused by chronic bronchitis, or by asthma, which is a reaction to inhaled allergens such as house dust mites. Lungworms can also cause transient coughing in cats. Although cats sometimes do suffer from pneumonia, it is more common for them to get pleural effusions – an accumulation of fluid around the lungs. This can be due to an injury, tumours, feline coronavirus infection (see page 132), heart disease, or a buildup of pus caused by a bacterial infection. Blood tests and radiographs are usually necessary to establish the cause of a chest problem, which can then be treated or controlled with drugs such as antibiotics or anti-inflammatories.

Right: Chest X-rays can be useful for diagnosing respiratory problems in cats. This X-ray shows that this cat has fluid on the lungs. The fluid may be caused by a number of conditions such as injury, infections or heart disease.

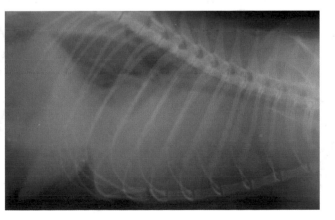

Common Skin Problems

Dermatitis ✦
Causes of skin problems

Left: Ringworm is a fungal infection that grows on the cat's hairs. It is quite common in kittens.

Feline allergic dermatitis is by far the most common skin problem in cats. The skin irritation is caused by an allergic reaction, and in the vast majority of cases this is brought on by flea bites. Anyone who has been licked by a cat knows how abrasive its tongue is, and a cat can quickly produce scabby or highly inflamed patches by licking irritated skin. Such patches often take the form of miliary dermatitis – multiple small scabs along the back – but can cause baldness, mainly on the tummy.

Any cat with skin irritation should initially be treated for fleas (see page 128). Even an occasional flea bite can start off the condition. If you do not see the fleas themselves, you may well notice the dark specks of flea dirt. You can easily distinguish these from grit by putting them on to a damp piece of cotton wool – flea droppings consist mainly of dried blood and they dissolve to leave a red halo. Other possible triggers of allergic dermatitis include dietary allergies and atopy – a reaction to inhaled substances – but these are much less common.

Anti-inflammatory drugs, and possibly antibiotics, may be necessary to get the problem under control. Evening primrose oil contains large amounts of gamma linolenic acid, which helps to reduce the level of itchiness in the skin in many cats. The oil can safely be given for extended periods to cats with this condition if the cat is relatively easy to dose with medicine, but it will only be effective for as long as it is given.

To keep a skin condition from recurring, however, the triggering factor must be identified and removed.

Below and right: Ringworm can be passed from cats to humans. In cats, it tends to look like a scaly, bald patch (right), but in humans the typical ring-shaped lesion is more easily visible (below). The relatively hair-free skin of humans makes the condition easy to treat.

COMMON CAUSES OF SKIN DISEASE IN CATS

✦ Parasites (see page 128) – lice as well as fleas may attach themselves to the hairs of the host animal and suck blood. The eggs are stuck firmly to the hairs and are visible as nits. A tiny mite called *Cheyletiella* may also set up home on the surface of the skin, causing some scurfiness and itchiness. Safe and effective products for controlling skin parasites can be obtained from your veterinarian.

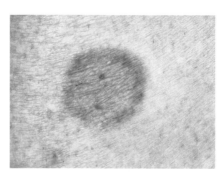

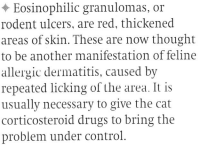

Left: Abscesses caused by bites are common in cats. Infection is injected under the skin by the attacker's sharp canine teeth and builds up until the abscess bursts open. Regular bathing in a solution of one teaspoon of salt in bowl of water will help, but antibiotics may also be needed.

Below: Rodent ulcers on the lips can be caused by repeated licking, triggered by a skin problem. They usually respond to treatment with anti-inflammatory drugs.

✦ Eosinophilic granulomas, or rodent ulcers, are red, thickened areas of skin. These are now thought to be another manifestation of feline allergic dermatitis, caused by repeated licking of the area. It is usually necessary to give the cat corticosteroid drugs to bring the problem under control.

✦ Skin infections often occur secondarily to some other condition, such as allergic dermatitis, but once established, the underlying problem will not respond to treatment until the secondary infection is cleared.

✦ Abscesses under the skin following on from puncture wounds, especially those resulting from fights, are one of the most common skin conditions that vets are called upon to treat.

✦ Ringworm is a fungal infection of the hair, causing patches of scaliness and hair loss, especially around the head and forelimbs. Some long-haired cats can carry the fungus with very little in the way of clinical signs. It is not uncommon in kittens, and is easily passed on to other cats and to humans. There is a very effective drug for treating the condition, but it has to be given for several weeks to allow

it to grow into the hair and eliminate the infection.

✦ Solar dermatitis is an inflammation of the unprotected extremities, especially the ear tips and nose of white cats, caused by exposure to the ultraviolet radiation in sunlight. In some cases it can undergo a cancerous transformation and require immediate removal. White cats should be kept indoors

when the sun is particularly strong, or their bare skin protected with a non-toxic sun block.

✦ Skin tumours are common, and are often harmless, but any lumps should be checked over by a veterinarian. If there is any doubt, they should be removed, and a specimen sent off to a laboratory for analysis by a pathologist to see if they are likely to cause further problems.

Diets & Disease

Prescription diets ✦
Obesity and weight loss ✦
Liver disease

A healthy diet, suitable for the particular needs of your cat at its stage of life, is an important part of keeping your cat healthy. There is now a wide range of high-quality complete cat foods available, and your veterinarian will help you decide which is best for your cat. The needs of a growing kitten are different from those of a sedate, neutered adult, and nutritional needs change again when the cat becomes elderly.

Below: Feeding low-calorie complete food is the best way to get your cat to lose weight. Any special diet should be given under veterinary supervision.

Left: Although cats do not suffer from coronary heart disease or strokes in the same way as humans, obesity can still pose a health risk. Cats are generally quite good at regulating their food intake, but inactive cats or those fed on a high-energy diet (such as many of the dried cat foods) can easily become overweight.

Prescription diets, supplied under the supervision of your veterinarian, can also play a major role in the treatment and control of many diseases, and a range of good products is now available. Examples of the types of problems that can be helped by prescription diets include:

✦ Kidney disease (see page 130). This can be helped by a diet that is low in phosphorus, together with moderately restricted levels of good-quality protein.
✦ Lower urinary tract disease (see page 130). The diet required depends upon the type of crystals forming in the urine, but most commonly should low in magnesium and designed to produce an acidic urine.
✦ Skin problems, which are sometimes due to a dietary allergy, and respond to a low-allergy diet.
✦ Digestive upsets, which need a diet that can be easily absorbed and is non-irritant to the bowel.

OBESITY AND DIET
Although cats are generally less greedy than dogs, obesity is still fairly common and can lead to health problems such as diabetes and respiratory and joint disorders. Neutered cats are

more prone to putting on weight than entire ones. Also, many cats are now fed on dry foods that are good for their teeth but often high in calories, thus encouraging weight gain.

It is far better to try to prevent a cat from eating too much than to wait until you have an overweight pet on your hands. Fat animals become inactive and have a wonderful layer of insulation around them, so that they burn up far fewer calories than a lean animal of a similar size. Weigh your cat regularly and put it on a lower calorie diet if you see its weight beginning to creep up. Many excellent reduced-calorie dry and canned foods are now available for cats.

Prescription weight-control diets are suitable for cats that become significantly overweight, and many owners have successfully achieved weight losses for their pets with these products. However, cats can be stubborn, and they should not suddenly be starved, so any change to a new diet is best carried out gradually.

LIVER DISEASE

As the processing factory of the body, the liver plays an essential role in the cat's metabolism. Liver disease tends to cause rather non-specific signs, such as lethargy, vomiting, poor appetite, diarrhoea and weight loss. More specific symptoms can include an enlargement of the liver itself and jaundice, a yellow discoloration of the body tissues due to a build-up of bile pigments in the body. Some major causes include the following:
✦ Lymphocytic cholangitis – an inflammation of the liver, thought to be caused by a disorder of the cat's immune system.
✦ Cholangiohepatitis – another form of liver inflammation most commonly caused by a bacterial infection that invades the bile ducts within the liver.
✦ Hepatopathy – many poisons affect the liver of cats, including plants, household and garden chemicals, and drugs such as paracetemol. Some cats have died because of their owners dosing them with drugs not intended for use in that species.

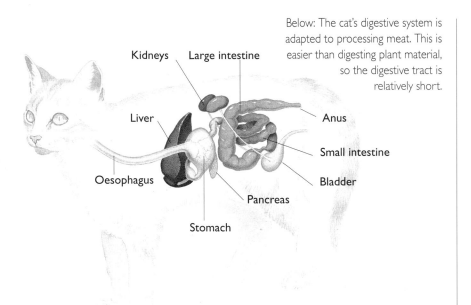

Below: The cat's digestive system is adapted to processing meat. This is easier than digesting plant material, so the digestive tract is relatively short.

Kidneys   Large intestine
Liver
Anus
Small intestine
Oesophagus
Bladder
Pancreas
Stomach

✦ Hepatic lipoidosis – which can follow on from a period of starvation, or from other metabolic diseases such as diabetes mellitus (see page 131). Fat is laid down in the liver and can cause serious interference with its normal function.
✦ Liver tumours – the liver is a common site for secondary tumours that have spread from another site in the body. It is also quite common for primary tumours to develop in the liver or in closely related structures such as the pancreas.

DIAGNOSING LIVER DISEASE

Blood tests and other examinations, such as X-rays, ultrasound and even taking a biopsy specimen of liver tissue surgically, all help the vet to reach an accurate diagnosis. Once the cause of the problem has been established, steps can be taken to correct it and to provide supportive treatment as necessary for the cat.

Fortunately, the liver has a good capacity for regeneration, but if chronic liver disease does continue, the normal liver will eventually become replaced by fibrous tissue, a process known as liver cirrhosis. Cats with liver disease need to be fed a low-fat, easily digestible diet, little and often. In particularly severe cases, the cat may need to be hospitalized for a time and fed liquid food via a fine tube that is passed through the nostril and down into the stomach.

Right: Getting a cat to stand still on weighing scales can be tricky. A better way is to weigh your cat in its carrier and then weigh the carrier separately. Weighing your cat regularly and recording its weight can help to identify problems early.

Ears, Eyes, Mouth & Teeth

Ear infections ✦ Eye problems ✦ Dental disease

Above: Ear mites are the commonest cause of ear irritation in cats. Treatment must be continued long enough to kill off the eggs as well as the adult mites.

Above: In a normal, healthy cat, the cornea should be transparent, with no cloudiness, the iris should be an even, bright colour, and the conjunctiva should be only slightly pink.

Below: A sore tongue or mouth can be caused by a wide range of problems and can seriously impede a cat's ability to feed and groom itself.

Ear infections are fairly common in cats. They can lead to the development of inflammatory polyps, which grow down the ear canal and sometimes even into the Eustachian tube and the back of the throat. By far the most common cause of external ear problems in cats are ear mites (see page 127). These parasites are often passed from a mother to her kittens and cause the production of large amounts of dark, crumbly wax.

If infection crosses the ear drum, it can gain a hold in the deeper structures of the ear, resulting in deafness and interfering with the organ of balance in the inner ear. This can cause the cat to become uncoordinated and to develop a head tilt to the affected side. Some cases respond to medical treatment with ear drops and oral antibiotics, but sometimes surgical drainage is required.

Below: A build-up of tartar on the teeth usually stems from the cat eating a soft diet that does not exercise its teeth properly. Dry food will help but regular brushing is best.

Congenital deafness does occur in some cats, especially in blue-eyed white cats. Affected cats can usually manage perfectly well if kept indoors away from traffic, but should not be used for breeding.

EYE CONDITIONS

The most common eye problem in cats is conjunctivitis, which may be linked to a more general condition such as cat flu, or can be due to direct infection, irritation or injury. Treatment usually involves the administration of suitable eye drops.

Corneal ulceration can result from a more serious injury to the eye and, if it penetrates the cornea completely, can lead to blindness. It can cause inflammation of the deeper structures of the eye, known as uveitis, a condition that can also result from systemic infections, such as feline infectious peritonitis (see page 125) and toxoplasmosis (see page 124).

A cataract is a cloudiness of the lens of the eye. It can develop with age, or be secondary to some other problem such as an injury or diabetes.

One condition that affects the eyes but is not a direct result of an eye problem, is the protrusion of the third eyelid across the eye. This looks like a skin appearing across one side of the eye and may tend to come and go. It is due to a paralysis, usually temporary, of the nerve that controls the third eyelid, and this is most commonly due to a viral infection. Although it may take several weeks to correct itself completely, it almost always does return to normal.

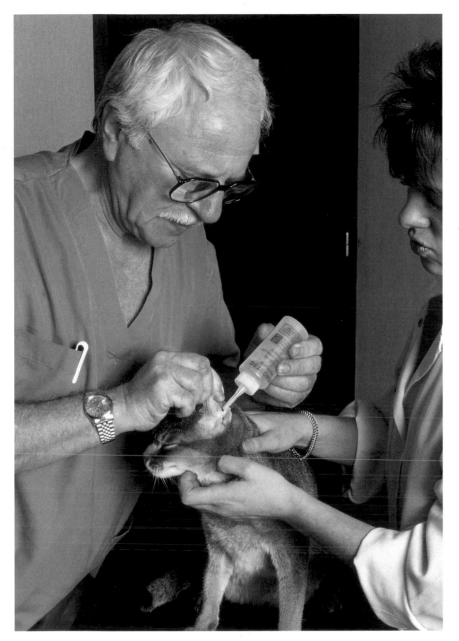

Above: If a cat's gums become inflamed, the teeth should be descaled under anaesthetic to prevent more serious complications.

Left: Drops are the first course of treatment administered for ear infections.

Below: Any eye problems should be treated promptly to avoid long-term damage.

Any eye problems should receive prompt veterinary attention, not only because the eye is so sensitive, but also because neglect may result in permanent damage to the cat's vision.

ORAL DISEASE

A sore mouth quickly stops a cat from grooming itself and eating its food so that it rapidly loses condition. It may also drool saliva, paw at its mouth and have bad breath. Many systemic diseases, such as kidney failure and some viral infections, cause ulceration of the mouth, as can chronic stomatitis. This is a poorly understood condition that can be due to several causes, including infection with feline immunodeficiency virus (see page 128) and poor dental hygiene. More often, the cause cannot be identified and the condition has to be kept under control with antibiotic and anti-inflammatory drugs.

Dental disease is very common in middle-aged and older cats. The major triggering factor is the accumulation of soft plaque and harder mineral-based calculus on the teeth, causing gingivitis, an inflammation of the gums. This leads to the formation of pockets, where food becomes trapped and infection gains a hold. In time, the periodontal membrane that holds the tooth in its bony socket becomes loosened and the tooth eventually falls out, although it may cause considerable discomfort before it does.

Preventative dental care can help to delay the onset of disease. Canned cat foods do little to exercise the teeth, and special dry foods have been developed that have a brushing action as the cat chews. Some owners manage to clean their cats' teeth regularly with special enzymatic cat toothpaste and this is certainly worthwhile. You have more chance of succeeding if you begin to brush your cat's teeth from an early age, before the gums start to become sore.

Nursing a Sick Cat

Post-operative care ◆ Feeding ◆ Giving medicines

*A*lways pay close attention to the instructions that you are given when you collect your cat after an operation and do not hesitate to telephone the surgery when you get back home if you realize there is something you have not understood. General tips include:

◆ Give any prescribed medications as directed. Contact the surgery if you are unable to administer them or if the cat seems to have any reaction.

◆ Do not give any food until the cat is fully awake. Then give just a small, easily digestible meal, such as white meat or fish with rice.

◆ Check any dressings or casts regularly to ensure that they are not overly tight or causing excessive discomfort. Dressings will probably need to be removed after a few days, or changed regularly. Watch out for any unusual smell or discharge.

◆ Contact your veterinary surgeon if the wound becomes increasingly reddened, swollen and hot, or if there is a significant amount of discharge or blood. Given the chance, a cat will always lick a wound, but if this becomes excessive, the licking may make it sore, or the cat may even pull out the stitches. It is sometimes necessary to fit the cat with an Elizabethan collar that prevents it from getting to the wound.

◆ Sutures are usually removed seven to ten days after the operation, although in some cases they may need to be left longer. Sometimes, only absorbable sutures are used under the skin, and they may not need to be taken out.

FEEDING A SICK CAT

Cats are often very fussy about what they will eat, especially when they are unwell. A wide range of prescription

Above: Sometimes it is necessary to use an Elizabethan collar to prevent a cat from getting to a wound. Most cats hate the collar at first but do gradually get used to it.

Below: Cats do not tolerate bandages well so they have to be stuck firmly to the limb. Bandaged cats should usually be kept indoors so that the dressing stays dry.

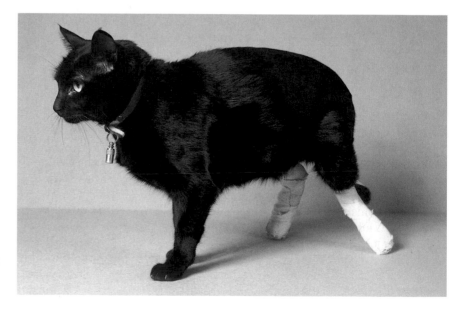

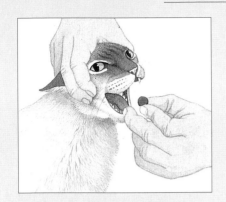

TABLETS

If the tablets can be given with food, crush one in a small amount of strong-smelling food and offer it to the cat when it is hungry. If you have to administer the tablet whole, lubricate it with a little butter, and use your left hand (if you are right-handed) to grasp the cat's head and bend it back as far as possible. The mouth will then drop open a little, and you can use one finger of the other hand to pull the lower jaw down. Quickly push the tablet right to the back of the cat's throat – you can use a special pill holder if you do not want to risk getting bitten. If possible, have someone else steadying the cat as you give the pills. If the cat does start to struggle violently, wrap its legs in a towel to prevent it from scratching.

LIQUIDS

Bend the head back in a similar manner and dribble the drops into the side of the mouth. Allow time for the cat to swallow, or the medicine may be accidentally inhaled.

EYE OINTMENT

Pull down the lower lid with one finger and drop the liquid or ointment into the space between the eyelid and the eye. Avoid touching the end of the dropper itself, or the surface of the dropper on to the eye. Discard any eye preparations a maximum of six weeks after opening the pack.

EAR DROPS

Get someone to hold the cat firmly at its shoulders. If necessary, wrap its legs in a towel to prevent scratching. Hold the ear flap firmly between the finger and thumb of one hand and use your other hand to squeeze the bottle so that the drops drip down into the ear. Keep hold of the ear flap firmly until you have inserted all the drops and massaged the side of the ear canal to encourage the drops to run down well into the ear and to help loosen any discharge within the ear. Let go of the ear flap, and wipe away any excess drops around the top of the ear canal.

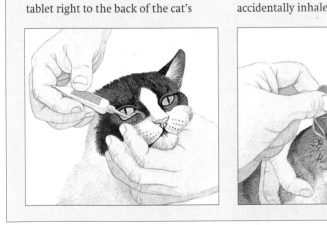

diets is now available to help treat many conditions, including some high-energy liquid foods specifically designed to tempt the cat that is unwilling to eat. Getting a sick cat to eat may be hard, especially if the cat has a sore mouth. If your pet has cat flu, it may be unable to smell the food properly. The following tips may help:
✦ Most cats prefer to have food that is warmed to body temperature to make it smell more strongly. The opening of a new can excites many cats and may be more tempting than an opened can taken from the refrigerator.
✦ Try different formulations and brands. For example, most prescription diets are available in either canned or dry form and in different varieties. Your vet may be able to supply you with a different brand if your cat refuses the first food it is offered.
✦ Change over gradually. If your cat is already eating its existing diet, you may be able to fool it into accepting the new diet by gradually adding an increased proportion to the normal food. Aim to feed only the prescribed food in the long run.
✦ Handfeeding may help to entice your cat to eat. Liquid foods can be given by syringe.
✦ Clean the cat's eyes and nose of any discharges with damp cotton wool to improve its sense of smell.
✦ A cat with cat flu may be helped if it is taken into a warm, moist environment such as a bathroom.

Feline First Aid

Immediate action ◆ What to do in emergencies

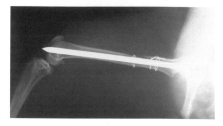

If your cat is involved in an accident of any sort, there are three things that should be done immediately. First, remove your cat from further danger without putting yourself at risk. Second, take any immediate first aid steps necessary to preserve life. Third, contact a veterinary surgeon for further advice and assistance. Do not give anything by mouth in case the cat needs to have a

Below: Shock is a major killer after a serious injury. Once any bleeding has been dealt with, keep the cat warm and comfortable.

general anaesthetic. Always keep a secure cat carrier at home in case it is needed, but in an emergency a sturdy cardboard box will do. If the cat struggles when someone attempts to pick it up, throw a towel over it and pick it up as a bundle, placing the cat and the towel in the carrier together. As a last resort, the cat can be wrapped in a large towel or blanket and carried.

All the following conditions require immediate veterinary attention, but the first aid tips given may improve your cat's chances of survival:

Above: A cat may break bones in a fall or road accident. If a fracture is suspected, the owner should not attempt to treat the broken bone but should get the cat to a vet as soon as possible. X-rays will reveal the exact site of the damage. The top X-ray shows a broken femur and the bottom X-ray shows the repair of the bone with a metal pin.

BLEEDING
It may be possible to apply a pressure bandage to try to staunch the flow of blood. Ideally, you should apply a swab of sterile gauze, or some similar material, and then firmly apply a bandage over that. Do not worry about making the bandage too tight – it will need to be removed as soon as you arrive at the veterinary surgery.

BURNS
These can result from heat, electrical burns or contact with corrosive chemicals. Turn off the electric current at the mains before attending to an electrocuted cat. Flush any type of burn very liberally under cold running water to cool down the damaged tissues and wash off any chemical contamination. With chemical burns, prevent the cat from licking itself while it is being taken to the vet.

CHOKING
If the cat is unconscious, you may be able to pull the tongue forward out of the mouth, and perhaps even grasp any foreign body visible. In a conscious cat, try sharply compressing the chest between your hands in the

hope that the rapid exhalation of air will force the offending item out of the throat. Alternatively, reach into the mouth with tweezers.

DROWNING

If the cat is unconscious, hanging it upside down and gently swinging it back and forth may be particularly effective in helping to drain water out of the lungs. Even if the cat does recover from the original accident, there is still a chance of pneumonia developing as a result of the fact that water has been inhaled into the lungs.

FITS

It is best not to disturb a cat while it is having a fit – just make sure it is out of harm's way, preferably in a dark and quiet room, and keep it under close observation. If the fit lasts for more than about five minutes, or if the cat keeps having fits in quick succession, then urgent veterinary attention is required. Otherwise, the cat should be checked over once the convulsions have ceased.

FRACTURES, DISLOCATIONS AND SPRAINS

Do not attempt to apply a splint or bandage, as the cat will invariably struggle and you could end up making the original problem worse. Keep the cat closely confined and resist the temptation to give any painkillers unless under veterinary advice. Cold compresses held on a sprained joint may be of benefit.

Above: An unconscious cat should be put in the recovery position, ideally with the body slightly higher than the head to allow any fluid to drain from the mouth. Pull the tongue forward so that it does not obstruct breathing.

INJURIES

Minor wounds can be bathed in a solution of one teaspoonful of salt dissolved in a pint of warm water. Wounds commonly become infected,

Above: Keep the cat as flat as possible when lifting, and support it from below.

REMEMBER THE ABC OF FIRST AID

✦ **A** Ensure that the **Airways** are clear, especially if the cat is unconscious. Clear any fluid or debris from the mouth and pull the tongue forward, but be very careful to avoid getting bitten.

✦ **B** If the cat is not **Breathing**, attempt artificial respiration by compressing the chest with your hand once every couple of seconds to force air out of the lungs.

✦ **C** Try to maintain the **Circulation**. Stop serious bleeding by applying firm pressure with a bandage over the wound.

---

especially those caused by a bite from another cat. Seek veterinary attention if any of the following apply:
✦ The wound is gaping open and looks as if it may require stitching.
✦ The wound penetrates a critical area such as the chest or abdomen.
✦ The wound becomes inflamed, smelly and begins to discharge.
✦ The cat seems unwell or refuses offers of food.

POISONING

Unless the substance that has caused the poisoning is caustic, try to make the cat vomit while the substance is still in the stomach. You can do this by dosing the cat with a small crystal of old-fashioned washing soda dissolved in water, or a strong solution of salt water. Keep relevant information about the nature of the poison, such as the packet in the case of pesticides, and contact your vet without delay. If your cat has contaminated its coat with a harmful substance, physically prevent it from grooming itself until its coat has been thoroughly cleaned. If the cat is poisoned by a caustic substance, take it straight to the vet.

Complementary Therapies

Herbal medicine ✦ Homeopathy ✦ Flower remedies

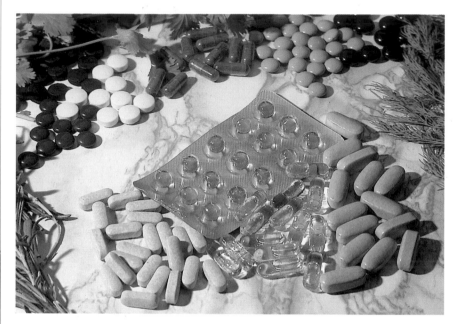

Left: Herbal medicines can be used to treat cats but only under the supervision of a qualified practitioner, or you may do more harm than good.

Conventional treatments do not always offer the perfect cure, and there is an increasing use of complementary medicine for humans and animals. Complementary medicine is often seen as being safe, free of side effects and as taking a broader view of the well-being of the patient as an entity, rather than just treating a specific set of symptoms.

To some extent this is true, and certain forms of complementary treatment have undoubtedly been shown to be effective – others are more controversial. Many owners like using complementary remedies because they can be obtained without the need to consult a vet. Although this may be fine for minor ailments, it is always best to take the advice of a qualified veterinary practitioner, who can carry out a proper examination of the patient to ensure that any serious problems are identified and the correct treatment is given. It is easy to cause considerable suffering and pain, as well as extra cost in the long run, through failing to obtain the correct treatment. If you want to try complementary medicine, look for a vet with an interest in such treatments in your area.

HERBAL REMEDIES
These have been used for thousands of years, and many modern drugs are based upon compounds that have been isolated from plant extracts. While conventional wisdom dictates that it is preferable to use highly purified compounds, which can be administered in precisely controlled quantities, herbalists feel that plants often contain a more natural mixture of drugs that may act in harmony to cause a more gentle action, with fewer side effects.

PHYSIOTHERAPY
Physiotherapy and other forms of manipulation, such as osteopathy and chiropractic, have a clearly identified role in conditions such as back pain in humans. Although their use in treating animals is more difficult, there are certainly cases where they can be beneficial.

ACUPUNCTURE
This involves stimulating certain points of the body, usually with needles, and it certainly has a measurable effect – some operations, even on animals, have been carried out solely under acupuncture. It is thought

Right: Treatment by a qualified animal physiotherapist can be of benefit for cats.

that acupuncture works by stimulating the production of chemicals called endorphins, a natural form of painkiller, within the body under treatment. Acupuncture is particularly useful for conditions involving chronic pain, such as arthritis.

HOMEOPATHY

There is plenty of anecdotal evidence to support the value of homeopathy, but no scientific proof that is generally accepted. Many people confuse homeopathic remedies with herbal ones, as the compounds used are often very similar, but the principles of treatment are very different.

Homeopathy is supposed to work on the principle of 'like cures like'. This means that compounds are chosen, which when given in normal doses would cause the same signs as the patient is exhibiting, but when diluted thousands of times, to the point where they can no longer be chemically detected in the product, leave behind some form of energy that cures the illness. From a purely scientific point of view, homeopathic remedies have no measurable active compound in them, so at least cannot be blamed for causing, rather than curing, problems.

FLOWER REMEDIES

Flower remedies are based upon the theories proposed by Dr Edward Bach, using certain plant petals that have been 'energized' by floating in water when exposed to sunlight. The water

FLOWER REMEDIES

♦

Rescue remedy contains a mixture of five essences, and is particularly useful in an emergency situation to counteract the effects of shock, collapse and trauma.

Mimulus is helpful for specific phobias, such as fear of noises or of being left alone, as well as for general shyness and timidity.

Impatiens is used to treat patients exhibiting signs of irritability, impatience and overreaction to certain stimuli.

Below: Deadly nightshade is the source of a homeopathic remedy called Belladonna, as well as the conventional medicine, atropine.

is then preserved with brandy and given to help cure problems, particularly emotional ones. Sceptics may argue that the brandy has more effect than the energized water!

HERBAL REMEDIES

♦

Calendula, or pot marigold, has a very useful antiseptic action, and can be applied externally to help soothe wounds and certain types of skin problem.

Peppermint, or the milder spearmint, is used as an infusion to relax the digestive tract of animals suffering from digestive upsets.

Dandelion has a diuretic action, and the leaves are rich in potassium. This helps to relieve the side effects of potassium loss associated with the use of synthetic diuretics to remove excess fluid from the body.

Garlic has several actions upon the body. It acts as an antiseptic within the bowel; it discourages blood clotting and parasites such as worms and fleas. Purists prefer the use of freshly crushed cloves rather than manufactured preparations, such as tablets and capsules, despite the smell!

Evening primrose oil has been used for many years, but has now been scientifically proven to help animals suffering from allergic skin disorders if given orally in large doses. This is due to a substance called gamma linolenic acid, which is found in this plant.

Nettle leaves are rich in iron and minerals, so are a good tonic for animals suffering from anaemia. They also help to ease arthritis because they increase the excretion of uric acid through the kidneys. The nettle sting contains histamine, and it is one of the wonders of nature that wherever nettles grow, there are usually dock leaves, which have an antihistaminic effect and thus help to alleviate the itching caused by nettle stings.

HOMEOPATHIC REMEDIES

♦

Arnica, derived from the plant *Arnica montana*, is probably the best known of all homeopathic remedies. It is used to counteract the effects of injury, reducing swelling and bruising and to help promote rapid healing. It is available in tablet and ointment form.

Homeopathic sulphur is commonly used to help animals with chronic skin problems, particularly if the skin is red and inflamed. The typical patient will have a dry and smelly coat, be overweight, and of a stubborn temperament.

Rhus toxidodendron is another homeopathic remedy of plant origin, and is used in cases where there has been damage to muscle tissue. It is said to be particularly effective for animals that show signs of stiffness after rest.

Parting with your Pet

Quality of life ✦ Euthanasia ✦ Grieving ✦ Cancer treatments

If your cat should be diagnosed as suffering from an incurable condition, you may have to face a difficult decision – should you put your pet to sleep? Factors such as the cost of on-going treatment and coping with problems such as incontinence need to be taken into account, but for most owners the important consideration is whether their cat is enjoying a reasonable quality of life.

If the cat is eating well, is responding to attention from its owners, is reasonably active, and is not suffering discomfort from some specific side effect of the illness, such as repeated vomiting, it is likely that the cat is still getting some enjoyment out of life. If the cat is listless, uninterested in its surroundings and off its food, euthanasia may be the kindest option if no improvement can be expected from treatment.

A FINAL INJECTION

Euthanasia is generally carried out by the intravenous injection of a concentrated barbiturate solution into the body. Previously, smaller doses of this type of drug were used as an anaesthetic, and the cat literally 'goes off to sleep' within a matter of seconds, after which the heart stops beating and breathing ceases. Many vets are happy for owners to stay with their cats when they are given the injection so that they can see just how peaceful the process actually is. The animal does not suffer any pain.

Most owners want to know that their pet will be decently disposed of, and most veterinary surgeries will

arrange to have them cremated, although you may wish to make arrangements to bury your cat at home or in a pet cemetery.

Some owners find it helpful to get a new cat quickly; others prefer to wait for a while. Either way, you should appreciate that it is normal to feel some degree of bereavement after the loss of a pet, and some people grieve as deeply as if they had lost a close relative. There are even pet bereavement counsellors that specialize in helping owners to cope with the loss of a pet.

CANCER

The diagnosis of a malignant tumour is not necessarily a death sentence for your cat. There are several types of treatment that can be used to try to cure certain types of cancer, or at least to give the animal a worthwhile extra lease of life.

Surgical removal can reduce the size of the tumour and be followed up by other forms of treatment. It may result in a complete cure of the disease if all the affected tissue is completely removed.

Chemotherapy involves the use of drugs to control cancer. This is particularly effective in many cases of lymphosarcoma, commonly caused by feline leukaemia virus. A combination of drugs is used to minimize their effectiveness with the minimum of side effects.

Radiotherapy can only be used at specialized centres, but can be very effective for tumours such as certain types of skin cancer.

Top right: Losing a pet that you may have looked after for many years is always a blow, but if you have more than one cat the impact will be somewhat reduced.

Left: With a good diet, regular vaccinations and preventative veterinary care, there is no reason why a domestic cat should not live well into its teens.

Pet was never mourned as you
Purrer of the spotless hue,
Plumy tail, and wistful gaze,
While you humoured our queer ways.

THOMAS HARDY, LAST WORDS TO A DUMB FRIEND, *1925*

Below: If your much-loved feline companion does become so ill that it is no longer getting any enjoyment from life, euthanasia is sometimes the kindest course of action.

LIFE OF A CAT

A kitten is born blind and helpless, wholly reliant for food and warmth on its mother. But in a matter of weeks it is able to run, jump, eat solid food and groom itself. Lively play helps to develop the kitten's physical coordination, and often mirrors later hunting actions.

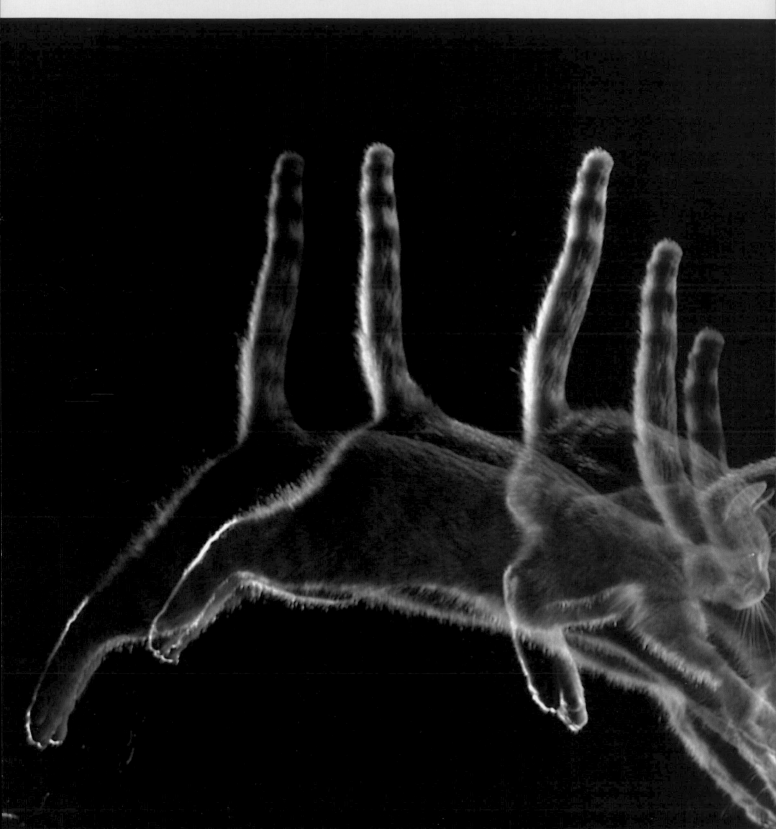

Once full grown, an adult cat may spend much of its time asleep. In the wild, sleeping helps conserve energy – the more energy a cat uses, the more prey it has to catch. And, of course, pet cats that go outdoors still follow their instincts and hunt prey, even though they do not need the extra food.

Tearaway kitten or staid mother of fifty,
Persian, Chinchilla, Siamese
Or backstreet brawler — you all have a tiger in your blood
And eye opaque as the sacred mysteries.

C. Day-Lewis, The Best Cat Stories, 1969

But the kitten, how she starts,
Crouches, stretches, paws, and darts!
First at one, and then its fellow,
Just as light and just as yellow.

WILLIAM WORDSWORTH,
THE KITTEN AND FALLING LEAVES, *1804*

Of all Nature's lovely shows, and they not a few, surely that of a cat
playing with her kittens or educating them is the prettiest.

EDITH CARRINGTON, THE CAT: HER PLACE IN SOCIETY AND TREATMENT, *1896*

A cat can lie softly in absolute comfort on the most unforgiving of surfaces.

THEOCRITUS, IDYLS XV,
C. 270 BC

They call me cruel. Do I know if mouse or songbird feels?
I only know they make light and salutary meals.

C. S. CALVERLEY, FLY LEAVES: SAD MEMORIES, 1872

Now she proceeds to clean
herself all over, having a just
sense of the demands of her
elegant person — beginning
judiciously with her paws, and
fetching amazing tongues at
her hind-hips.

LEIGH HUNT, THE CAT BY THE FIRE,
1830

PART 4

CAT BREEDS

*I*n many countries cats have now overtaken dogs as the most popular domestic pets. The majority of these cats are non-pedigrees or 'moggies', but there is also a wide range of pedigree breeds, with a variety of fur lengths, colours and patterns. If you are considering purchasing a pedigree kitten, try not to make your choice on looks alone. Under that appealing furry exterior is a personality and character unique to each breed. The needs of different breeds do vary and not all will suit every household. The following pages should help you make your choice. For some owners, part of the pleasure of owning pedigree cats is taking part in shows. Cat shows are competitive events, but they also give other enthusiasts, exhibitors and members of the public the chance to see the increasingly exciting range of pedigree cat breeds that are now available.

Showing Cats

Cat shows ✦ Judging ✦ Preparing for a show

Although cats in various shapes, colours and sizes have been recorded throughout history, it was not until the late 1800s that an interest in cat shows developed and a formal Cat Fancy – an organization for cat lovers – was started.

The world's first proper cat show was held in London's Crystal Palace in 1871 and it attracted 160 entrants. This show demonstrated the need for some type of formal registration body, and a system was devised to record the details of the parentage of pedigree cats. Each breed was given a 'standard of points': guidelines for the judges on the desired characteristics of that breed.

As the popularity of cats increased, the Cat Fancy spread to the rest of Europe and to North America. Now there are cat fancies all over the world, including Russia and the Far East. Cats began to be imported and exported between countries, increasing not only the variety of breeds and colours available, but also adding 'hybrid vigour' to the gene pool.

A CAT SHOW TODAY

A visit to any all-breed, championship show today will bewilder non-experts. Most people recognize Persians and Siamese, but there are many other breeds, colours and patterns to choose from. For anyone contemplating buying a pedigree kitten, a cat show provides a perfect 'shop window' of the varieties available and a chance to chat with owners and breeders.

There are two ways of judging cats. Most common is a system known as ring judging, used in North America and many European countries. The judge is seated at a table and stewards bring each exhibit individually for the judge to give a, usually verbal, appraisal. A written assessment is placed on the cat's pen shortly afterwards. Owners, exhibitors and the general public are allowed to watch the proceedings.

Left: Pens at shows in North America are allowed to be decorated. This superb example of a white Persian seems to have taken all the awards.

Above: Entrants at the National Cat Club Show in Britain wait in their show pens to be visited by the judges.

In other countries, including the UK, the cats are all penned according to breed, colour and sex, and the judge, accompanied by a steward, visits each in turn. Neither the owner nor members of the public are allowed into the hall until judging of the main 'open' class has taken place.

The aim of both systems is the same, however. Cats of each breed, and usually of each colour, are judged according to a strict standard of points. The judges decide on the best entire adult male and female of each breed, and award a certificate. Similar titles are used for the neuters. Three certificates awarded by judges at three different shows will give the cat the title of Champion.

At the end of the day at many championship shows, the best adult, neuter and kitten of each breed is reassessed and a panel of judges decides on the best of each. These are

then judged against each other to award the title 'Best in the Show'. Champions can compete further at later shows for the title of Grand Champion. At most shows there are also classes for the 'moggie', so any cat owner can enjoy the fun of exhibiting at a show.

WHAT THE JUDGES LOOK FOR

The judges are well versed in breed standards, but this is not all they seek in the perfect cat. While type and coat colour are all-important, temperament also plays a large part in the final decision. However beautiful a cat, if it is aggressive or bites the judge, it will be marked down against

Above: In the European ring-judging show system, each entrant is brought to the judge for individual appraisal.

Left: Every aspect of a cat must be looked at. Here a show judge checks a contestant's head to make sure it is of the approved shape and type.

a similar specimen with a sweeter disposition. Ill temper is not a trait to be encouraged in any breed. It is equally important that the cat should be in good health, free from parasites, with a coat that shines and radiates well-being. To achieve this, the cat needs a good diet, a happy home and regular grooming.

Showing cats

PREPARING YOUR CAT

Each breed of cat needs different forms of preparation for a show, mainly dependent on the length and colour of its coat.

Sleek, short-haired breeds, such as the Foreigns, Burmese, Siamese and Orientals, need little special preparation. The darker colours may benefit from a bran bath the night before, followed by a rub with bay rum to add extra shine. On the day of the show, a polish with a silk scarf or a piece of chamois leather will add an extra gleam to the cat's coat.

Long-haired cats are usually bathed a few days before the show. Persians

Above: A bran bath helps to remove any grease or dandruff from the fur of a short-haired cat. Warm the bran slightly first and then rub it into the coat, against the fur. Leave for a while, then brush out thoroughly.

Left: Long-haired and pale-coloured cats need shampooing before a show.

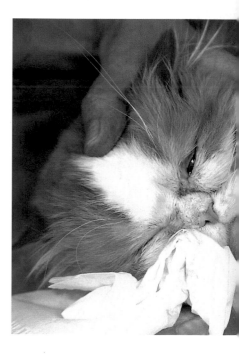

Left: After shampooing, rinse well and apply conditioner to make the coat easier to comb. Rinse again, making sure that no traces of soap or conditioner remain. Wrap the cat in a towel and gently pat it dry. Keep it warm and out of draughts while its fur is wet.

are often given a dusting of talcum powder to 'bulk' up the coat, but all traces must be thoroughly brushed out before judging. Do not use talcum powder on short-haired cats. Any white or paler-coated varieties also benefit from a bath.

On the day of the show, the cat, whether short- or long-haired, should have a clean, sparkling coat, free from moulting hairs and dander, clean ears and nose, and bright eyes. And, most importantly for the judge, claws should be clipped to avoid accidents.

Right: Unless your cat is frightened by the noise of a hair dryer, this is an ideal way to dry its coat after bathing. Do not use the dryer at full heat and hold it at a safe distance from the cat.

Right: Once the fur is completely dry, comb it through gently so that it stands out around the cat's body.

Below: Check that the cat's eyes are clean. Some, particularly Persians, may suffer from watery eyes, which stains the fur around the eyes. Wipe gently with moist cottonwool.

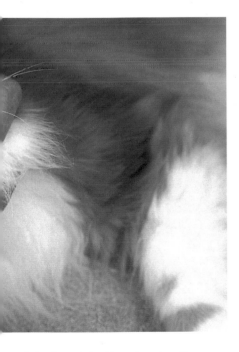

Right: Short-haired breeds such as Siamese do not need much grooming, but a good brushing will help to remove any loose hairs. A final rub with a silk cloth or chamois leather will give an additional gleam and help the fur to lie smoothly.

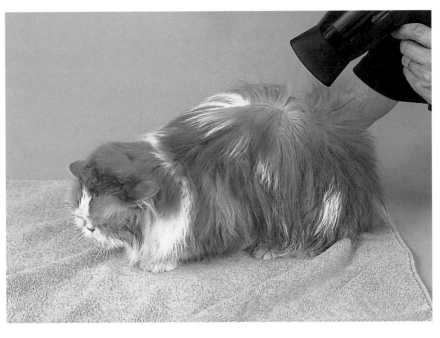

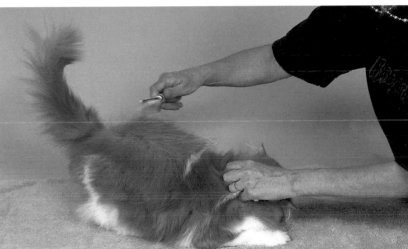

Coat Types

Length and colour ✦ Choosing a breed

Pedigree cat breeds are usually grouped into seven sections: Longhairs (Persians), Semi-longhairs, British Shorthairs, Foreign Short-hairs, Orientals, Burmese and Siamese. For simplicity, the breeds in this book have been arranged phenotypically (by appearance) rather than genotypically (by their genetic make up), which usually governs which section they will be registered under at a show. The Balinese, for example, looks like a Semi-longhair, but is registered and judged with the Siamese, its founder breed.

SELFS AND NON-SELFS

Within the Persian, British and Oriental sections, the breeds are subdivided into self and non-self groups. The selfs are cats with a plain coat colour, such as black, blue or chocolate. This should be of a uniform colour and density right down to the root of each hair, without any markings or shading. The non-self are cats with patterned, ticked, tipped or shaded coats. Burmese are different. The plain-coated varieties appear to be self-coloured, but they are not. Burmese kittens are born with very pale fur, which darkens as they mature, and the undercoat is paler.

Certain coat colours are referred to as 'dilute'. These are created by the presence of a recessive dilution gene that reduces the strength of a colour; so that, for example, red becomes cream and chocolate becomes lilac.

Some breeds, such as the Burmilla (see page 200) were created by an accidental mating. Others are produced as a result of deliberate breeding programmes, using particular breeds to introduce desired characteristics. The practice of bringing a different breed

Above: Longhair, or Persian, cats have a long, luxuriant coat, which needs daily grooming. These cats are available with a wide range of self and non-self coat colours.

Above: The Abyssinian is an example of a short-haired cat. The fur is short and close lying, with a fine texture. Short-haired cats need little in the way of grooming except when moulting.

Left: The Maine Coon is a semi-longhair. Like other semi-longhaired cats its coat is medium length and, although it does require some grooming, it does not need daily attention like the Persians.

into a breeding programme is known as outcrossing and has been used to create breeds such as the Colourpoint Persian (see page 172).

CHOOSING A PEDIGREE CAT

Think carefully before choosing a pedigree cat and make sure you select one with the characteristics that suit you. Go to a cat show and see which breed takes your fancy. Talk to the breeders and, most important, go and visit your chosen breed in a domestic situation before you make your final decision as to which cat to buy.

In general, Persians and British Shorthairs are quiet, gentle, undemanding – and often lazy. If you want an active breed, these are not the cats for you. On the plus side, they do not generally pine if their owner is out for long periods.

At the other end of the scale, Burmese, Siamese and Orientals need attention and can be extremely demanding. They are intelligent, inquisitive and active, and they do not like to be left alone for any length of time. In between are the Semi-longhairs and Foreign Shorthairs. They are active and outgoing but less so than Siamese, Burmese and Orientals.

The following pages provide a guide to the different breeds. Their grooming needs are listed as follows:
✦ Daily grooming – you should spend at least ten minutes a day brushing and combing the cat or its coat will become knotted and matted.
✦ Frequent grooming – once a week, possibly more when moulting.
✦ Regular grooming – every few weeks, more when moulting.
✦ Little grooming required – stroking removes most of the loose fur and an occasional brush or comb in the moulting season is usually enough.

Above: A tipped coat is made up of white or pale-coloured hairs, each tipped with a darker colour.

Above: A shaded coat is made up of pale hairs, each with a dark section. The dark colour reaches about half way down the length of the hair.

Above: A ticked coat is made up of hairs that have two or three bands of colour along their length.

Far left: The Russian Blue is an example of a self-coloured cat – the colour of each hair is solid from the tip to the root.

Left: The Maine Coon tabby has a patterned or non-self coat. It has a mixture of solid and ticked hairs.

Black

History
While black long-haired cats have been known since the 16th century, it was not until the late 19th century that the first long-haired cats were imported from Persia to Europe. These early Persians were quite different from the cats that grace the show bench today – their faces were longer, their ears larger and they had a rangier shape. Over the years, selective breeding has produced the cobby, stocky body and open face familiar today.

Temperament
Quiet, gentle and affectionate. The Black Persian fits into most domestic situations well. Like all domestic breeds, it enjoys human company, but is generally happy to be left while the owner is at work.

Body
Medium sized, well muscled and cobby, with small, wide-set ears and a short, open face. The tail is short, with bushy, well-plumed fur. Legs should be short, thick and strong, with rounded paws and tufted toes.

Coat
Long and luxuriant, with a softer undercoat. In an adult, the coat should be a dense, solid black, with no sign of

rustiness. Kittens may have pale, 'ghost' tabby markings up to the age of about six months.

Eyes
Large and round; deep orange or copper in colour.

Breed Assessment
GROOMING Daily grooming
VOICE Quiet
ACTIVITY LEVEL Low
COUNTRY OF ORIGIN Persia (Iran)
BREED RECOGNIZED IN All countries

CAT BREEDS
Longhairs (Persian)

162

Breed Assessment
GROOMING Daily grooming
VOICE Quiet
ACTIVITY LEVEL Low
COUNTRY OF ORIGIN Persia (Iran)
BREED RECOGNIZED IN All countries

Blue

History
Genetically the dilute (see page 160) form of black, the Blue Persian is an old-established colour. It was purported to be Queen Victoria's favourite breed and today is still one of the most popular and recognizable Persians.

Temperament
Gentle, affectionate, quiet and loving. This is a companionable cat, but it does not usually pine when its owners are away from home for a few hours.

Body
Medium sized, well muscled and stocky but elegant in shape. Its head is round, with a short face and small, neat, wide-set ears. The tail is short and bushy and the legs are short and strong, with rounded paws and tufted toes.

Coat
Long, thick and luxuriant, with a dense, soft undercoat. The colour should be pale to medium blue, solid to the roots, and without any shading or marking.

Eyes
Large and round; deep orange or copper in colour.

Cream

History
When Cream Persians were first seen at the end of the end of the 19th century, their pale coats did not impress the Victorians, who dismissed them as rather poorly coloured reds. American breeders, however, considered the pale coat attractive and established the colour. In the 1920s the Cream was brought back to Europe and may now be any colour from buff to pale honey. Today, the Cream is one of the most sought-after of all the Persian colours.

Temperament
Sweet-natured, quiet, loving and affectionate, the Cream Persian makes an ideal pet.

Body
Medium sized, cobby but elegant, with a round, full-cheeked face and small, neat ears. The tail should be full, bushy and well plumed, and the legs short and stocky, with rounded paws and tufted toes.

Coat
Long and luxuriant, with a soft, silky texture and a softer undercoat. The colour should be a pale to medium cream, sound to the roots and with no shading or markings.

Eyes
Large and round; deep orange or copper in colour.

Breed Assessment
GROOMING Daily grooming
VOICE Quiet
ACTIVITY LEVEL Low
COUNTRY OF ORIGIN Persia (Iran)
BREED RECOGNIZED IN All countries

Red

History
Although the Red is one of the older colours of Persian, good examples are extremely scarce since it is difficult to breed with a solid coat and no tabby markings. Litters tend to have at least one heavily marked kitten. Before a proper standard of points was set up, 'ghost' tabby markings were acceptable.

Temperament
Sweet-natured, gentle, loving and affectionate.

Body
Medium sized, well muscled and cobby, with small, wide-set ears and a short, open face. The tail is short and bushy; the legs are short and strong, with rounded paws and tufted toes.

Coat
Ideally, a deep, rich red, free of white hairs. The colour should be sound to the roots and free of tabby markings, although some slight shading on the forehead and legs is permissible.

Eyes
Large and round; deep orange or copper in colour.

Breed Assessment
GROOMING Daily grooming
VOICE Quiet
ACTIVITY LEVEL Low
COUNTRY OF ORIGIN Persia (Iran)
BREED RECOGNIZED IN All countries

Chocolate

History
A relative newcomer to the Persian group, the Chocolate is a by-product of the Colourpoint (see page 172) breeding programme. Early Chocolates were rather rangy and did not usually have the massive coat so typical of Persians. Selective breeding has ensured that those seen in shows today conform to the general standard for Persians.

Temperament
Gentle and affectionate; the Chocolate often has a more outgoing personality than the Black or Blue.

Body
Medium sized, well muscled, with a short face and small, wide-set ears. The tail is short and bushy and the legs short and strong, with rounded paws and tufted toes.

Coat
Long, thick and luxuriant, with a full undercoat. In an adult, the colour should be a warm, medium to dark chocolate, free of markings or shadings. Kittens may have a slight greying in the coat.

Eyes
Large and round; copper or deep orange in colour.

Breed Assessment
GROOMING Daily grooming
VOICE Quiet
ACTIVITY LEVEL Low
COUNTRY OF ORIGIN UK
BREED RECOGNIZED IN All countries

Breed Assessment
GROOMING Daily grooming
VOICE Quiet
ACTIVITY LEVEL Low
COUNTRY OF ORIGIN UK
BREED RECOGNIZED IN All countries

Lilac

History
Another of the newer colours of Persians, the Lilac is also the result of the Colourpoint (see page 172) breeding programme. Early Lilacs did not have the typically Persian body shape, but the Lilacs today conform to the general Persian standards and their delicate lilac hue has made them a most popular and unusual breed.

Temperament
Sweet-natured, gentle and affectionate. The Lilac is often more outgoing than other self-colour Persians.

Body
Medium sized and well muscled, with small, wide-set ears and a short, open face. The tail of the Lilac is short and bushy and the legs short and strong, with rounded paws and tufted toes.

Coat
Long and luxuriant, with a softer, dense undercoat. The colour should be a warm, even lilac, solid to the roots and free of any shading or markings.

Eyes
Large and round; copper or deep orange in colour.

White

History

The original white longhairs seen in Europe were from the Ankara region of Turkey and are what is known today as the Turkish Angora (see page 176). They had a rangier shape than the modern White Persian and did not have such a long coat. During Victorian times, when cats with much thicker, denser and more profuse coats were imported from Persia, they became more popular, but the earliest examples were not white. The modern White Persian breed is thought to be descended from a cross-mating of the original Turkish imports and those from Persia. Three different eye colours are acceptable – blue, orange or odd (one of each colour).

Temperament

Gentle, quiet and affectionate, the White Persian is generally an undemanding breed.

Body

Medium sized, well muscled and cobby, with small, neat ears and a thick, bushy tail. The legs are short, stout and strong, with rounded paws and tufted toes.

Coat

Long and luxuriant, with a dense, softer undercoat. The colour should be a pure white, with no shades or marks.

Eyes

Large and round; may be a pure deep blue or deep orange, or one of each.

Breed Assessment

GROOMING Daily grooming and a regular bath

VOICE Quiet

ACTIVITY LEVEL Low

COUNTRY OF ORIGIN UK

VARIETIES Blue-eyed White, Orange-eyed White, Odd-eyed White

BREED RECOGNIZED IN All countries

Orange-eyed White

Blue-eyed White

CAT BREEDS
*Longhairs
(Persian)*

165

Orange-eyed White

Odd-eyed White

Bi-colour

History
Bi-coloured cats (those with coats of a mixture of white and another colour) have existed for many centuries, but solid-coated varieties were always more popular. As interest in pedigree breeding (particularly of Persians) surged in the 20th century, it was inevitable that bi-colours would turn up as a product of breeding programmes involving whites and tortoiseshells. Bi-colours are now popular in the USA and Europe.

Temperament
Quiet, sweet-natured and affectionate. The Bi-colour is generally an undemanding breed.

Body
Well muscled and broad chested, with short, sturdy legs. This medium-sized breed has a short face with a round, wide head and small, neat, wide-set ears.

Coat
Luxuriant, silky and long. The markings are all-important and the face should show both the solid colour and white. An inverted 'V' in white on the face is favoured by many fancies. The breed standard allows for all degrees of white, from white feet, chest and belly to nearly all white, with coloured patches on the head and a coloured tail.

Eyes
Large and round; copper or deep orange in colour.

Bi-colour

Breed Assessment
GROOMING Daily grooming
VOICE Quiet
ACTIVITY LEVEL Low
COUNTRY OF ORIGIN UK
VARIETIES All colours accepted for the selfs
BREED RECOGNIZED IN All countries

Bi-colour

Tortie and White (Calico)

History
Similar to the Bi-colour, this multicoloured cat is a mixture of white and any of the accepted tortoiseshell colours. Originally named the Chintz in Britain, this variety of Persian is known as the Calico in the USA. Very popular as both a show cat and a pet, it is a charming and attractive breed.

Temperament
Friendly, sweet-natured and generally undemanding.

Body
Cobby, broad chested and medium sized, with a rounded head, short nose and small, neat, wide-set ears. The legs are short and sturdy.

Coat
Long, fine and thick. As with the Bi-colour, the standard for the breed allows for all degrees of white, from white feet, chest and belly to a nearly all-white coat, with coloured patches on the head and a coloured tail. All three colours should show clearly.

Eyes
Large and round; copper or deep orange in colour.

Breed Assessment
GROOMING Daily grooming
VOICE Quiet
ACTIVITY LEVEL Low
COUNTRY OF ORIGIN UK
VARIETIES All colours accepted for the selfs as well as their tortie-tabby variations. Silver not accepted in Britain
BREED RECOGNIZED IN All countries

Tabby and White

History
Another of the Bi-Colour variations, but there is some tabby patterning on the coloured patches.

Temperament
Sweet-natured, loving and gentle.

Body
Cobby and muscular, with short, sturdy limbs and a broad, round head. Ears are small, neat and wide set.

Coat
Long, thick and luxuriant. The colour should be a mixture of white and tabby on the body and face, as for the Tortie and White.

Blue Tabby and White

Eyes
Large and round; the colour may vary from shades of green to copper.

Breed Assessment
GROOMING Daily grooming
VOICE Quiet
ACTIVITY LEVEL Low
COUNTRY OF ORIGIN UK
VARIETIES Brown, Blue, Chocolate, Lilac, Red and Cream
BREED RECOGNIZED IN All countries

Brown Tabby and White

Chinchilla

History
The Chinchilla is probably the most popular of all the Persians. The combination of its pure white coat, delicately tipped with black to produce a silvery colour that almost sparkles, and the typical emerald-green eyes, give this unique breed an almost fairy-like appearance. The Chinchilla was first shown at a major cat show in 1894 at Crystal Palace in London, making it one of the very first artificially created colours.

Temperament
Sweet-natured, loving and affectionate. Chinchillas are usually more outgoing and extrovert than other varieties of Persian.

Body
Cobby and medium sized, with a round, broad head. Its small, wide-set ears should be well tufted and the short, brick-red nose is distinctively outlined in black. The Chinchilla is sometimes more finely boned and elegant than other Persians.

Coat
Silky, long and dense. The top coat should be evenly but lightly tipped in black, overlaying a pure white undercoat to give a sparkling appearance.

Eyes
Large and round; deep emerald green outlined in black.

Breed Assessment
GROOMING Daily grooming and a regular bath
VOICE Quiet
ACTIVITY LEVEL Low to moderate
COUNTRY OF ORIGIN UK and USA
BREED RECOGNIZED IN All countries

Chinchilla mother and kitten

Golden Persian

History
This breed originated in the USA from certain lines of Chinchilla that carried the non-silver gene. It was first seen in Europe in the 1970s. Originally called the Golden Chinchilla, it has now been renamed the Golden Persian. It is accepted and recognized as a separate breed in all countries and is a popular addition to the Persian group.

Temperament
Loving, sweet-natured, intelligent and friendly.

Body
Cobby and medium sized, with sturdy legs. The head is broad and round, with small, tufted ears and a snub nose.

Coat
Dense, long and silky. Like the Chinchilla, it has a tipped coat. The tipping should be seal brown or black, overlaying a pale apricot undercoat.

Eyes
Large and round; green or blue-green in colour.

Breed Assessment
GROOMING Daily grooming
VOICE Quiet
ACTIVITY LEVEL Low to moderate
COUNTRY OF ORIGIN USA
BREED RECOGNIZED IN All countries

Golden Persian kitten

Golden Persian

Shaded Silver

History
A relative of the Chinchilla (see page 168), the Shaded Silver has a more heavily tipped coat. Although it does not have a large following of admirers, probably because of the more glamorous looks of the Chinchilla, it is still a most attractive breed.

Temperament
Affectionate, friendly and sweet-natured. Like the Chinchilla, this breed is usually more outgoing and adventurous than most Persians.

Body
Cobby and medium sized, with short, sturdy legs. The head should be round and broad, with small, wide-set, well-tufted ears.

Coat
Silky, long and thick. Although the undercoat is white, the tipping reaches farther down the hair shaft than in the Chinchilla, giving this cat a much darker look.

Eyes
Large and round; emerald or blue-green in colour and outlined in black.

Breed Assessment
GROOMING Daily grooming
VOICE Quiet
ACTIVITY LEVEL Low to moderate
COUNTRY OF ORIGIN UK
BREED RECOGNIZED IN All countries

Pewter

History
Another of the shaded varieties of Persian, this cat is similar to the Cameo, but less heavily tipped than the Smoke. Originally the result of a mating between a Chinchilla and a self-colour Persian, it is becoming increasingly popular.

Temperament
Sweet-natured, affectionate and generally undemanding.

Body
Cobby, with firm, short legs. The head is round and broad, with a snub nose and small, neat, wide-set ears.

Coat
Silky, long and dense. The colour should be an evenly shaded black overlaying a white undercoat, giving the impression that the cat is wearing a pewter mantle.

Eyes
Large and round; copper or orange in colour.

Breed Assessment
GROOMING Daily grooming
VOICE Quiet
ACTIVITY LEVEL Low
COUNTRY OF ORIGIN UK
BREED RECOGNIZED IN All countries

Cameo

History
One of the most popular of all the tipped varieties (see page 160), this attractive cat has a coat that is more lightly tipped than the Smoke – and is sometimes as light as the Chinchilla. It has a pale undercoat, which should be as close to white as possible, contrasting with the darker tips of the hairs. A dedicated breeding programme did not begin until the 1950s, when the colour became popular in the USA.

Temperament
Affectionate and sweet-natured. This breed is generally undemanding.

Body
Well muscled and medium sized, with a deep, broad chest and short, sturdy legs. The head is round and wide, with a short face and small, neat, wide-set ears.

Coat
Luxuriant, long, dense and silky. There are two densities of tipping allowed, both of which should have an undercoat that is as pure white as possible: the Shell is shaded lightly toward the tips, while the Shaded is more heavily marked.

Eyes
Large and round; copper or deep orange in colour.

Breed Assessment
GROOMING: Daily grooming
VOICE Quiet
ACTIVITY LEVEL Low
COUNTRY OF ORIGIN USA
VARIETIES Red, Cream, Blue-cream and Tortie are available in Shell and Shaded Cameos
BREED RECOGNIZED IN All countries

Smoke

History
Although it may look like a self colour, this popular and attractive breed is actually the most densely coloured tipped Persian. The white undercoat below the darker colour is revealed only when the cat is moving. This breed was first mentioned in the 1860s, but almost died out before a revival took place in the 1960s. It is still not particularly common.

Temperament
Generally undemanding, sweet-natured and affectionate.

Body
Cobby and medium sized, with short, sturdy legs. The head is round and broad, with a snub nose and small, wide-set, tufted ears.

Coat
Silky, long and thick, with evenly distributed colour, without tabby markings, overlaying the undercoat. The undercoat should be as near to white as possible, while reflecting the main colour.

Eyes
Large and round; deep orange or copper in colour.

Breed Assessment
GROOMING Daily grooming
VOICE Quiet
ACTIVITY LEVEL Low
COUNTRY OF ORIGIN UK
VARIETIES Black, Blue, Chocolate, Lilac, Red, Cream and the four colours of Tortie
BREED RECOGNIZED IN All countries

Colourpoint (Himalayan)

History
One of the 'genetically manufactured' varieties, this cat first emerged in the late 1940s in North America and Sweden. The 'Himalayan' coat pattern, more usually associated with the Siamese, is easily the most distinctive feature of this breed. (The term 'Himalayan' is used for any animal with a restricted coat pattern – a pale coat and colour only on cooler parts such as ears, muzzle, paws and tail.) The Colourpoint Persian is an extremely popular cat and is available in a range of colours and patterns, not all of which are officially recognized by all the relevant authorities. In North America, this breed is known as the Himalayan.

Blue Colourpoint

Cream Colourpoint

Temperament
Affectionate and sweet-natured. With its Siamese background, the Colourpoint is often more outgoing and extrovert than the self-colour Persians. Those who admire this cat believe that it combines the good points of both Persians and Siamese, having the inquisitive instincts of the Siamese and the gentle nature of the Persian breeds.

Body
Cobby and medium sized, with short, sturdy legs. The head is broad and round, with a short face and small, neat, wide-set ears.

Coat
Silky, long and thick. The body colour should be as light as possible.

Eyes
Large, round and full; brilliant blue in colour.

Breed Assessment
GROOMING Daily grooming and occasional bathing
VOICE Quiet
ACTIVITY LEVEL Low to moderate
COUNTRIES OF ORIGIN USA and Sweden
VARIETIES Seal, Blue, Chocolate, Lilac, Red, Cream and the associated colours of Tortie, Tabby and Tortie-Tabby (Torbie in the USA)
BREED RECOGNIZED IN All countries

Tabby Colourpoint

Tortoiseshell

History
A delightful breed in its own right, the Tortoiseshell is used in breeding programmes to produce the self Red and Cream Persians. It is usually a female-only variety.

Temperament
Affectionate and sweet-natured. This breed does have a wilful streak that is common to cats with the tortoiseshell pattern, hence the nickname 'naughty torties'.

Body
Cobby, broad chested and of medium size, with short, sturdy legs. The head is broad and round, with a short nose and small, wide set ears.

Coat
Thick, long and fine. The colours should be evenly mixed and well broken throughout the coat.

Eyes
Large and round; deep orange or copper in colour.

Breed Assessment
GROOMING Daily grooming
VOICE Quiet
ACTIVITY LEVEL Low
COUNTRY OF ORIGIN UK
VARIETIES Black, Chocolate and Lilac
BREED RECOGNIZED IN All countries

Blue Cream

History
Usually a female-only variety, the Blue Cream was originally the product of mating Blue and Cream Persians. There are slight differences in the standards required for the colour distribution. In North America the colours should be patched, but European authorities prefer them to be gently intermingled.

Temperament
Sweet-natured and affectionate. This is generally an undemanding breed.

Body
Broad chested, well muscled and of medium size, with short, sturdy legs. The head is wide and round, with a short face and small, neat, low-set ears.

Coat
Luxuriant, long and silky. The mixture of pale cream and pastel blue should be clearly patched for North American standards, but well mingled in Europe.

Eyes
Round, full and large; the colour should be deep orange or copper.

Breed Assessment
GROOMING Daily grooming
VOICE Quiet
ACTIVITY LEVEL Low
COUNTRY OF ORIGIN UK
BREED RECOGNIZED IN All countries

CAT BREEDS
*Longhairs
(Persian)*

173

Tabby

History
The tabby coat, which echoes the tabby patterning of the wild ancestors of domestic breeds, has been seen for centuries. Brown Tabby Persians were one of the first varieties of Longhairs to be seen in Europe. They were brought to Britain in Victorian times and are documented as having been exhibited at the first official cat show in 1871. This variety is now available in many colours other than brown, including tortie-tabby, the most popular of which today is probably the Silver Tabby.

Temperament
Generally undemanding, sweet-natured and affectionate.

Body
Muscular and cobby, with short, sturdy legs. This breed has a short face, a round, broad head and small neat, well-tufted and low-set ears.

Coat
Dense, but long and silky with distinct darker tabby markings. There should be 'oyster' markings on the flanks, a 'butterfly' on each shoulder and an 'M' marking on the head.

Eyes
Large and round; the colour should be orange or copper in all colours except in the silver, which should have green or hazel eyes.

Brown Tabby

Breed Assessment
GROOMING Daily grooming
VOICE Quiet
ACTIVITY LEVEL Low
COUNTRY OF ORIGIN Persia (Iran).
VARIETIES Silver, Blue, Chocolate, Lilac, Red, Brown and associated colours of Tortie-Tabby (Torbie in the USA)
BREED RECOGNIZED IN All countries

Silver Tabby

American Curl

History
The American Curl is a recent arrival in Europe. The original Curl, found in California in 1981, was a stray cat with strangely curled-back ears. Her new owners gave her the name 'Shulamith' and later that year she became pregnant. When her kittens were born, two of them had the same curiously shaped ears as their mother. A sensible breeding programme was established and the breed was eventually recognized by various American cat societies. It remains more popular in the USA than elsewhere and is comparatively rare in other countries. A shorthair variety is available, but it has not established itself with the popularity of the semi-longhair.

Temperament
Friendly, intelligent and playful. A very adaptable breed, the American Curl is not over demanding and will fit into most domestic situations.

Body
Medium sized and elegant, with a well-proportioned body. The most important point is that the ears should curl back to make a smooth arc.

Coat
The tail and ears should be well furred, while the main body should have silky, medium-length fur that lies close to the body. All colours and patterns are acceptable.

White American Curl

Eyes
Variable, but should complement the coat colour.

Breed Assessment
GROOMING Semi-longhair needs frequent grooming; Shorthair needs regular grooming, more when moulting
VOICE Quiet
ACTIVITY LEVEL Moderate to high
COUNTRY OF ORIGIN USA
VARIETIES Semi-Longhair and Shorthair are available
BREED RECOGNIZED IN USA

CAT BREEDS
Semi-longhairs

175

Red Tabby and White American Curl

Angora (Oriental Longhair)

History
Angoras were the first long-haired cats to be brought to
Western Europe. Some were imported from Ankara in
Turkey in the 19th century, but they lost popularity as
the more fully coated Persian cats arrived and by the early
1900s had virtually disappeared. Today, the Angora has
been genetically 're-created' by breeders of Orientals in
Britain, and is a semi-longhaired version of the Oriental.
It is also known as the Javanese or Mandarin and as the
Oriental Longhair in the USA. The original Angora cats
were rediscovered in 1962 in Ankara zoo in Turkey, where
a breeding project was established. Some of the results
were taken to the USA, where they are classified as the
Turkish Angora to distinguish their pure blood lines from
the British re-created version.

Temperament
Lively, intelligent and companionable. This breed will
suit most family situations.

Body
Long, lean, lithe and elegant, with a well-balanced
appearance. Essentially this breed is a long-haired
Oriental and so conforms to their standard of points.
The legs are slim, with small, rounded feet.

Coat
Long, silky, and glossy with a definite sheen. The tail is
long, tapering and plume-like.

Lilac Angora

Eyes
Almond shaped and green
in colour. In white varieties,
however, may be blue or
odd-eyed.

Breed Assessment
GROOMING Regular grooming
VOICE Loud and talkative
ACTIVITY LEVEL Very high
COUNTRY OF ORIGIN UK
VARIETIES Many different colours
available, including Black, Blue,
Chocolate, Lilac, Red, Cream,
Cinnamon, Caramel, Fawn,
Shaded, Smoke, Tortie, Tabby,
Silver Tabby and White
BREED RECOGNIZED IN
All countries

Chocolate Angora and Fawn Angora

Balinese

History
The Balinese originated from a natural mutation that resulted in semi-longhaired kittens occasionally appearing in litters of Siamese. In the late 1940s, a litter containing semi-longhaired kittens was born to a Siamese in California and the owner decided to develop them as a breed. Two of this original litter were mated to each other and the resulting progeny were true to type; they all had long, silky coats with the 'Himalayan' coat restriction so typical of the Siamese – that is, darker points restricted to the cooler parts of their bodies such as face, ears, paws and tail. By 1963, this breed had become so popular that the Balinese was granted championship status in America and, in the 1980s, was afforded the same official status in Europe. The breed was named Balinese after Siamese breeders objected to the original designation of Longhair Siamese as being confusing.

Temperament
Lively and companionable, with an outgoing personality. The Balinese may be slightly quieter in voice and less demanding than its short-haired counterparts, the Siamese.

Body
Graceful and lithe, with all the elegance of the Siamese. The head is long and straight and ears large, wide set and sometimes tufted. The legs are long, slim and elegant.

Coat
Medium-length fur lying close to the body. The tail should be plume-like.

Blue Point Balinese

Chocolate Tortie Point Balinese

Eyes
Widely spaced, with an Oriental, almond shape; deep blue in colour.

Breed Assessment
GROOMING Regular grooming
VOICE Loud and talkative
ACTIVITY LEVEL Very high
COUNTRY OF ORIGIN USA
VARIETIES Seal Point, Blue Point, Chocolate Point, Lilac Point, Red Point, Cream Point, Caramel Point, Tabby Point (acceptable in all the previous colour variations), Tortie Point (acceptable in all the previous colour variations) and Tortie-Tabby Point. In the USA the Red, Cream, Tabby and Tortie are known as Javanese, and the Tortie-Tabby as a Torbie Javanese
BREED RECOGNIZED IN All countries

Seal Point Balinese

Birman

History
The Birman has a unique and interesting history. Said to be the sacred temple cats of Burma – although these origins are also claimed for the Burmese breed – Birmans have pure white paws, explained by a delightful legend. Many years ago, bandits were attacking the Khmer temple in Burma, which housed a golden image of the blue-eyed goddess Tsun-Kyan-Kse. One of the priests was injured and as he lay dying, his faithful cat came and gently rested its paws on his chest, offering him companionship in his last hours. As the priest died, the cat was transformed. Its fur turned golden like the goddess, its eyes blue and the extremities of the body darkened. Its paws turned to the purest white as a symbol of the cat's devotion to his dying master and to this day white paws are this breed's most distinctive feature. A further legend says that every time a Birman cat dies, the soul of a priest accompanies it to heaven. First imported to Europe by way of France, the Birman is now a popular breed throughout the world and is available in a variety of colours and patterns.

Tortoiseshell Birman

Birman Seal Point

Coat
Medium length and silky with a ruff. The darker-coloured points are restricted to the face, ears, tail and legs and all the paws are white.

Eyes
Roundish in shape; as deep a blue as possible in colour.

Breed Assessment
GROOMING Frequent grooming
VOICE Talkative
ACTIVITY LEVEL Moderate to high
COUNTRY OF ORIGIN Burma
VARIETIES Seal, Blue, Chocolate, Lilac, Red, Cream, Tortie (acceptable in all colour variations), Tabby (acceptable in all colour variations) and Tortie-Tabby
BREED RECOGNIZED IN All countries

Temperament
Intelligent, affectionate and sweet-natured. The Birman makes the most delightful pet for almost any household and enjoys the companionship of both humans and other animals. If the owner is out at work all day, the Birman should have a feline companion.

Body
Long bodied and elegant but solidly built. The Birman has a broad, rounded face, a tapered, longish nose and wide-set, medium-sized ears. The legs are thickset and of medium length, and the tail should be bushy and in proportion to the body.

Tabby Birman

Cymric

History
Despite its name, which derives from *Cymru*, the Celtic name for Wales, the Cymric originates from the Isle of Man rather than Wales and is actually the semi-longhaired version of the Manx cat (see page 196). Because of its glamorous coat, the Cymric has become a most popular breed in the USA. The breed is not recognized in Britain, although it is elsewhere in Europe, and a structured breeding programme has not as yet been implemented.

Temperament
Friendly, intelligent and quiet. This cat is generally a good family pet.

Body
Solidly built and chunky. The general body type is that of a modified British/American Shorthair; the main difference, other than the fact that the Cymric is tailless, is that the hind legs are longer than the front ones, giving the cat a 'rabbity' gait. The Cat Fanciers' Association standards in America call for a show specimen to be completely tailless (Rumpy) but, as with the Manx, Stumpy and Tailed versions crop up in any litter. These may not be shown.

Coat
Long and thick. The Cymric's coat is not as long and silky as most of the breeds found in this section, but is much thicker and longer than that of the Manx. It is accepted in all colours and patterns.

Eyes
Large and round. The colour should complement the cat's coat colour.

Breed Assessment
GROOMING Daily grooming
VOICE Quiet
ACTIVITY LEVEL Moderate to high
COUNTRIES OF ORIGIN Isle of Man, UK and USA
VARIETIES All colours and patterns accepted, except the Siamese/Himalayan patterning
BREED RECOGNIZED IN Europe and the USA

Red Tabby Cymric

Cream Cymric

Red Cymric

Maine Coon

History
Probably one of the largest breeds of cat known, this gentle giant is often claimed to be the original 'all-American' breed, but history suggests otherwise. It is said that this breed may have been sent to America from France by Marie Antoinette, when she hoped to flee across the Atlantic to escape the French Revolution. The first part of its name derives from the American state of Maine, where the cat was first seen, while its luxuriant raccoon-like tail provides the second part.

Temperament
Sweet-natured, friendly, intelligent and playful. The Maine Coon is good with children and makes an ideal family pet.

Brown Tabby
Maine Coon

Red Tabby and White Maine Coon

Body
Solid, muscular and medium to large in size. The head is medium length with a squared-off muzzle and large ears held wide and tall. It has a long, tapering tail, sturdy legs and rounded paws.

Coat
Long, heavy and silky. The unusual waterproof top coat should be glossy, with shorter fur on the head, increasing in length down to the hindquarters and tail. The Maine Coon does not need as much grooming as some other semi-longhair breeds.

Eyes
Round and full, set wide apart. They may be green, gold or copper in colour, although blue or odd eyes are allowed in whites.

Breed Assessment
GROOMING Frequent grooming
VOICE Chirpy and talkative
ACTIVITY LEVEL Moderate to high. Enjoys outdoor life and hunting
COUNTRY OF ORIGIN USA
VARIETIES All colours and patterns are accepted except chocolate, lilac and Siamese/Himalayan patterning
BREED RECOGNIZED IN All countries

Silver Tabby and White
Maine Coon

Norwegian Forest Cat

History
This very popular breed was first exported from Norway only in the 1970s, making it a relative newcomer to the cat fancy. Historically, Norse legends refer to the *Skogatt*, a mountain-dwelling fairy cat with an ability to climb sheer rock faces that other cats could not manage. Certainly, the Norwegian Forest Cat is a most adept climber, with a somewhat ethereal appearance, so perhaps the legend is based on fact. Folk tales also mention huge cats which served Freya, the Norse goddess of love and beauty.

Temperament
Outgoing, friendly and somewhat independent. This cat makes a wonderful family pet.

Body
Strongly built but with an elegant look. Similar in size to the Maine Coone, the Norwegian Forest is a larger than average cat and has a long, sturdy body, long legs and a bushy tail. Its head is long, with a triangular shape and straight profile. The ears are high set, with tufted tops.

Coat
Long and glossy. The thick, water-repellent top coat covers a woolly undercoat. The coat is longest around the legs, chest and head, giving rise to an impressive ruff.

Eyes
Large and open in shape; any colour is acceptable.

Blue Tabby and White Norwegian Forest Cat

Breed Assessment
GROOMING Frequent grooming
VOICE Quiet
ACTIVITY LEVEL Moderate to high. Enjoys outdoor life and hunting
COUNTRY OF ORIGIN Norway
VARIETIES All colours and patterns are accepted except chocolate, lilac and Himalayan (Siamese) patterning
BREED RECOGNIZED IN All countries

Brown Tabby Norwegian Forest Cat with kitten

Norwegian Forest kitten

Ragdoll

History
The often-quoted story about the origins of this American breed is a genetic impossibility. Ragdolls were said to have come from a white Persian-style cat that was struck by a car while pregnant and broke her pelvis. It was claimed that the damage sustained in this accident resulted in her kittens being excessively limp when held and feeling no pain. Rumours that these cats can be thrown around like a rag doll are equally untrue but have given rise to the breed's name. While the exact background of the Ragdoll is unknown, it seems to have arisen in California during the 1960s and is likely to have been related to Birmans. It took some years before any authority would take the Ragdoll seriously as a breed.

Temperament
Sweet-natured, quiet, loving and very relaxed. The Ragdoll is generally undemanding and makes an excellent pet.

Seal Colourpoint Ragdoll

Body
Broad chested, long and muscular. This breed has sturdy, medium-length legs, round, tufted paws and a long, tapering tail. The head is broad, with well-rounded cheeks. The ears are medium sized and set wide apart on a flat skull.

Coat
Silky but dense. The fur of the Ragdoll should be medium length and close lying, apart from the hairs around the legs and tail, which should be well plumed. The neck should also have a small but definite ruff.

Eyes
Medium in size and set wide apart; the colour should be blue, the more intense the better.

Bi-Colour Ragdoll

Breed Assessment
GROOMING Frequent grooming
VOICE Quiet
ACTIVITY LEVEL Moderate
COUNTRY OF ORIGIN USA
VARIETIES The Ragdoll is available in three distinct patterns – Colourpointed, Mitted and Bi-Colour. Seal, Blue, Chocolate and Lilac are all acceptable colours for each of these patterns
BREED RECOGNIZED IN
All countries

Seal Mitted Ragdoll

Somali

History
The Somali is essentially the semi-longhaired version of the Abyssinian (see page 199) and for years was considered the unwanted 'poor relation' of this old-established breed. Indeed, breeders who encountered a 'fluffy' kitten in an Abyssinian litter would tend to ignore its existence and re-home it as a pet. It was not until the 1960s that an American breeder thought to breed them in their own right. They established a firm following in the USA and by 1978 were given championship status. Somalis arrived in mainland Europe in the late 1970s and, in 1981, a pair was taken to England, where they are a popular breed.

Temperament
Intelligent, companionable and outgoing. But like its Abyssinian relative, the Somali does not always mix well with other breeds of cat.

Body
Firm and muscular. The Somali is a medium-sized, well-proportioned cat of foreign type, with long legs and a tapering tail; its gently contoured head has a moderate wedge and the ears are wide set, large and tufted.

Coat
Dense, soft and fine. One of the ticked (see page 161) varieties of cats, the Somali has a triple-banded, medium-length coat. The fur should show a definite ruff around the neck, and the tail should be full and well plumed, giving it a typical 'foxy' look.

Eyes
Large and almond shaped; they may be green, amber or hazel in colour.

Usual Somali and kitten

Breed Assessment
GROOMING Regular grooming
VOICE Quiet
ACTIVITY LEVEL High
COUNTRY OF ORIGIN USA
VARIETIES Usual, Sorrel, Chocolate, Blue, Lilac, Fawn, Red, Cream, Torties (in all colours), Silver (in all colours) and Tortie Silver (in all colours)
BREED RECOGNIZED IN All countries

Fawn Silver Somali

Usual Somali

Tiffanie (UK)

History
The Tiffanie is a cat of Burmese type, but with semi-longhaired fur. It is a fairly recent by-product of the Burmilla/Asian breeding programme (see page 200) and is available in all the colours accepted for that group. By mating Burmilla to Burmilla it was inevitable that the long-haired gene would eventually manifest itself, resulting in the breed known in the UK as the Tiffanie. The cat recognized as the Tiffany in the USA is a totally unrelated breed, not to be confused with the UK Tiffanie.

Temperament
Friendly, outgoing and intelligent. The Tiffanie falls midway between the restrained longhair and the lively Burmese. Like the Burmilla, it has been bred for temperament as well as appearance and this is written in its standard of points (see page 156).

Chocolate Smoke Tiffanie

Body
Elegant, firm and muscular. The Tiffanie has the well-balanced proportions of the Burmese.

Coat
Long, fine and silky. This texture should be particularly noticeable on the neck ruff. The tail should be medium or long and highly plumed.

Eyes
Wide set, full and expressive. The eyes should be slightly slanted and neither too almond nor too round in shape. The colour may be green, yellow or chartreuse, depending on the coat colour.

Chocolate Silver Tiffanie

Breed Assessment
GROOMING Regular grooming
VOICE Fairly quiet
ACTIVITY LEVEL Very high
COUNTRY OF ORIGIN Britain
VARIETIES The Tiffanie is available in all the colours and patterns accepted for the Burmilla/Asian group – self, shaded and tabby colourings of Black, Chocolate, Red, Blue, Lilac, Cream, Caramel, Apricot, Black Tortie, Chocolate Tortie, Blue Tortie, Lilac Tortie and Caramel Tortie
BREED RECOGNIZED IN UK

Brown Smoke Tiffanie

Turkish Van

History
This is an old, original breed that arose from generations of local matings, rather than from deliberate action by breeders. The Turkish Van comes from the upland areas of inner Turkey around the Lake Van region – hence its name. It is also known as the Turkish swimming cat because, true to its lakeside origins, it has a natural love of water and unlike most cats enjoys swimming. Popular on both sides of the Atlantic, the Turkish Van was first seen in Western Europe in the 1950s. The auburn and white pattern is the typical form, but the breed is now accepted (though not without some controversy) in several shades. However, in Turkey pure white examples of the breed are preferred.

Temperament
Quiet voiced, friendly, sweet-natured and intelligent.

Body
Long bodied and sturdy with strong legs. Its tufted paws are neatly shaped and the tail should be in proportion to the body length. The head is wedge shaped, with a long, straight nose. The ears are medium sized, high set and well feathered.

Coat
Long, soft and silky. The distinctive pattern should be restricted to the head, which should have a white blaze and tail. The rest of the coat should be chalk-white, with no trace of yellowing or other shading.

Eyes
Large and oval; the colour should be a medium/light amber, except in the blue-eyed and odd-eyed varieties.

Auburn Turkish Van

Breed Assessment
GROOMING Frequent grooming, but usually less in summer
VOICE Quiet
ACTIVITY LEVEL Moderate to high. This breed enjoys swimming and splashing about
COUNTRY OF ORIGIN Turkey
VARIETIES Auburn and Cream, both of which are accepted with amber, blue or odd-eyed coloration. Some associations recognize black, blue, torties and tabbies
BREED RECOGNIZED IN All countries

Turkish Van and kittens

British Black

History
The British Shorthair is said to have been introduced into Britain by the invading Romans, although it is usually thought of as the 'native' British cat. Within this short-haired group, many colours and patterns are available and the British Black, with its dense, glossy coat, is a popular variety.

Temperament
Sweet-natured, gentle and generally undemanding.

Body
Broad chested, cobby and solidly built. The ears are small, neat and wide set.

Coat
Glossy, short and dense; the colour should be solid black to the roots, without any rusty tinge.

Eyes
Large, round and wide set; the colour should be deep orange or copper.

Breed Assessment
GROOMING Regular grooming
VOICE Quiet
ACTIVITY LEVEL Moderate
COUNTRY OF ORIGIN UK
BREED RECOGNIZED IN All countries

British Cream

History
The shorter summer coat of this breed tends to show vestigial tabby markings inherited from the early Creams. This fault has been reduced during an extensive selective breeding programme, but this colour still remains one of the most problematic to breed with a clear coat.

Temperament
Affectionate, sweet-natured and generally undemanding.

Body
Solid, cobby and broad chested, with short, sturdy legs. The short, round head has small, neat, wide-set ears.

British Cream

Coat
Plush, short and dense. The colour should be an even, pale-toned cream, with as few markings as possible.

Eyes
Large, round and wide set; deep orange or copper in colour.

Breed Assessment
GROOMING Regular grooming
VOICE Quiet
ACTIVITY LEVEL Moderate
COUNTRY OF ORIGIN UK
BREED RECOGNIZED IN All countries

British Cream

British Blue

History
Probably the best known and most popular of this group, the British Blue is also one of the longest established of the Self Colours. It was developed from blue non-pedigrees in the late 19th century. A decline in the numbers of first-class studs during World War II led to some outcrossing (see page 160) to blue longhairs and it was some years before the breed could be returned to its previous glory. A similar breed, known as the Chartreuse (see page 238), is seen in Europe. In North America and some European countries the Chartreuse is treated as a separate breed.

Temperament
Sweet-natured, loving, gentle and undemanding. This breed is more prone to laziness than other shorthairs. Because it tends to be rather greedy, a close watch should be kept on its weight.

British Blue

Body
A solid, sturdy breed, with short, strong legs. The head is full cheeked and round with small, neat, wide set ears.

Coat
Dense, short and plush, with a 'crispness' to the touch. The colour should be a medium to light blue, with no silver or shading, and solid to the roots.

British Blue kitten

Eyes
Large, round and wide set; deep orange or copper in colour.

British Blue

Breed Assessment
GROOMING Regular grooming
VOICE Quiet
ACTIVITY LEVEL Moderate
COUNTRY OF ORIGIN UK
BREED RECOGNIZED IN All countries

CAT BREEDS
Shorthairs (British and American)

187

British Chocolate

History
Regularly utilized as an outcross for the Colourpointed breeding programme (see page 191), the Chocolate is itself a result of that programme. The Chocolate often carries the restricted 'himalayan' coat pattern gene (see page 172), and so is of great value in the breeding of the different colours of Colourpointed.

Temperament
Affectionate, sweet-natured and generally undemanding. This breed does tend to be rather greedy, so a close watch should be kept on its weight.

Body
Solid, cobby and broad chested, with short, sturdy legs. The face is full cheeked and round in shape, with small, neat, wide-set ears.

Coat
Thick, plush and short. The colour should be a rich, even chocolate, with no markings or shading, and the hairs should be solid to the roots.

British Chocolate

Eyes
Large, round and wide set; deep orange or copper in colour.

Breed Assessment
GROOMING Regular grooming
VOICE Quiet
ACTIVITY LEVEL Moderate
COUNTRY OF ORIGIN UK
BREED RECOGNIZED IN All countries

British Chocolate
kitten

British Chocolate

British Lilac

History
Often seen on the show benches, the Lilac is a more recent development, resulting, like the Chocolate, from the Colourpointed breeding programme (see page 191). While many breeders look on this breed as a useful addition to the gene pool for the Colourpoint series, it is also a most attractive cat in its own right.

Temperament
Affectionate, friendly, gentle and generally undemanding. Like the Chocolate, the Lilac can be rather greedy and a close watch should be kept on its weight.

Body
Solid, cobby and broad chested, with short, sturdy legs. The round, full-cheeked head has small, neat, wide-set ears, which lie low on the head.

Coat
Thick, short and plush. The colour should be an even pink-tinged, frosty grey, solid to the roots, without any markings or shadings.

Eyes
Large and round; deep orange or copper in colour.

Breed Assessment
GROOMING Regular grooming
VOICE Quiet
ACTIVITY LEVEL Moderate
COUNTRY OF ORIGIN UK
BREED RECOGNIZED IN All countries

British Lilac

British Lilac

CAT BREEDS
Shorthairs
(British and American)

189

British White

History

Although having the physical appearance of a lustrous white coat, the kittens of this variety can betray their parental genotype by slight 'thumb print' head markings, reflecting their base colour. For example, a white kitten carrying the blue gene can show pale blue markings. As with the White Persians, the British White comes in three varieties, Blue-Eyed, Orange-Eyed, or Odd-Eyed (one of each colour). If allowed access to a garden, this breed will require occasional bathing to retain its colour.

Temperament

Affectionate, sweet-natured and generally undemanding. Like other British shorthairs, this breed is greedy and a watch should be kept on its weight.

Body

Broad chested, solid and cobby, with short, sturdy legs. The head is well rounded, full cheeked, and the ears are small, neat and wide set.

Coat

Plush, dense and short. The fur should be a brilliant, pure white with no yellowing or markings, although slight head marks are allowable in kittens.

Eyes

Large and round; the colour should be brilliant sapphire blue, deep orange or copper, or the cat should have one eye of each colour.

British Odd-eyed White

Breed Assessment

GROOMING Regular grooming
VOICE Quiet
ACTIVITY LEVEL Moderate
COUNTRY OF ORIGIN UK
BREED RECOGNIZED IN All countries

British Orange-eyed White

British Bi-colour

History
The Bi-coloured British Shorthair breed first appeared in the late 19th century. With its distinctive coat, which is a mixture of white and any of the solid colours, the British Bi-colour has always been more popular than the Bi-Colour Persian.

Temperament
Generally undemanding, affectionate and sweet-natured.

Body
Sturdy and broad chested, with short, strong legs. The head is full cheeked and round, with small, wide-set ears.

Coat
Plush, short and dense. Between a third and half of the coat should be white and symmetry in the markings is desirable but not essential.

Eyes
Large, round, lustrous and wide set; deep gold or copper in colour.

Breed Assessment
GROOMING Regular grooming
VOICE Quiet
ACTIVITY LEVEL Moderate
COUNTRY OF ORIGIN UK
VARIETIES Black, Blue, Chocolate, Lilac, Red, Cream and the spectrum of tortie colours
BREED RECOGNIZED IN All countries

British Colourpointed

History
The restricted 'Himalayan' coat pattern (see page 172) of the Siamese was first introduced into the British Shorthairs in the 1970s in a breeding programme involving Colourpoint Longhairs. The Persians were used, since they were closer to the British in body type than the Siamese. Early British Colourpointeds tended to have a rather fluffy coat, because of their Persian ancestry. These cats have now been mated back to British, resulting in a cat of true British type but with the colourpoint pattern.

Temperament
Generally undemanding and relaxed. Sweet-natured, affectionate and gentle, the Colourpointed is sometimes more outgoing than other British colours.

Body
A cobby, sturdy breed, with a broad chest and short, strong legs. The head is round, broad and full cheeked, with small, neat, wide-set ears.

Coat
Short and dense, with a plush feel. The coloured points, restricted to the face, ears, legs and tail, should clearly contrast with the pale body colour.

Eyes
Large, round and lustrous; blue in colour.

Breed Assessment
GROOMING Regular grooming
VOICE Quiet
ACTIVITY LEVEL Moderate
COUNTRY OF ORIGIN UK
VARIETIES Seal, Blue, Chocolate, Lilac, Red, Cream, all the colours of Tortie, Tabby and Tortie-Tabby, and the Silver/Smoke versions of all of these
BREED RECOGNIZED IN All countries

British Smoke

History
The British Smoke first appeared in the late 19th century and was almost certainly a cross between Silver Tabbies and self-coloured British Shorthairs. Although the cat may appear to be a self colour at first, the pale, silvery undercoat is revealed when the fur is moved. It is this that gave rise to the breed's name and that has guaranteed its long-lasting popularity.

Temperament
Sweet natured and loving. This breed is generally undemanding, except for its hearty appetite.

Body
Broad chested and sturdy, with short, strong legs. The head is broad and full cheeked, with small, wide-set ears.

Coat
Short and dense with a plush feel. The pale, silvery undercoat lies close to the skin.

Eyes
Large, round and lustrous; copper, gold or orange in colour.

Breed Assessment
GROOMING Regular grooming
VOICE Quiet
ACTIVITY LEVEL Moderate
COUNTRY OF ORIGIN UK
VARIETIES Black, Blue, Chocolate, Lilac, Red, Cream and the Tortie varieties of the self colours
BREED RECOGNIZED IN Most countries

British Tipped

History
One of the more recently developed patterns, the British Tipped was not officially recognized until 1978. It is now becoming increasingly popular. This breed, with its distinctive tipped coat, is the result of a long and rather complicated breeding programme, which involved crossing British Shorthair Blues (see page 187) and Smokes with the longhaired Chinchilla (see page 168) over several generations.

Temperament
Generally undemanding, sweet-natured and affectionate. This cat likes its food and easily becomes overweight.

Body
Solidly built and broad chested, with short, sturdy legs. Its head should be broad and round, with small, neat, wide-set ears. The Tipped is sometimes more lightly boned than other varieties of British.

Coat
Dense and short with a plush feel. The pale, silvery undercoat should be lightly and evenly tipped with one of the accepted colours. The tipping gives a sparkling appearance as the cat moves.

Eyes
Large and round; usually copper or orange in colour, but the Black Tipped and Golden should have green eyes.

Breed Assessment
GROOMING Regular grooming
VOICE Quiet
ACTIVITY LEVEL Moderate
COUNTRY OF ORIGIN UK
VARIETIES Black, Blue, Chocolate, Lilac, Red, Cream, Tortie and the non-silver variety, Golden
BREED RECOGNIZED IN All countries

British Tabby

History
Tabby markings are shown on Ancient Egyptian paintings of cats, and Shorthaired Brown Tabbies are one of the oldest known breeds. It is generally thought that the cats travelled from mainland Europe to Britain with the invading legions of Imperial Rome in the 1st century AD. It is available in the classic and mackerel pattern and in many colours, but the silver is probably the most popular.

Temperament
Sweet-natured, affectionate and gentle. Tabbies are often more outgoing than their self-coloured counterparts.

Body
Broad-chested, solid and muscular breed with short, sturdy legs; silver varieties are sometimes more lightly boned. The head is full cheeked, round and broad with small, neat, wide-set ears.

Coat
Dense, short and plush. The base colour should be pale, reflecting the main colour; in the silver the base colour should have a definite silvery tone. The Classic Tabby should have a distinct 'M' marking on the forehead, with 'oyster' markings on the flanks and a 'butterfly' pattern over the shoulders; the tail should be well ringed. The Mackerel pattern should have similar markings, as well as a series of vertical, patterned lines on the body.

British Silver Tabbies

Eyes
Large, round and lustrous; they should be deep orange or copper in most varieties, but the Black/Silver should have hazel or green eyes.

Breed Assessment
GROOMING Regular grooming
VOICE Quiet
ACTIVITY LEVEL Moderate
COUNTRY OF ORIGIN UK
VARIETIES Brown, Blue, Chocolate, Lilac, Red, Cream, Tortie and the associated colours of Silver
BREED RECOGNIZED IN All countries

CAT BREEDS
Shorthairs (British and American)

193

British Tortie Tabby

British Red Tabby

British Silver Tabby

British Spotted

History
With a coat reminiscent of those seen in wild cats, the Spotted is a variety of British Tabby, but distinct enough to have its own classification. This is an extremely popular breed, especially in the Silver colours, which are the most glamorous. Its beautiful coat, combined with its sweet nature, makes it one of the most attractive of the British Shorthairs.

Temperament
Generally undemanding and affectionate. The spotted is usually more outgoing than the solid colours.

Body
Cobby, solid and muscular, with short, sturdy legs. The head is round, broad and full cheeked with small, neat, wide-set ears. The Silver varieties are sometimes more lightly boned than the other colours.

Coat
Dense, short and plush. Clearly defined dark spots should be numerous and well distributed over the coat and the head should have a 'M' mark on the forehead, overlaying a pale background colour. In the Silvers the background colour should show a pale silvering.

Eyes
Large, round and lustrous. The colour should be deep orange or copper in all varieties except the Black/Silver, which should have green or hazel eyes.

Breed Assessment
GROOMING Regular grooming
VOICE Quiet
ACTIVITY LEVEL Moderate
COUNTRY OF ORIGIN UK
VARIETIES Brown, Blue, Chocolate, Lilac, Red, Cream, Tortie and the Silver varieties of these
BREED RECOGNIZED IN All countries

British Tortoiseshell (and Blue-Cream)

History
The combination of colours in its coat, which are never exactly replicated in any two cats, make this an attractive and individual breed. Available in many different colours, the British Tortoiseshell is usually a female-only variety, as with all Torties. Male kittens are occasionally born but usually prove to be sterile.

Temperament
Affectionate and sweet-natured. As with all Torties, this breed is usually more demanding than other Shorthairs.

Body
Broad chested, solid and cobby, with short, sturdy legs. The head is round and broad, with small, neat ears.

Coat
Dense, short and plush. The coat should be an evenly mingled mixture of the base colour with red or cream. There should not be large patches of any colour, but a small blaze down the nose is acceptable.

Eyes
Large, round and lustrous; deep gold or copper.

Breed Assessment
GROOMING Regular grooming
VOICE Quiet
ACTIVITY LEVEL Moderate
COUNTRY OF ORIGIN UK
VARIETIES Black, Blue, Chocolate and Lilac. The Blue is known as Blue-Cream
BREED RECOGNIZED IN
All countries

American Shorthair

History
A close relative of the British Shorthair, this breed was probably introduced to America by English settlers who travelled over in the *Mayflower* in 1602. Other ancestral cats would have come over with the French and Dutch. As the settlers' cats adapted to the new home, with its harsher winters and competing carnivores, they became different from their European forebears. The domestic cats in North America became increasingly large and solid, with thick, dense coats. In 1904, American breeders began work to establish a definite breed, based on the best qualities of the local cats. At first, any cat which met the standard could be registered as belonging to the breed, but this practice has now been discontinued. The breed was known as the Domestic Shorthair until 1965, when it was renamed to distinguish it from the British Shorthair and to set it apart from ordinary domestic cats.

Temperament
Outgoing, intelligent, affectionate and good-natured. This breed is a good hunter.

Body
Muscular and heavy bodied. The general body type is that of the British, but rangier, with longer legs and larger head and ears.

Coat
Short, dense and thicker than the British Shorthair coat.

Eyes
Large and lustrous. The colour of the eyes depends on the coat colour.

Silver Classic Tabby American Shorthair

Breed Assessment
GROOMING Regular grooming
VOICE Quiet
ACTIVITY LEVEL Moderate to high
COUNTRY OF ORIGIN USA
VARIETIES Accepted in all colours and patterns
BREED RECOGNIZED IN USA

CAT BREEDS
Shorthairs (British and American)

195

Red Tabby American Shorthair

Red Tabby American Shorthair

Manx

History

As with many of the tailless or short-tailed varieties of cat, rumours and stories abound regarding the genetic roots of this species. Many of the breeds with shortened tails, or no tails at all, stem from the Far East and one legend does indeed state that the cats first arrived in the Isle of Man on East India Company ships trading with the Far East. Another legend relates that the cats swam ashore from a wrecked galleon of the Spanish Armada in 1588. A third holds that the Manx cat was late getting into the Ark and that Noah slammed the door on its tail. It is most likely that the cat was the result of a random mutation on the Isle of Man rather than arriving from elsewhere. One of the earliest breeds of cats to be recognized, the Manx is now bred worldwide.

Temperament

Affectionate, sweet-natured and intelligent.

Body

Well rounded, with hind legs that are longer than the front legs, causing a unique rabbity gait. The head is medium long and round, with prominent cheeks and a straight, wide nose. The most obvious feature of the true Manx, or Rumpy, is that it lacks a tail. But not all Manx cats are totally tailless – the Stumpy has a small, vestigial tail and tailed Manx are also seen; both of the latter are used in Manx breeding programmes.

Coat

Short, very thick and double coated. All colours and patterns are acceptable, except the colourpointed pattern.

Eyes

Large and round; the colour should be in keeping with the coat colour.

Red Tabby and White Manx

Breed Assessment

GROOMING Daily grooming
VOICE Quiet
ACTIVITY LEVEL Moderate to high
COUNTRY OF ORIGIN Isle of Man, UK
VARIETIES All colours and patterns
BREED RECOGNIZED IN All countries

White Tailed Manx

Colour Manx

White Stumpy Manx

Exotic Shorthair

History
The Exotic Shorthair was originally bred in the 1960s in the USA from American Shorthairs and Persians. This breeding programme was later echoed in Britain with British Shorthairs and Persians. The breed remains something of an enigma because, although it should conform in type to the standards accepted for Persians, it has a short coat. This makes it an ideal choice for anyone who likes the short face and cobby type of the Persian but could not cope with its grooming requirements.

Temperament
Sweet-natured, friendly, affectionate and generally undemanding.

Body
Well muscled, cobby and medium sized. The chest is broad and the legs thick and short. The head is massive and round, with a short, snub nose and neat, wide-set ears.

Coat
Soft, dense and plush. The coat is slightly longer than that of the British Shorthairs.

Eyes
Large, round and wide set; the colour should complement the coat colour.

Breed Assessment
GROOMING Frequent grooming
VOICE Quiet
ACTIVITY LEVEL Low to moderate
COUNTRY OF ORIGIN USA
VARIETIES All Persian colours and patterns, and spotted tabbies
BREED RECOGNIZED IN All countries

Red Tabby Exotic Shorthair

Blue Bi-colour Exotic Shorthair

Blue-Cream Tortie-Tabby Exotic Shorthair

Scottish Fold

History
The forward-folding ears of this breed originated from a natural mutation first seen in a farm cat in Scotland in the 1960s. When this cat produced two kittens, also with folded ears, a local shepherd took one and became interested in developing a new breed. In 1971, several individuals were sent to the USA, where they became established as a popular breed. Elsewhere, some authorities have refused to register the Folds because the gene that causes the folded ears can also give rise to skeletal deformities. These problems can be prevented by avoiding too close an inbreeding and only mating Scottish Folds with non-folded cats.

Temperament
Sweet-natured and gentle.

Body
Stocky and broad chested like other British cats, but with a somewhat flatter skull. The skull shape and the distinctive folded ears give the headed an attractively rounded look. This cat seems to have perfectly normal hearing despite the curiously folded ears.

Coat
Dense, thick and resilient. The coat of this breed is similar to that of the Manx. Long-haired varieties of Scottish Fold are also available.

Eyes
Unusually large and round giving this breed an almost owl-like appearance; the colour should complement the coat colour.

Breed Assessment
GROOMING Regular grooming
VOICE Quiet
ACTIVITY LEVEL Moderate
COUNTRY OF ORIGIN UK
VARIETIES All colours and patterns are accepted
BREED RECOGNIZED IN USA and Europe

Black Bi-colour Scottish Fold

Blue Bi-colour Scottish Fold

Blue-Cream Scottish Fold

Abyssinian

History

The Abyssinian is an old, established breed that has not changed radically over the years – except that it is now available in a variety of colours. The original Abyssinians are thought to have been brought over to Europe from Africa by soldiers returning from the Anglo-Abyssinian War, which ended in 1868.

Mummified cats found in Egyptian tombs have a similar shape to the Abyssinian, and the Abyssinian's distinctive ticked coat is similar to that of some African wild cats. Abyssinians were accepted as a breed in Europe by the late 1880s and in 1907 some individuals were taken to North America.

Temperament

Intelligent, friendly and outgoing. These cats need human and feline companionship, but they do not always mix well with other breeds of cat.

Body

Elegant and graceful, with long, slender legs and a tapering tail. The head is wedge shaped and often has a dark line behind the eyes. The ears are large and cup shaped with distinctive tufted tips.

Coat

Short and close lying. The hairs should have at least four bands of colour and should feel fine in texture but not soft to the touch. There are now several colours, in addition to the original Usual or Ruddy.

Sorrel Abyssinian

Eyes

Large and almond shaped, set wide apart; the colour may be amber, hazel or green.

Breed Assessment

GROOMING Infrequent grooming, except when moulting
VOICE Quiet
ACTIVITY LEVEL High
COUNTRY OF ORIGIN Abyssinia (Ethiopia)
VARIETIES Usual, Sorrel, Blue, Chocolate, Lilac, Fawn, Red, Cream, Silver (in all base colours), Tortie (in all base and silver colours)
BREED RECOGNIZED IN All countries

Blue Abyssinian

Usual Abyssinian

Burmilla

History
The origins of this recent and enchanting breed read almost like a modern-day fairy story. Baroness Miranda von Kirchberg had a Chinchilla male cat and a Burmese female, which was on heat and was shut into the study prior to visiting her appointed Burmese mate. The housekeeper heard the Chinchilla crying for his beloved Burmese and scratching at the study door trying to find her, so she let him in. The result of this accidental mating is now history: in 1981 a litter of quite charming kittens was born. The Baroness nicknamed them 'Burmillas'. Such was their beauty that she decided to instigate a sensible breeding programme. That programme has given rise to the group that now includes the Asians (see pages 201-02), Bombay (see page 203) and Tiffanie (see page 184).

Temperament
Sweet-natured, friendly, affectionate and intelligent. This breed loves human company and is less demanding than the Burmese, but more outgoing than the Chinchilla.

Body
Well muscled and sturdy, with the elegant look of a Burmese type. The hind legs are slightly longer than the front, and the tail tapers, though its length is in proportion to the body. The head has a gently rounded dome and a wedge-shaped muzzle. The ears are medium sized and wide set.

Coat
Short, fine and close lying. The undercoat should be as pale as possible, with even tipping over the rest of the body and a distinct 'M' marking on the forehead.

Eyes
Moderate Oriental shape, neither almond nor round; may be any colour from yellow through to green, depending on the coat colour.

Breed Assessment
GROOMING Little grooming required
VOICE Talkative
ACTIVITY LEVEL High
COUNTRY OF ORIGIN UK
VARIETIES Black, Blue, Chocolate, Lilac, Caramel, Red, Cream, Apricot and the associated Torties; they are accepted in silver and standard versions
BREED RECOGNIZED IN Europe (including UK)

Brown Shaded Silver Burmilla

Black Shaded Silver Burmilla

Asian Smoke

History

This breed shares its origins with the Burmilla and, similarly, early generations were outcrossed with Burmese (see page 226) and Chinchillas (see page 168). Along with other breeds that share these origins, it is often placed in the group now known as 'Asian'. Baroness von Kirchberg, who first bred these cats, named them 'Burmoiré' because their pale, silvery undercoat, darker top coat and very faint tabby markings, were reminiscent of the watered silk known as moiré. As the popularity of the Asian group increased, a more descriptive and less romantic name was thought to be appropriate. Genetically a shaded, non-agouti variety of the Asian, the breed is now called the Asian Smoke.

Temperament

Sweet-natured, friendly, intelligent, playful and athletic.

Body

A shorthaired cat of Burmese type. The body is medium length and well muscled, the hind legs are longer than the front, and the tail tapers to a rounded tip. The head is wedge shaped and should have a gently rounded dome, with medium-sized, wide-set ears.

Coat

Short, sleek and close lying. It is important that the paler undercoat should comprise at least one-third, but no more than half, of each hair shaft, the remaining part being of the darker, base colour.

Eyes

Slightly Oriental in set, full and expressive and set well apart. The colour may vary from yellow, through chartreuse to green.

Chocolate Asian Smoke

Breed Assessment

GROOMING Little grooming required
VOICE Talkative
ACTIVITY LEVEL High
COUNTRY OF ORIGIN UK
VARIETIES Black, Blue, Chocolate, Lilac, Caramel, Red, Cream, Apricot and the associated Torties; may be Full or Burmese expressions
BREED RECOGNIZED IN UK

CAT BREEDS
Shorthairs (Foreign)

201

Chocolate Asian Smoke

Asian Tabby

History
This is another member of the Asian group, which was established by an accidental mating of a Chinchilla to a Burmese in 1981 (see page 200). It was realized from the beginning that this cross would result in myriad fur lengths, colours and patterns in future generations. The Asian Tabby is the short-haired, agouti variation and is one of the most popular of the Asian group, with a wide range of colours and patterns now available.

Temperament
Generally sweet-natured, friendly, intelligent, playful and athletic.

Body
Like all Asians, a short-haired cat of Burmese type. The body is medium length, well muscled and sturdy. The rear legs are slightly longer than the front and the tail is in proportion to the body and tapers to a rounded tip. The wedge-shaped head has a gently rounded dome, with medium-sized wide-set ears.

Coat
Short, sleek and close lying. It may have ticked, spotted, mackerel, or classic tabby markings, but whatever the colour or pattern, it is important that the base colour and markings should balance overall.

Eyes
Full and expressive, set wide apart and slightly Oriental in shape. The colour may be yellow, chartreuse or green, depending on the coat colour.

Brown Asian Ticked Tabby

Breed Assessment
GROOMING Little grooming required
VOICE Talkative
ACTIVITY LEVEL High
COUNTRY OF ORIGIN UK
VARIETIES Classic, Spotted, Mackerel or Ticked; the colours can be Black, Blue, Chocolate, Lilac, Caramel, Red, Cream, Apricot and all of the associated Tortie colours; these colours and markings may be accepted in silver or standard versions and in Full or Burmese expression
BREED RECOGNIZED IN U.K.

Black Asian Ticked Tabby

Bombay (and Asian Self)

History
The best known of the Asian Selfs is the black variety called the Bombay. In Britain, this breed was produced from the Burmilla/Asian breeding programme. In the USA, the Bombay was the result of a mating between a Burmese and a domestic black shorthair, which has produced a slightly different looking cat. Known as 'the patent leather kid with the copper penny eyes', it has very bright eyes and a jet-black coat famous for its sheen and texture.

Temperament
Intelligent, outgoing, affectionate and athletic.

Body
Like all Asians, basically a cat of Burmese type but with a different coloured coat. It has a medium-sized, well-muscled body, with a wedge-shaped head and rounded dome. The ears are medium sized and wide set. The hind legs are slightly longer than the front. The tail is in proportion to the body and tapers to the tip.

Bombay

Coat
Sleek, shiny and close lying. Colouring should be solid to the roots and as even as possible, although some tabby markings are acceptable in the paler colours. For the Bombay, a deep jet-black that is solid to the roots is essential.

Eyes
Large. Colour should be gold, yellow, chartreuse or green, or copper in USA.

Breed Assessment
GROOMING Little grooming required
VOICE Talkative
ACTIVITY LEVEL High
COUNTRY OF ORIGIN UK or USA
VARIETIES Black for the Bombay, and self colours of Blue, Chocolate, Lilac, Red, Cream, Caramel and Apricot
BREED RECOGNIZED IN UK and USA (Bombay only)

Bombay

Bengal

History
The result of an experimental mating between a domestic female shorthair and an Asian Leopard Cat, the first Bengal kittens were born in the USA in the 1960s. Two decades later a full breeding plan was devised, which involved the Egyptian Mau (see page 208) and Indian street cats. This resulted in the breed now known as the Bengal, which has a delightful 'fireside moggie' temperament but the looks of a true wild cat.

Temperament
Intelligent, sweet-natured, playful and loving.

Body
Large and muscular, with a rounded head, prominent whisker pads and small, wide-set, round-tipped ears.

Coat
Unusually soft in texture, resembling the feel of a wild cat pelt. The pattern may be either spotted or marbled. Cats with a pearly grey ground to the markings are known as Snow Bengals.

Eyes
Large and oval, with an almond slant; blue, blue-green or green in the Snow Bengals; for the other colours, the eyes can be any hue from gold through to green.

Breed Assessment
GROOMING Little grooming required
VOICE Quiet
ACTIVITY LEVEL High; fond of water, so should have some available in the form of a dripping tap, bath or hand basin
COUNTRY OF ORIGIN USA
VARIETIES The Bengal may be either spotted or marbled in pattern and is available in Brown, with either the Siamese/Himalayan gene (blue-eyed Snow) or the Burmese or Tonkinese pattern (Snow with any other eye colour)
BREED RECOGNIZED IN All countries

Spotted Bengal

Marble Bengal (left) Spotted Bengal (right)

AOC-eyed Snow Marble Bengal

Cornish Rex

History

A natural mutation, the Cornish Rex was first discovered in 1950, when a kitten with strange, curly fur was born to a farm cat in Cornwall, England. At a vet's suggestion, this kitten was mated back to its mother and two of the resulting litter were born with the curly coats that are now associated with this breed. In 1957, the Cornish Rex was taken to the USA, where breeders have produced a cat that is more slender than the British variety.

Temperament

Intelligent, friendly, lively and playful. The Cornish Rex has a mischievous side to its character. These cats can tend to gluttony and owners need to keep an eye on the diet or they will end up with a plump cat, rather than the rangy slender shape of the typical Rex.

Red Cornish Rex

Tortie and White Cornish Rex

Body

Muscular, medium sized and slender. This cat has a long, wedge-shaped head, flat skull and large ears set high.

Coat

Short, fine and soft in texture. The curly coat has no guard hairs and should wave, giving a rippled look.

Eyes

Oval and medium sized; any colour is acceptable.

Breed Assessment

GROOMING Little grooming required
VOICE Talkative
ACTIVITY LEVEL High
COUNTRY OF ORIGIN UK
VARIETIES All colours and patterns acceptable
BREED RECOGNIZED IN All countries

CAT BREEDS
Shorthairs (Foreign)

205

Bi-Colour Cornish Rex

Devon Rex

History
Unrelated to the Cornish Rex (see page 205), the Devon Rex is the result of a natural mutation first seen in a stray tom found in Devon in 1960. When he mated with another local stray, their litter included one curly-coated kitten. When this kitten was mated with a Cornish Rex, however, normal kittens were produced, showing that, despite their apparent similarity, the curly coats of the two breeds were produced by different genes. Inbreeding was needed to perpetuate the gene, before the cats were bred out to short-haired, Siamese and other breeds to introduce diversity to the colour of the coat. The Devon Rex was first recognized as a breed in 1967.

Temperament
Friendly, intelligent, mischievous and playful. The Devon Rex rarely sits still and is renowned for its curiosity and investigative activity. This breed has a tendency to overeat, so owners need to keep a watch on its diet.

Blue Tabby Devon Rex

Devon Rex kittens

Body
Medium sized with a slender, firm, muscular body and long legs. The head should be wedge shaped, with large, low-set ears and full cheeks. The face shape, together with the large eyes, give this breed the typical 'pixie' expression that has become its hallmark.

Coat
Short, fine and curled or waved and not as dense as the coat of the Cornish. This breed of Rex cat has guard hairs, but they are wavy, like the other hairs of its fur. It should never appear to be bald. The whiskers are as curly as the rest of the coat, but may be brittle and are often lost. Cats with paler-coloured coats may require sun block on the ears in the summer months.

Eyes
Large and wide set; any colour is acceptable.

Breed Assessment
GROOMING Little grooming required
VOICE Talkative
ACTIVITY LEVEL High
COUNTRY OF ORIGIN UK
VARIETIES All coat colours and patterns are acceptable
BREED RECOGNIZED IN All countries

Black Smoke Devon Rex

Other Rexes

Although the Cornish and Devon Rexes are the best known of the curly-coated cats, other similar random mutations have been seen in different parts of the world from time to time. Many of these quickly died out, usually because of insufficient interest in establishing a proper breeding programme. Among those that enjoyed only

Selkirk Rex

Long-haired Selkirk Rex

short-lived existence were the Italian, Ohio, Oregon and Prussian Rexes. A cat known as the Urals Rex was discovered in the early 1990s in Russia. It is not yet known if a breeding programme has been established to keep this strain going.

The German Rex, which derives from a stray found among the ruins of East Berlin in the 1940s, differs from the Cornish Rex in that its coat has no guard hairs and, with its thicker, denser undercoat, appears woollier. Serious breeding programmes in both Germany and the USA during the 1950s popularized this breed and it has been more long-lived than many Rexes.

However, it has been found that the coat mutation is identical to that of the Cornish, though its body form is distinct. With the increased popularity of the Cornish Rex in recent years, the German line has declined. Although it is still recognized by FIFe (the Federation Internationale Féline), the German Rex is rarely seen on the European show benches today.

The Selkirk Rex is named after the Selkirk Mountains in Wyoming, USA, where the first was born in a litter at a pet rescue centre in 1987. Thanks to its unusual coat, the kitten was noticed by a breeder. A concentrated breeding programme was initiated in Montana, where the cat was crossbred with a variety of other cats. This gave rise to the breed's chunky build and short-muzzled, round head.

The recessive gene for long hair was present from the start, and long-haired Selkirks are extremely striking. This breed is now very popular in both the US and Canada, where it has gained the nickname of 'Sheepcat' because of its thick, curly coat. It is said to be the only genetically dominant variety of Rex.

Breeders are still divided on the subject of Rexes. Some dislike their wavy coats; others defend these cats, admiring their affectionate, playful personalities.

Black German Rex

Egyptian Mau

History

Mau is the Egyptian word for cat and this breed is the result of breeding programmes to re-create the cats shown in Ancient Egyptian tomb paintings. In particular, the characteristic markings on the forehead are said to resemble the scarab beetle held sacred by the Ancient Egyptians. The breed began in 1953, when a Russian princess living in Rome acquired a spotted cat from Cairo. She mated this with a cat belonging to the Egyptian ambassador and produced a litter, one of which was mated back to its mother. A few years later the princess left Italy for the USA, where her cats formed the basis of the breed. By 1968, the breed was officially recognized in the USA and in the late 1970s it arrived in Europe. Some confusion has been caused by the use of the word Mau to describe the oriental Spotted Tabbies found in Britain.

Silver Egyptian Mau

Temperament

Companionable, intelligent, outgoing and adventurous.

Body

Long bodied and elegant. The Egyptian Mau is a modified Siamese/Oriental type, with a more rounded face than most Orientals. It is a most attractive cat, with a distinctive, spotted coat.

Coat

Smooth, short and close lying, with clearly defined spots. There should be a distinctive 'M' mark on the forehead.

Eyes

Almond shaped, but not too Oriental; pale green in colour.

Breed Assessment

GROOMING Little grooming required
VOICE Fairly quiet
ACTIVITY LEVEL High
COUNTRY OF ORIGIN USA
VARIETIES Black, Smoke, Pewter, Bronze and Silver
BREED RECOGNIZED IN USA

Silver Egyptian Mau

Japanese Bobtail

History

The Bobtail is an ancient breed that may have been introduced into Japan from China a thousand years ago, or may have existed even earlier. At first, only the nobility were allowed to own Bobtails, which they walked on leads, but in the 17th century there was an urgent need for cats as pest controllers and ownership spread. The most favoured form is the three-coloured or *Mi-Ke*, which is believed to be lucky and is linked to the legendary Beckoning Cat (see page 245) of Japan. Images and statues of the Beckoning Cat with one paw raised are also believed to bring good luck. In 1968, the breed was taken to the USA, where the cats were selectively bred to produce a lighter and more delicate creature than the native Japanese cats. This breed is increasingly popular in the USA and Japan, but is little known elsewhere.

Temperament

Companionable, friendly and intelligent.

Body

Medium sized and well muscled. Like the Manx, the Bobtail has hind legs that are longer than the fore legs, giving it an unusual gait. The head should be triangular in shape. The most distinctive factor of this breed is its short 'bobbed' tail, which is curled when the cat is at rest, but held upright when it is moving. It is curious that both the two best-known tailless, or semi-tailless breeds, the Bobtail and the Manx, originate from islands, and it is thought that they arose from a mutation caused by a limited gene pool.

Mi-Ke (three-coloured) Japanese Bobtail

Coat

Short and close lying. Characteristically, the fur should radiate at the base of the tail. A semi-longhaired variety is also available.

Eyes

Large and oval; the colour should complement the coat.

Breed Assessment

GROOMING Regular grooming; more frequent for semi-longhairs

VOICE Talkative

ACTIVITY LEVEL Moderate

COUNTRY OF ORIGIN Japan

VARIETIES The classic version is black, red or tortie and white, but other colours are acceptable

BREED RECOGNIZED IN USA and Japan

Red and White Japanese Bobtail

Korat

History
One of the oldest known breeds, the Korat is considered to be sacred and a harbinger of good fortune in its native Thailand. A pair of Korats was a traditional gift for a bride. The breed is believed to have originated in Korat, an eastern province of the country. It was first taken to the USA in the late 1950s and a breeding programme was started. Korats did not reach Europe until the 1970s. Although not seen in large numbers on the show bench, this breed has a firm following of dedicated breeders.

Temperament
Intelligent, quiet, gentle and loving. The Korat enjoys the company of another similar cat.

Body
Elegant, medium sized and muscular. Its heart-shaped face and large ears give this breed its typically sweet expression.

Coat
Short and close lying. The coat should have the distinctive feature of being 'broken' – that is, slightly, but noticeably, standing up along the spine.

Korat

Eyes
Large, round and lustrous. As kittens, the eyes are sometimes yellow and may not develop into the correct green hue until cats are two or three years old.

Breed Assessment
GROOMING Little grooming required
VOICE Quiet
ACTIVITY LEVEL High
COUNTRY OF ORIGIN Thailand
VARIETIES Only the original Blue is recognized.
BREED RECOGNIZED IN All countries

Korat

Ocicat

History
In the 1960s, a breeding programme was set up in the USA to create an Abyssinian-point Siamese. The second generation produced a beautiful golden-spotted male among a litter of mixed tabbies. The kitten looked just like a young ocelot and this was the beginning of the breed now known as the Ocicat. The breed is most popular in the USA but is attracting admirers elsewhere.

Temperament
Friendly, intelligent and companionable.

Body
Well muscled and solid. This is a long cat with a broad head and a slight squareness to the jaw, resulting in its characteristic muzzle. The large, wide-set, tufted ears may give it the look of a wild cat, but this is a purely domestic breed, with a pedigree ancestry.

Lilac Ocicat

Black Silver Ocicat

Breed Assessment
GROOMING Little grooming required
VOICE Talkative
ACTIVITY LEVEL High
COUNTRY OF ORIGIN USA
VARIETIES Brown, Blue, Chocolate, Lilac, Cinnamon, Fawn and the Silver varieties of these colours
BREED RECOGNIZED IN All countries

Coat
Sleek, short, smooth and well spotted. The face should show an 'M' marking on the forehead and there should be a 'broken bracelet' marking at the throat and scattered spots on the body. The tail should show rings and spots of darker colour.

Eyes
Large, wide set and almond shaped; the colour may be anything except blue.

Cinnamon Ocicat

Russian Blue

Russian Blue

History
This breed was originally named the 'Archangel Cat', for it is believed to have originated in the port of Archangel (now Arkhangel'sk) in northern Russia. It is most likely that it was brought to Europe in the 19th century by seafarers travelling from this sub-Arctic city. The Russian Blue also arrived in North America around the turn of the century. It became a popular breed in the West where, because of confusion with the British Blue, it became known as the Foreign Blue. It did not regain its true name until 1939. Although Blue is considered, and accepted as, the typical colour for this breed, both black and white Russians have been known. This is because during World War II the breed became so scarce that it almost died out and it was maintained only by outcrossing (see page 161) to British Blues and Blue Point Siamese.

Temperament
Intelligent, sweet-natured and gentle. This breed is generally fairly quiet.

Body
Medium to large sized, an elegant and graceful breed with long, slim legs. When they move, these cats look almost like a ballerina *en pointe*. The head is straight in profile, with prominent whisker pads and large ears, set high on a flat skull.

Coat
Fine, soft and silky, with a plush feel. This breed has an unusually thick double coat, which has a fine sheen created by the delicate silver tips to the guard hairs. The down hairs of the undercoat are particularly water resistant. The dense fur of the Russian Blue probably results from the bitterly cold winter weather in its native Arkhangel'sk.

Eyes
Almond shaped and wide set; vivid green in colour.

Breed Assessment
GROOMING Little grooming required but possibly more when moulting
VOICE Quiet
ACTIVITY LEVEL Moderate
COUNTRY OF ORIGIN Russia
VARIETIES Blue, Black and White
BREED RECOGNIZED IN All countries (Blue only)

Russian Blue

Singapura

History

The history of this breed before 1975, when it was first imported into the USA, is obscure. According to the breeders who took it to the USA, the breed originated among the small, feral cats of Singapore, known locally as 'drain cats' because they sheltered in the city drains and sewers. Some believe that oriental-type pet cats, perhaps from ships visiting the port, also played a part in the background of the actual specimens taken to North America. Once in the USA, the breed was established and came to Europe in the 1980s. Although still far from numerous, the Singapura is increasingly popular in Europe and the USA.

Temperament

Intelligent, friendly and playful. The Singapura is outgoing and can be talkative.

Body

Elegant, with a tapering tail and long, slim legs. The head is rounded, with a blunt muzzle and large, pointed ears. The Singapura is known as the smallest breed of domestic cat, but sensibly constructed breeding programmes have been implemented to ensure that today's examples have a heavy feel, despite being only small to medium in size.

Coat

Smooth and silky. The coat should be short, sleek and dense, with even ticking.

Singapura

Eyes

Large and almond shaped, with a slight upward tilt. They may be green, yellow or hazel in colour and are outlined in black.

Breed Assessment

GROOMING Little grooming required

VOICE Talkative

ACTIVITY LEVEL High to very high

COUNTRY OF ORIGIN Singapore

VARIETIES Brown ticked (known as Sepia Agouti in the USA)

BREED RECOGNIZED IN All countries

CAT BREEDS
*Shorthairs
(Foreign)*

213

Singapura

Sphynx

History
The natural mutation for the nearly hairless Sphynx first occurred in Canada in 1966, when a pet cat gave birth to a hairless male kitten. However, most Sphynx today are descended from three hairless kittens found in Toronto in 1978. The Sphynx's popularity waned in North America in the late 1970s but increased in Europe, where new breeding programmes were instigated in both Holland and France. The breed is now popular in North America and Europe, but it remains rare.

Temperament
Mischievous, friendly and intelligent. The Sphynx is said to be unusually sociable.

Body
Elegant, with long, slim legs and a medium-sized, muscular body. The head is longer than it is wide and is set on a slender neck. The ears are large, wide set and broad at the base.

Coat
Although at first glance the Sphynx may seem to be hairless, it is evenly covered in a very fine, downy fur

Blue Sphynx

that is often denser and more apparent on the tail and legs. The fur has been likened to the bloom on peach skin and is very soft to the touch. It is important that the pattern and pigmentation should be clearly visible on the skin. Some asthmatics who are allergic to cat hair find they can tolerate this breed quite happily because of its minimal amount of fur.

Eyes
Medium sized and lemon shaped. Eyes can be any colour but should complement the skin colour.

Breed Assessment
GROOMING Occasional rub with a chamois leather or hand
VOICE Quiet
ACTIVITY LEVEL High
COUNTRY OF ORIGIN Canada
VARIETIES All colours and patterns are acceptable.
BREED RECOGNIZED IN All countries (not by GCCF in UK)
SPECIAL NEEDS Care must be taken to protect the Sphynx from sunburn. The Sphynx may also suffer from greasy skin and need regular bathing

Blue Bi-colour Sphynx

CAT BREEDS
Shorthairs (Foreign)

214

Tabby and White Snowshoe

Snowshoe

History
Often mistakenly described as being a short-haired Birman (see page 178), this breed is the result of matings between American Shorthair Bi-Colours and Siamese. The original hybrids that gave rise to this breed were produced in the USA in the 1960s, but it was nearly 20 years before any major authority recognized the Snowshoe and even now it is not accepted everywhere.

Temperament
Sweet-natured, friendly and intelligent. The Snowshoe loves company.

Body
Elegant, sturdy and well built. The body is of medium to large size, with a triangular, wedge-shaped head that should not be as elongated as that of the Siamese. The ears should be medium in size and should clearly continue upward in line with the side of the face.

Coat
Sleek, short and close lying. The body colour should be pale, with the darker base colour restricted to the face, ears, tail and legs. The muzzle and paws must be white, and it is desirable for the face to show an inverted 'V' between the eyes.

Eyes
Large and almond shaped; the eyes should be a brilliant blue in colour.

Breed Assessment
GROOMING Little grooming required
VOICE Softly talkative
ACTIVITY LEVEL High
COUNTRY OF ORIGIN USA
VARIETIES Seal, Blue and Tabby
BREED RECOGNIZED IN USA and Europe

Seal Point Snowshoe

Tonkinese

History

Cats similar to the Tonkinese are thought to have been brought to the West from Burma as early as the 1880s, but their distinctive features were bred out as part of the Burmese breeding programme. It was in the 1960s that a mating between Burmese and Siamese in the USA produced the Tonkinese, originally known as the Golden Siamese, seen today. The breed was also developed in Canada and was first recognized in Canada and the USA. It is now popular in Europe, too. The Tonkinese should be a balance between the two founder breeds, with all the character and personality of both but with the more robust, well-built body of the Burmese. For this reason, they are ideal for anyone looking for a cat of the old-fashioned 'apple headed' Siamese type.

Temperament

Intelligent, inquisitive, friendly and outgoing. The Tonkinese has a quieter voice than either the Siamese or Burmese.

Chocolate Tonkinese

Body

Well balanced and muscular. Without showing a tendency to the type of either of the foundation breeds, the appearance of the Tonkinese should lie squarely between the two.

Coat

Close lying, fine and short, with a definite sheen. The darker points should blend into the paler body colour.

Eyes

Fuller than the eyes of Siamese but not round. For perfection they should be a bluish green or aquamarine in colour, but shades from green to light blue are acceptable.

Lilac Tonkinese

Breed Assessment

GROOMING Little grooming required
VOICE Talkative
ACTIVITY LEVEL Very high
COUNTRY OF ORIGIN USA
VARIETIES Brown, Blue, Chocolate, Lilac, Red, Cream and the associated torties, tabbies and tortie-tabbies.
BREED RECOGNIZED IN All countries

Cream Tonkinese

American Wirehair

History
Although at first glance similar in appearance to the Rex varieties, the American Wirehair is genetically unique. It resulted from a natural mutation that was first seen in a kitten born to a farm cat in New York State in the mid-1960s. The kitten was acquired by a breeder, who began a breeding programme during which it was found that the wirehair gene was dominant. At first the show standards for the breed were identical to those for the American Shorthair, except for the coat, but this changed as breeders recognized consistent characteristics emerging. The American Wirehair has become a popular breed in the USA, and it is known in Canada, Germany and Japan. However, it has yet to be seen in Britain, Australia and other countries.

Temperament
Affectionate, friendly and sweet-natured. This breed is also known for its inquisitive nature.

Body
Elegant, well muscled and medium sized. The American Wirehair is of modified foreign type. It has a round head, with high cheekbones and a pronounced muzzle, topped by large, high-set ears.

Coat
Thick, coarse, short and tightly crimped, with something of the feel of a young lamb's coat when touched. The guard hairs typically turn over into a hook.

Brown Tabby and White American Wirehair

Eyes
Almond shaped; any colour is acceptable but should complement the coat colour.

Breed Assessment
GROOMING Little grooming required. Paler-coated varieties may need sun block if allowed outside in the summer.
VOICE Quiet
ACTIVITY LEVEL High
COUNTRY OF ORIGIN USA
VARIETIES All colours and patterns accepted
BREED RECOGNIZED IN USA, Canada and Europe (not UK)

CAT BREEDS
Shorthairs (Foreign)

217

Brown Patched Tabby and White American Wirehair

Havana

History
Not to be confused with the quite separate American breed known as the Havana Brown, the Havana is a chocolate-brown cat of Siamese type. Developed in Britain in the 1950s from a mating of a Siamese to a domestic shorthaired half-Siamese, the first Havana was born in 1952 and the breed was granted official recognition in 1958.

Temperament
Intelligent, sociable, outgoing and athletic. The Havana will pine if left alone for long periods.

Body
Medium sized, muscular but elegant. This cat is similar to a Siamese, with a long, slim body, long whip-like tail and long, slender legs. The head is a triangular wedge shape, straight in profile, with large, wide-set ears.

Coat
Short, sleek and close lying. It should be a warm, chestnut-brown colour, solid to the roots without any shading or barring.

Eyes
Oriental in shape and slanting toward the nose; colour should be a clear, vivid green.

Breed Assessment
GROOMING Little grooming required
VOICE Talkative
ACTIVITY LEVEL Very high
COUNTRY OF ORIGIN UK
BREED RECOGNIZED IN All countries

CAT BREEDS
Orientals

218

Black

History
In the 1960s, a breeding programme was begun to produce a plain-coated cat of Siamese type, without the restricted coat pattern. Although it is reported that a Siamese-type cat with a solid black coat existed in Germany before World War II, the glamorous Oriental Black known today is the result of much hard work on the part of dedicated breeders.

Temperament
Intelligent, affectionate, athletic and outgoing. This cat pines if left alone and enjoys the company of another cat with a similar temperament.

Body
Elegant, long and slim. This medium-sized cat has a long whip-like tail and long, slender legs. The head is a triangular wedge shape, with a straight profile and large, wide-set ears.

Coat
Short, sleek and close lying. The colour should be jet-black, solid to the roots with no shading or markings.

Eyes
Oriental in shape and slanting toward the nose. As with nearly all Orientals, the colour should be a clear green.

Breed Assessment
GROOMING Little grooming required
VOICE Talkative
ACTIVITY LEVEL Very high
COUNTRY OF ORIGIN UK
BREED RECOGNIZED IN All countries

Blue (and Lilac)

History
Not until 1962 did a breeder start a programme aiming at producing solid-coloured cats of Siamese body shape. By 1965, white cats of Oriental shape were appearing at cat shows as experimentals, and other colours were quick to follow. Both the Blue and the Lilac Oriental Shorthairs originate from the breeding plan devised to produce the Havana. While the first generation were all black, later generations, which encountered the recessive gene, produced some blue kittens. The Blue, when mated to a cat carrying the chocolate gene, results in Lilac.

Temperament
Intelligent, affectionate, outgoing and athletic.

Body
Long, slim and elegant. Like the Siamese, these Orientals are well muscled, with long, slim legs, a slender neck and a long whip-like tail. The head is a triangular wedge shape, with a straight profile and large, wide-set ears.

Coat
Short, sleek and close lying. The Blue is a medium/light blue with no silvering and the Lilac a frosty grey with a distinct pinky tinge. In both colours the fur should be solid to the roots.

Eyes
Oriental in shape and slanting toward the nose; the colour should be clear, vivid green.

Lilac Oriental

Breed Assessment
GROOMING Little grooming required
VOICE Talkative
ACTIVITY LEVEL Very high
COUNTRY OF ORIGIN UK
BREED RECOGNIZED IN All countries. The Lilac is sometimes known as Lavender

CAT BREEDS
Orientals

219

Blue Oriental

Red (& Cream)

History
These two colours of Oriental are becoming increasingly popular. When a Red is mated to an Oriental carrying the blue gene, which acts as a modifier, the paler-coated, cool-toned Cream Oriental is produced.

Temperament
Intelligent, friendly, outgoing and athletic. Like all Orientals, it does not like to be left alone too long and enjoys the company of humans and other cats.

Body
Medium sized, slim, elegant and muscular. This cat is of the Siamese type, with a whip-like tail and long, slender limbs. The head is a triangular wedge shape, with a straight profile and large, wide-set ears.

Coat
Short, sleek and close lying. The Red is a warm, rich red, solid to the roots. The Cream is a even, cool-toned hue. The coat should be as clear of tabby markings as possible.

Eyes
Oriental in shape and slanting toward the nose; vivid green in colour.

Breed Assessment
GROOMING Little grooming required
VOICE Talkative
ACTIVITY LEVEL Very high
COUNTRY OF ORIGIN UK
BREED RECOGNIZED IN All countries

Foreign White

History
First seen in the 1960s, the white is the only Oriental self colour with blue eyes. To ensure that the eyes stay a piercing blue, this Oriental is usually mated with a Siamese, rather than another Oriental.

Temperament
Intelligent, friendly, extrovert and outgoing. This cat does not like being left alone and may pine if without company for any length of time.

Body
Medium sized, long, slim and elegant. With its long, slender legs and whip-like tail, the Foreign White is similar in shape to the Siamese. The head is a triangular wedge shape, with a straight profile and large, wide-set ears.

Coat
Sleek, short and close lying. The coat of this breed should be a pure, brilliant white.

Eyes
Oriental in shape, slanting toward the nose; a clear, brilliant blue in colour.

Breed Assessment
GROOMING Little grooming required
VOICE Talkative
ACTIVITY LEVEL Very high
COUNTRY OF ORIGIN UK
BREED RECOGNIZED IN All countries

New Oriental Self Colours

History
There are several welcome additions to the spectrum of Oriental colours available. The Cinnamon resulted from the introduction of the sorrel colour gene to Siamese, which were then mated to Abyssinians. The dilute (see page 160) version of this is known as the Fawn. The Caramel was first seen in 1974, when an English breeder was experimenting with various new colours, including silver, and two curiously coloured kittens were born. This colour is now known as Caramel.

Temperament
Intelligent, affectionate, extrovert and athletic. These cats like human and feline company and do not like to be left alone too long.

Body
Elegant, long, slim and lithe. These Orientals have a Siamese shape, with long, slender limbs and a long, whip-like tail. The head is a triangular wedge shape, with a straight profile and large, wide-set ears.

Coat
Short, sleek and close lying. The Cinnamon is a warm, even brown that is solid to the roots, with no shading or markings. The Fawn is a warm, rosy mushroom colour. The Caramel is a cool-toned bluish beige, while the

Cinnamon Oriental

sex-linked version of Caramel, Apricot, is a hot cream with a soft metallic sheen.

Eyes
Oriental in shape and slanting toward the nose; clear green in colour.

Breed Assessment
GROOMING Little grooming required
VOICE Talkative
ACTIVITY LEVEL Very high
COUNTRY OF ORIGIN UK
BREED RECOGNIZED IN All countries

Caramel Shaded Oriental

Tabby (Spotted)

History
Originally known in Britain as the Egyptian Mau, the name of this breed was changed in 1978 to Oriental Spotted Tabby to avoid confusion with the unrelated American breed of the same name (see page 208). First seen in the late 1960s, the Spotted was the first of the Oriental Tabbies to be officially recognized.

Temperament
Intelligent, affectionate, extrovert and friendly.

Body
Medium sized, elegant and slim but well muscled. This cat is of the Siamese type, with a whip-like tail and long, slim legs. The head is a triangular wedge shape and the ears are large and wide set.

Coat
Short, sleek and close lying. There should be clearly defined solid-coloured spots on an agouti background.

Eyes
Oriental in shape and slanting toward the nose; should be green in colour.

Breed Assessment
GROOMING Little grooming required
VOICE Talkative
ACTIVITY LEVEL Very high
COUNTRY OF ORIGIN UK
VARIETIES Brown, Blue, Chocolate, Lilac, Red, Cream, Apricot, Cinnamon, Caramel, Fawn, and the same in Silver, Tortie, and Tortie-Silver
BREED RECOGNIZED IN All countries (but not all colours)

Chocolate Spotted
Oriental Tabby

Brown Spotted
Oriental Tabby

Red Spotted Oriental Tabby

Tabby (Classic and Mackerel)

History
The Oriental Tabby originated from matings between Orientals and Tabby Point Siamese. The silver gene has been introduced by mating back to the Chinchilla to produce the most popular Silver Tabby.

Temperament
Intelligent, affectionate, extrovert and friendly. Just like its Siamese cousins, this breed loves human and feline company and tends to pine if left alone.

Body
Elegant, medium sized and well muscled. This cat is of the Siamese type, with a svelte body, whip-like tail and long, slim legs. The head is the typical triangular wedge shape and the ears are large and wide set.

Coat
Short, sleek and close lying. The solid-coloured markings should be clearly defined and set off against a background of agouti fur.

Eyes
Wide set, Oriental in shape and slanting toward the nose; a brilliant, clear green in colour.

Breed Assessment
GROOMING Little grooming required
VOICE Talkative
ACTIVITY LEVEL Very high
COUNTRY OF ORIGIN UK
VARIETIES Brown, Blue, Chocolate, Lilac, Red, Cream, Apricot, Cinnamon, Caramel, Fawn and the same in Silver, Tortie and Silver Tortie
BREED RECOGNIZED IN All countries (but not all colours)

Tabby (Ticked)

History
This popular variety of Tabby was first granted championship status in 1993. The evenly ticked coat is reminiscent of the wild ancestors of all the domestic breeds. The gene for ticking was introduced early in the history of this breed by matings between Siamese and the ticked Abyssinian.

Temperament
Intelligent, friendly, affectionate and extrovert.

Body
Elegant, medium sized and well muscled. Similar to the Siamese in shape, this cat is long and slender, with a whip-like tail and long, slim legs. The head is a triangular wedge shape, with large, wide-set ears.

Coat
Short, sleek and close lying. The fur should be evenly ticked and have at least two or three bands of colour on each hair.

Eyes
Oriental in shape, and slanting toward the nose; the colour should be clear green.

Breed Assessment
GROOMING Little grooming required
VOICE Talkative
ACTIVITY LEVEL Very high
COUNTRY OF ORIGIN Britain
VARIETIES Brown, Blue, Chocolate, Lilac, Red, Cream, Apricot, Cinnamon, Caramel, Fawn, and the same in Silver, Tortie and Silver Tortie
BREED RECOGNIZED IN All countries (but not all colours)

Tortoiseshell

History
As with all Tortoiseshells, this is usually a female-only variety. Occasionally a male will be born but it is usually found to be sterile. The Oriental Tortoiseshell was first bred in Britain and arose as part of the breeding programme devised to produce the Red and Cream self colours.

Temperament
Intelligent, friendly, outgoing and extrovert. Known as the 'naughty tortie', the Tortoiseshell is often more wilful than other colours and patterns. Like all Orientals, this cat enjoys company and does not like to be left alone for long periods of time. If the owner is out at work for hours each day, a second cat of similar temperament is essential.

Body
Elegant, medium sized but muscular. Similar to the Siamese in shape, this cat has a whip-like tail and long, slender legs. The head is a triangular wedge shape, and the ears large and wide set.

Coat
Short, sleek and close lying. The colours should be mingled or patched with red, cream or apricot, while the base colour should be solid to the roots without any tabby markings.

Eyes
The eyes should be Oriental in shape and slanting slightly down toward the nose; a clear green in colour.

Breed Assessment
GROOMING Little grooming required
VOICE Talkative
ACTIVITY LEVEL Very high
COUNTRY OF ORIGIN UK
VARIETIES Black, Blue, Chocolate, Lilac, Cinnamon, Caramel and Fawn
BREED RECOGNIZED IN All countries (but not all colours).

Blue Tortoiseshell Oriental

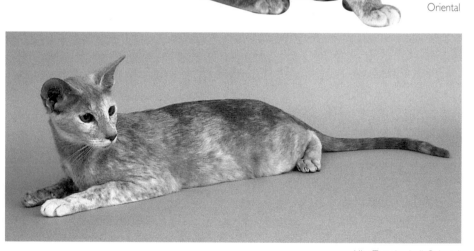
Lilac Tortoiseshell Oriental

Chocolate Tortoiseshell Oriental

Shaded (and Smoke)

History
The Shaded was the result of an accidental mating between a Chinchilla and a Chocolate Point Siamese. The offspring of this match had dark coats, shading to a paler silver colour near to the skin. Together with the amusing, almost clown-like facial markings, this made for a most attractive cat. This first Shaded was mated to a Red Point Siamese, carrying the blue gene, which resulted in the non-agouti silver version known as the Smoke.

Temperament
Intelligent, friendly, outgoing and athletic. Like all other Orientals, the Shaded and Smoke love human and feline company and do not like to be left alone for long periods of time.

Body
Long and slim but well muscled. Siamese in shape, the Shaded and Smoke have long, slim legs and a whip-like tail. The head is a triangular wedge shape, with a straight profile and large, wide-set ears.

Coat
Short, sleek and close lying. The Shaded is an agouti cat, with a silvery white undercoat overlaid with standard or silver colours. The Smoke is the non-agouti, silver variety.

Eyes
Oriental in shape and slanting down toward the nose; clear green in colour.

Caramel Shaded Oriental

Breed Assessment
GROOMING Little grooming required
VOICE Talkative
ACTIVITY LEVEL Very high
COUNTRY OF ORIGIN UK
VARIETIES Available in all colours accepted in Orientals
BREED RECOGNIZED IN All countries (but not all colours)

CAT BREEDS
Orientals

225

Black Smoke Oriental

Brown Burmese (Sable Burmese)

History

The Burmese was first brought to California from the Far East in the 1930s. A dark brown cat resembling a Siamese but with no restricted points, it was the subject of great interest. Since there was no other Burmese in the USA at the time, this female cat, named Wong Mau, was mated to a Seal Point Siamese. The kittens were, of course, hybrids but, when one of the Wong Mau's sons was mated back to her, the resulting litter contained some plain-coated, dark brown kittens just like herself. These became the basis for the Burmese breed. A pair was first brought to Europe in 1948 and today the Burmese is a most popular breed. The Brown is known as the Sable Burmese in the USA.

Temperament

Intelligent, friendly, extrovert and outgoing. The Burmese is very much a 'people cat' and does not like being left alone for long periods. It also loves the company of other cats, preferably another Burmese or Siamese. If living in overcrowded conditions, however, the Burmese tends to become territorial.

Body

Elegant, but sturdy and well muscled. The head of this medium-sized cat has a rounded dome with wide-set ears. In profile, there should be a distinct nose break and firm chin. The legs are slender and the tail should be in proportion to the body and taper to a rounded tip.

Coat

Short, glossy and close lying. The colour should be an even rich, warm, seal brown.

Eyes

Large, lustrous and wide set, slightly slanting toward the nose. While a golden yellow colour is preferred, almost any shade of yellow from chartreuse to amber is accepted.

Brown Burmese

Breed Assessment

GROOMING Little grooming required
VOICE Talkative
ACTIVITY LEVEL Very high
COUNTRIES OF ORIGIN Burma and USA
BREED RECOGNIZED IN All countries

Brown Burmese

Blue Burmese

History
The first Blue Burmese was born in Britain in 1955 from a mating of two Browns. It was aptly named Sealcoat Blue Surprise. It had always been thought that Burmese and Siamese had a similar genetic colour inheritance pattern and as the Blue Point Siamese had been around for many years, it was inevitable that a blue version of Burmese would eventually be seen. Nevertheless, this new colour created much interest.

Temperament
Intelligent, friendly, extrovert and outgoing. The Blue Burmese is a 'people cat' and does not like being left alone for long periods. It also loves the company of other cats, preferably another Burmese or Siamese. If living in overcrowded conditions, however, the Burmese tends to become territorial.

Body
Medium sized, well muscled and sturdy. The head is round and domed with medium-sized, wide-set ears. In profile, the nose should make a distinct break and the chin should be firm. The legs are slender and the tail should be in proportion to the body length and taper to a rounded tip.

Coat
Short, glossy and close lying. The colour should be an even, soft silvery grey, with pronounced silvering on the paws, ears and face.

Eyes
Large and lustrous; wide set, slanting slightly toward the nose. Although golden yellow is the preferred colour, eyes in all shades from yellow through to amber are accepted at shows.

Blue Burmese

Breed Assessment
GROOMING Little grooming required
VOICE Talkative
ACTIVITY LEVEL Very high
COUNTRY OF ORIGIN UK
BREED RECOGNIZED IN All countries

Blue Burmese

Chocolate Burmese (Champagne)

History
A popular breed on both sides of the Atlantic, the Chocolate is a dilute colour (see page 160) first seen in the USA, where it is known as the Champagne.

Temperament
Intelligent, friendly and playful. It is sometimes found that the dilute colours are less extrovert than the other colours, but the Chocolate is typically outgoing. As with all Burmese, it does not like being left alone and is happier if it has a feline companion, preferably a breed with a similar personality.

Body
Medium sized and elegant, but sturdy. This cat is well muscled with slender legs and a tapering tail, the length of which should be in proportion to the body. The head has a rounded dome and wide-set, medium-sized ears. In profile, there should be a distinct nose break and a firm chin.

Coat
Short, glossy and close lying. The colour should be an even milk chocolate, although there may be some shading on the back, head and tail.

Eyes
Large and lustrous. The eyes should be noticeably wide set and slightly slanting toward the nose. They may be almost any colour ranging from chartreuse yellow to amber, but a shade of bright golden yellow is usually preferred.

Breed Assessment
GROOMING Little grooming required
VOICE Talkative
ACTIVITY LEVEL Very high
COUNTRY OF ORIGIN USA
BREED RECOGNIZED IN All countries

Lilac Burmese (Platinum)

History
The Lilac is a popular addition to the array of Burmese colours and is produced from parents that carry the genes for both Blue and Chocolate. This dilute colour (see page 160) is known as Platinum in the USA, where the breed was first produced. Lilacs first came to Europe in the late 1960s and early 1970s.

Temperament
Intelligent, friendly and outgoing. Like other dilute colours, the Lilac has a tendency to be slightly less demanding than most Burmese.

Body
Medium sized, elegant and sturdy. This well-muscled cat has slender legs and a tapering tail, the length of which is in proportion to the body. The head has a rounded dome and shows a distinct nose break and firm chin in profile. The ears are medium sized and wide set.

Coat
Short, glossy and close lying. The colour should be an even, pale dove-grey, with a definite pinky tinge. The head, back and tail may be a slightly darker shade of grey.

Eyes
Large, wide set and slightly slanting toward the nose. Although golden yellow is the preferred colour, the eyes of this breed may be any shade from chartreuse yellow through to amber.

Breed Assessment
GROOMING Little grooming needed
VOICE Talkative
ACTIVITY LEVEL Very high
COUNTRY OF ORIGIN USA
BREED RECOGNIZED IN All countries

Red Burmese

History
From 1965 to 1975, breeders worked on a breeding programme aimed at bringing new sex-linked colours into the Burmese breed. By outcrossing to Red Point Siamese and Red Shorthairs, the red gene was introduced, producing Red, Cream and Tortie Burmese.

Temperament
Intelligent, friendly, companionable, lively and outgoing.

Body
Elegant, medium sized and well muscled, with slender legs and a tapering tail. The head has a rounded dome and, in profile, should show a firm chin and a distinct nose break. Ears are medium sized and wide set.

Coat
Short, glossy and close lying. The colour should be a rich tangerine, although slight tabby markings on the face are acceptable.

Eyes
Large and lustrous, slanting slightly toward the nose. The preferred colour is golden yellow, but all shades from yellow to amber are accepted.

Breed Assessment
GROOMING Little grooming required
VOICE Talkative
ACTIVITY LEVEL Very high
COUNTRY OF ORIGIN UK
BREED RECOGNIZED IN All countries

Breed Assessment
GROOMING Little grooming required
VOICE Talkative
ACTIVITY LEVEL Very high
COUNTRY OF ORIGIN Britain
BREED RECOGNIZED IN All countries

Cream Burmese

History
Like the Red, the Cream Burmese is a sex-linked colour created by Burmese breeders. The dilute (see page 160) version of Red, this attractive cat is now a popular variety of Burmese.

Temperament
Intelligent, friendly, lively and outgoing.

Body
Elegant, medium sized and well muscled, with slender legs and a tapering tail. The head has a rounded dome and, in profile, should show a firm chin and a distinct nose break. Ears are medium sized and wide set.

Coat
Short, sleek and glossy. The colour is an even cream, with faint tabby markings permissible on the face. The ears, face and paws should show a 'bloom', as if they have had a light dusting of talcum powder.

Eyes
Large, lustrous and wide set, slanting slightly toward the nose. Golden yellow is preferred, but any colour from chartreuse yellow to amber is accepted.

Tortoiseshell

History
The Tortoiseshell is the only patterned variety of Burmese and is available in four colours. Like the Red and Cream, it was developed as part of a special breeding programme mating Burmese with Red domestic shorthairs, which took place in Britain between 1965 and 1975. While it is recognized as a Burmese in most countries, the Tortoiseshell is known as the Malayan by some North American fancies. As with all Torties, it is usually a female-only breed. Few males have been recorded and those that are born are rarely fertile.

Temperament
Intelligent, friendly and fun loving. Probably the most extrovert and outgoing of all Burmese, the Tortoiseshell has not gained the nickname of 'naughty tortie' without good reason. Like all Burmese, it demands attention from its owners and does not like being left alone for any length of time. If this is a problem, a feline companion is advisable.

Body
Elegant, muscular and sturdy. This medium-sized cat has slender legs and a tapering tail of a length in proportion to its body. The head has a rounded dome and a distinct nose break and firm chin in profile. The ears are medium sized and wide set.

Lilac Tortie Burmese

Coat
Short, glossy and close lying. The colour should be a well-mingled mixture of red or cream on any of the four base colours.

Eyes
Large and lustrous. The preferred colour is golden yellow, but any shade from chartreuse yellow to amber is accepted.

Breed Assessment
GROOMING Little grooming required
VOICE Talkative
ACTIVITY LEVEL Very high
COUNTRY OF ORIGIN UK
VARIETIES Brown Tortie, Blue Tortie, Chocolate Tortie and Lilac Tortie
BREED RECOGNIZED IN All countries

Chocolate Tortie Burmese

Seal Point

History
Originally called the Royal Cat of Siam, the Siamese was revered in its native home of Thailand. Today, it is probably the most instantly recognizable of all the pedigree breeds, with its elegant, elongated shape, pale body colour and, most distinctive of all, the dark, seal-brown points restricted to the face, ears, legs and tail. The early Siamese were much chunkier than the svelte, lithe cat familiar today, which is the result of selective breeding. There is currently some interest in re-creating a Siamese of the chunkier, 'old-fashioned' type.

Temperament
Intelligent, outgoing, loyal and loving. Like all Siamese, the Seal Point is extremely friendly with its human owners and may demand attention whenever it is in the house. The Siamese is easily the loudest and most vocal of any cat. Its ability to keep up a continuous torrent of mews, yowls and calls in a variety of tones is legendary. Those who like Siamese find this compulsive chatter a great attraction.

Body
Elegant, slender and athletic. This is a medium-sized, muscular cat. The legs are long and slender and the tail long and whip-like. The head should be triangular in shape, with a long, straight profile, and the ears are large, wide based and wide set.

Coat
Short, fine and close lying. The body colour should be a pale, warm cream and the dark brown points should be restricted to the face, ears, legs and tail.

Seal Point Siamese

Eyes
Slightly slanting toward the nose, and Oriental in shape; the colour should be a deep, clear, brilliant blue.

Breed Assessment
GROOMING Little grooming required
VOICE Loud and extremely talkative
ACTIVITY LEVEL Very high
COUNTRY OF ORIGIN Siam (Thailand)
BREED RECOGNIZED IN All countries

CAT BREEDS
Siamese

231

Young Seal Point Siamese

Blue Point

History
First exhibited at a cat show in 1896, the Blue Point was was initially thought of as a poorly coloured Seal Point and was not immediately popular. It was not until the 1930s that a serious breeding programme was implemented to ensure that this colour continued. Official recognition followed in 1932 in the USA and in 1939 in Britain. It is likely that the blue gene was present in Siamese cats from the very beginning.

Temperament
Intelligent, playful, outgoing and friendly. The Blue Point is extremely gregarious and may demand attention whenever it is in the house. It does not like to be left alone for any length of time and it may be best to provide it with a feline companion, preferably of a similar breed.

Body
Long, slim, muscular and elegant. This is a medium-sized breed with long, slim legs and a long, whip-like tail. The head is triangular in shape, with a long, straight profile and large, wide-set ears.

Blue Point Siamese

Coat
Short, fine and close lying. The body colour should be glacial white, with light blue points restricted to the face, ears, legs and tail.

Eyes
Slightly Oriental in shape, and slanting toward the nose; a bright, clear, vivid blue in colour.

Breed Assessment
GROOMING Little grooming required
VOICE Loud and extremely talkative
ACTIVITY LEVEL Very high
COUNTRY OF ORIGIN UK
BREED RECOGNIZED IN All countries

Blue Point Siamese

Chocolate Point

History
The Chocolate Point was first seen about the same time as the Blue Point and was also thought to be a poorly coloured Seal Point. It took nearly 20 years of breeding before the colouring was considered worthy of having its own breed number and thus official recognition.

Temperament
Intelligent, friendly and playful. Like other Siamese, this cat is extremely vocal.

Body
Elegant, long and slim. This is a medium-sized, muscular breed with long, slim legs and a whip-like tail. The triangular-shaped head is long, with a straight profile and large, wide-set ears.

Coat
Short, sleek and close lying. The body should be a pale ivory, with the milk chocolate colour restricted to the face, ears, legs and tail.

Eyes
Slightly Oriental in shape, and slanting toward the nose; vivid, clear, bright blue in colour.

Breed Assessment
GROOMING Little grooming required
VOICE Loud and extremely talkative
ACTIVITY LEVEL Very high
COUNTRY OF ORIGIN Britain
BREED RECOGNIZED IN All countries

CAT BREEDS
Siamese

233

Breed Assessment
GROOMING Little grooming required
VOICE Loud and extremely talkative
ACTIVITY LEVEL Very high
COUNTRY OF ORIGIN UK
BREED RECOGNIZED IN All countries

Lilac Point (Frost Point)

History
A later development among the Siamese, the Lilac Point is said to originate from matings with Russian Blues in the late 1940s. However, as both Blue and Chocolate Point Siamese already existed at this time, it is equally possible that this recessive colour occurred naturally. The Lilac Point is known as the Frost Point in the USA.

Temperament
Intelligent, friendly, loving, outgoing and noisy.

Body
Medium sized, elegant and muscular, with long, slim legs and a whip-like tail. The triangular face has a long, straight profile and the ears are large and wide set.

Coat
Short, sleek and close lying. The coat on the body should be magnolia in hue, and definitely not an icy white. The coloured points are pinkish grey and are restricted to the face, ears, legs and tail.

Eyes
Oriental in shape, slightly slanting toward the nose; a deep, clear, vivid blue in colour.

Red Point *(Red Colorpoint Shorthair)*

History
Red Point Siamese were developed from a breeding programme that aimed to introduce the sex-linked colours into the Siamese coat pattern. A domestic tortoiseshell was mated to a Siamese and, in 1934, the first Red Point was seen on exhibition. This colour of Siamese was granted official recognition in 1966. In the USA it is known as the Red Colorpoint Shorthair.

Temperament
Intelligent, companionable, playful, outgoing.

Body
Elegant and medium sized, slender in both body and legs. The tail is long and whip-like and the head is triangular in shape, with a straight profile; the ears are large and low set.

Coat
Short, sleek and close lying. The body colour should be a warm, even white, with the rich, reddish gold points restricted to the face, ears, legs and tail.

Eyes
Slightly Oriental in shape and slanting toward the nose; the colour should be an intense, brilliant blue.

Breed Assessment
GROOMING Little grooming required
VOICE Loud and extremely talkative
ACTIVITY LEVEL Very high
COUNTRY OF ORIGIN UK
BREED RECOGNIZED IN
All countries

Breed Assessment
GROOMING Little grooming required
VOICE Loud and extremely talkative
ACTIVITY LEVEL Very high
COUNTRY OF ORIGIN UK
BREED RECOGNIZED IN All countries

Cream Point *(Cream Colorpoint Shorthair)*

History
The palest of all the Siamese colours, the dilute Cream (see page 160) was inevitable once the red gene had been introduced into the breeding programme. In the USA this breed is known as the Cream Colorpoint Shorthair.

Temperament
Intelligent, companionable, friendly and playful.

Body
Elegant, medium sized and slender. This cat has long, slim legs and a long, whip-like tail. The head is triangular in shape, with a straight profile and large, wide-set ears.

Coat
Short, sleek and close lying. The body is a creamy white, and points of a cool cream colour, with a distinctive 'powdery' look, are restricted to face, ears, legs and tail.

Eyes
Slightly Oriental in shape, and slanting toward the nose; the colour should be a clear, bright blue.

Tortie Point
(Tortie Colorpoint Shorthair)

History
The Tortie Point is known as the Tortie Colorpoint Shorthair in the USA. An attractive cat in its own right, it is part of the breeding programme for Red and Cream Points. As with all Tortoiseshell cats, it is usually a female-only variety. The occasional male that is born is usually found to be sterile.

Temperament
Intelligent, companionable, friendly and playful. Possibly even more extrovert than other Siamese colours, the Tortie is as mischievous as others of its coat pattern. Although lovable and affectionate, it does display a certain amount of wilfulness in its character.

Body
Elegant, with a long, slim, muscular body. This medium-sized cat has slim legs and a long, whip-like tail. The head is triangular in shape, with a straight profile and large, wide-set ears.

Coat
Short, sleek and close lying. The pale body colour should contrast clearly with the darker points. These are restricted to the face, ears, legs and tail and should be an evenly broken mixture of any of the recognized solid colours, well mingled with red or cream.

Blue Tortie Point Siamese

Eyes
Slightly Oriental in shape, and slanting toward the nose; the colour should be a deep, intense, brilliant blue.

Breed Assessment
GROOMING Little grooming needed
VOICE Loud and extremely talkative
ACTIVITY LEVEL Very high
COUNTRY OF ORIGIN UK
VARIETIES Seal, Blue, Chocolate, Lilac, Cinnamon, Caramel and Fawn
BREED RECOGNIZED IN All countries

CAT BREEDS
Siamese

235

Chocolate Tortie Point Siamese

Tabby Point (Lynx Colorpoint Shorthair)

History
Over the years, this breed has been given a variety of names. Originally called the Shadow Point, it was later named Lynx Point (the name Lynx Colorpoint Shorthair is still used in the USA), before the name Tabby Point was adopted. Although first recorded as far back as 1902, the first litter of Tabby Points was not shown until 1961, when it generated a great deal of interest. This breed is now available in a wide variety of colours and patterns.

Temperament
Intelligent, outgoing, loyal and loving. As with all Siamese, this cat does need company and does not like being left alone for any length of time. If the owner is out for long periods each day, this cat will appreciate a feline companion, ideally another Siamese or an Oriental.

Body
Medium sized, elegant and muscular. Both body and legs are long and slim and the tail is long and whip-like. The head is triangular in shape, with a straight profile and large, wide-set ears.

Chocolate Tabby Point Siamese

Coat
Short, sleek and close lying. The body colour should be pale, making a good contrast with the points. The tabby points, restricted to the face, ears, legs and tail, should feature clear tabby markings and there should be a well-defined 'M' marking on the forehead.

Eyes
Slightly Oriental in shape, and slanting toward the nose; the colour should be a deep, intense, brilliant blue.

Breed Assessment
GROOMING Regular grooming
VOICE Loud and extremely talkative
ACTIVITY LEVEL Very high
COUNTRY OF ORIGIN UK
VARIETIES Seal, Blue, Chocolate, Lilac, Red, Cream, Apricot, Cinnamon, Caramel, Fawn and the Tortie-Tabby (US Torbie) patterns of these
BREED RECOGNIZED IN All countries

Chocolate Tabby Point Siamese

New Colours of Siamese

The Cat Fancy (see page 156) originated in Britain and it is therefore appropriate that the newer colours of Siamese, one of the oldest known breeds, were developed there, too. Three new colours were accepted in 1993 and are currently still under preliminary status. These 'new' colours have probably been around for many years, but were simply mis-registered in the past. The colours that are seen today are mainly the result of deliberate breeding programmes that involved matings between Siamese and Orientals. The latter are cousins of the Siamese, but without the restricted coat pattern, and are available in a very wide range of colours.

The new colours that are currently accepted, although still without championship status, are Cinnamon, and the dilute (see page 160) of this colour, Fawn, together with Caramel and the sex-linked version of Caramel, Apricot. These colours are available not only in the plain points, but in the whole spectrum of Tortie, Tabby and Tortie-Tabby Points. All colours within this range are also seen in Silver, although these cats have yet to gain official recognition in either Europe or North America.

CAT BREEDS
Siamese

237

Fawn Point Siamese

Recent Developments

New breeds of cat appear from time to time. Some are mere 'passing fancies', but others may prove to be viable additions to the range of acceptable pedigree breeds. Few registration bodies currently recognize these rarer breeds, a selection of which is described below.

Californian Spangled

This relatively new breed is the result of an intensive breeding programme designed to produce a cat with markings like the now-endangered African leopard. Eight different lines of pedigree and non-pedigree domestic animal, including an Egyptian street cat, were involved in the programme. The Californian Spangled has distinctive black spots and a black-tipped tail. Its low-slung gait is reminiscent of the movements of a wild leopard. Much controversy surrounded its debut in 1986 when, instead of being launched at a major cat show, it was sold only through a mail-order catalogue. Viewed by many as a 'designer item', its price rocketed – although this was not the breeder's original intention. Different coloured varieties have been produced, including Black, Blue, Bronze, Brown, Charcoal, Gold, Red, Silver and White.

Californian Spangled

Chartreuse

Chartreuse

This blue-coated cat is similar to the British Blue (see page 187), but it has a lighter build and eyes the colour of the yellow or green Chartreuse liqueur. Its history is obscure, but it may date back as far as 1300. Some theories on its origins link it with the Carthusian monks, whose main monastery was La Grande Chartreuse on the Franco-Italian border, but, although this explains the name, it is a matter of pure conjecture. In the 1920s and '30s in France, two sisters took a great interest in the Chartreuse and began a breeding programme. But after the Second World War, so few of these cats remained that they had to recreate the breed using non-pedigree blue cats. However, many people regard the Chartreuse as a British Blue of rather inferior type.

American Bobtail

There are varying accounts of the origins of this short-tailed breed, which is quite separate from the genetically different, wild American bobcat. However, it is generally accepted that the American Bobtail is descended from a short-tailed kitten discovered near an Indian Reservation in Arizona in the 1960s. This kitten was crossed with a Siamese and some of the resulting litter had short tails. The young of one of these kittens were all short tailed and so the breed began. The Bobtail's shortened tail is reminiscent of the Stumpy Manx's tail, but is similar in length to that of the Japanese Bobtail, without its distinctive curl. A double-coated breed, the American

Bobtail has either long or semi-long fur. A generally friendly, calm and intelligent cat, it has a stocky build with a broad, rounded head and large eyes.

Karelian Bobtail

Another breed of obscure ancestry, this breed looks rather like a longer-haired variety of the Japanese Bobtail. The Karelian Bobtail first appeared on the show bench in Germany in 1995.

La Perm

The originator of this breed was found in a litter of ordinary cats on a farm near Dalles in Oregon in 1986.

This kitten was born bald but later grew the distinctive curly coat. The La Perm was accepted by TICA (The International Cat Association) in the USA in 1995, but does not have status with any of the other registering bodies. Its shaggy, curly coat and placid nature ensured its survival, but the numbers of the La Perm are limited.

Nebelung

This silver-tipped, long-coated version of the Russian Blue, was developed in the USA in the 1980s. It was recognized by TICA (The International Cat Association) in 1987 in two colours only – blue and white. So far, it is not accepted by other registering bodies.

Blue Nebelung

Munchkin

The breed takes its name from the 'small people' in *The Wizard of Oz*. A mutation discovered in the USA in 1983, the Munchkin has caused great controversy in the cat world. Seen as the feline equivalent of the Dachshund, it has unnaturally short legs and a long spine. It lacks the usual feline grace and its critics worry that it is unable to groom itself properly. It may also suffer from health problems related to its long back and short legs. Short-legged cats were reported in England in the 1930s and in Russia in the 1950s, but the lines were not perpetuated.

Ojos Azules

In 1984 a tortoiseshell cat with vivid blue eyes was found in New Mexico – its Spanish name means 'blue eyes'. Subsequent breeding showed the blue-eyed gene to be dominant. This rare breed is unusual, since blue eyes in cats are normally associated only with white-furred animals or those with the Himalayan (Siamese) restricted coat pattern. The Ojos Azules has yet to be proved a viable addition to the Cat Fancy and so, currently, has no official status.

Munchkin

Peke-faced Persian

This Persian cat gets its name from its extremely flat, short-nosed face, thought to be similar to that of a Pekingese dog. The flattened face is thought to cause health problems in this breed.

Sokoke

First discovered in East Africa in 1977, this cat has unusual tabby markings, giving it a 'wood grained' look. Its body is slender and elegant and it has a long, tapering tail. There has been much controversy regarding the Sokoke's ancestry. Although found as a tropical feral, the ease with which it became domesticated might suggest that its origins were from escaped domestic breeds. The main breeding programme for this cat is currently in Denmark.

Spotted Mist

This cat is the result of a breeding programme started in Australia in the late 1970s and was the country's first important pedigree cat breed. Produced by crossing Burmese with Abyssinians and domestic tabbies, the Spotted Mist is a cat of Burmese type, but with a short, dense, glossy coat that has a misty ground colour and spots on the sides, flanks and belly. The breed was officially recognized in Australia in 1986, since which time it has produced several champions.

Siberian

This large, strongly built cat comes from northern Russia, where its long, dense coat protects it from the harsh winter weather. A long-known breed, it is rumoured to be the ancestral basis of most present-day long-haired cats, such as Persians. There is currently increasing interest in the Siberian cat in Germany, as well as in its native Russia. A few Siberians were reported as having been imported into Britain in the late 1800s, but their popularity was short-lived and they were overtaken by the more glamorous and heavily coated Persians.

Ojos Azules

Siberian

Amazing Cats

There are millions of pet cats in the world and to their owners each is unique and special. However, there are a few cats that come to wider public notice because of their behaviour, their training, because they have famous owners, or simply by accident or fate. Others go down in the record books for being fatter, older or having more kittens than other cats.

There are even heroic cats. During the Second World War, a charitable organization awarded the animal equivalent of the Victoria Cross medal – the Dickin Medal – to animals associated with the armed forces that displayed conspicuous gallantry and devotion to duty. Many dogs, several horses and one cat were honoured with the Dickin Medal. Simon, the award-winning cat, served as a mouser on board HMS *Amethyst* during the Yangtse Incident in 1949 and was in the commander's cabin when the shell that wounded him exploded.

TV stars

Arthur, the white cat who could scoop his favourite brand of cat food out of a tin with his paw, starred in more than 300 television commercials between 1966 and 1975. His biography was published, and he became very famous before he died in 1976 at the grand age of 17. Ten years later, a skinny, white cat in poor condition called Snowy was 'discovered' by animal trainer Anne Heat in an animal rescue shelter. She nursed him back to health and began to train him to use his paw on command. Anne had spotted his exceptional temperament even when he was ill and knew he would be a calm, confident performer. When Arthur II retires, no doubt Arthur III will be waiting in the wings.

In the USA a parallel story has a hero called Morris, also an ex-stray found in a cat shelter and chosen to promote a brand of pet food. Like Arthur, his unflappable personality made him an ideal performer and he appeared in 40 commercials in 10 years.

Incredible journeys

There are many amazing stories of cats that move to new homes with their owners and then return to their original houses many miles away. Ninja, a male cat from Washington State, USA, went missing from his new home and turned up a year later in his old home – about 1,370 km (850 miles) away.

Winged cat

There have been several reports of cats with fur-covered wings in the last 100 years. One winged cat, said to have a wingspan of 58cm (23in), was shot in Sweden in 1949. The wings may, of course, be fakes, but it is possible that they are caused by a rare mutation.

Socks, so called because of his pure white feet, is the USA's First Cat. A homeless stray, he was rescued by the Clintons' neighbours before taking up residence with Chelsea, Hillary and the then Governor Clinton in Arkansas in 1991. In 1993, his diary 'Socks goes to Washington' was published and the cat is now said to receive 75,000 letters and parcels per week. He is not the first cat to be so popular in the White House. Theodore Roosevelt's cat, Tom Quartz, also had his biography published. There are other cats at high levels of government. In 1989 a black and white stray was taken in by staff at 10 Downing Street, residence of the British Prime Minister. Named Humphrey, the cat became an official civil servant, with the title Chief Mouser to the Cabinet Office, until his retirement in 1997.

A picture tells a thousand words

Cats have amazing resilience and powers of recovery. The epitome of misery and cruelty, this little kitten was rescued from the River Thames in London with half a brick tied around his neck. He lived to become a happy pet, but his picture highlights the plight of thousands of cats that are neglected, cruelly treated or abandoned.

Oldest cat

Ma, a female tabby from Devon in the UK was 34 when she died in 1957.

Amazing mothers

A tabby called Dusty, from Texas, USA, produced 420 kittens during her life. The oldest recorded feline mother is Kitty from Croxton, Staffordshire in the UK. She gave birth to her last kitten – the 218th – when she was 30 in 1987. A four-year-old Burmese queen called Tarawood Antigoe mated with a half-Siamese tom to produce a litter of 19 kittens, the largest litter ever recorded; 15 of the kittens survived.

Heaviest cat

The most reliable record of a severely obese cat belongs to Himmy, a neutered male tabby from Queensland, Australia, who is reported to have weighed 21.3kg (almost 47lb). He died of respiratory failure.

Smallest cat

The record for the smallest cat belongs to Tinker Toy, from Illinois, USA, who is 7cm (2¾ in) tall and 19cm (7½ in) long.

Champion mouser

The title of best mouser goes to Towser, a female tortoiseshell owned by a distillery in Tayside, UK. In 24 years, she caught 28,899 mice – an average of three a day.

Cat Myths & Legends

Ailurophilia means the love of cats while ailurophobia is the extreme dislike of cats. (*Ailauros* means ferret in Greek and ferrets were kept as rat-catchers before cats took over the role.) Cats have evoked extreme emotions since they began their association with humans in Ancient Egypt, hence their prominent place in myth and legend. At times they have been worshipped as gods or burned as devils. They have been seen as talismans, bringing good fortune, and associated with evil and bad luck. Napoléon Bonaparte was terrified of cats. One evening while in his quarters during a campaign, he began to shout for help. His aide rushed in and found the great man, sword in hand, confronting a tiny kitten.

BLACK CATS

✦ In many countries, including the UK, black cats are considered lucky and white cats unlucky – white being the colour of ghosts. However, the black cat did not always have such a good press. In medieval Europe, the black cat was linked to the devil, who was believed to borrow the cat's black coat before tormenting his victims.

✦ In other parts of the world, beliefs differ. In North America, the black cat is thought unlucky and the white cat lucky. Black is seen as a symbol of poverty and sickness in China, and it is the tortoiseshell cat that is considered lucky in Japan.

✦ A black cat walking in front of a bride and groom suggests that the couple will be happy. It is also considered a good omen if a black cat walks into a house.

✦ Sailors' wives used to keep black cats to ensure the safe return of their husbands. While having a black cat on board ship was considered lucky by sailors, saying the word 'cat' during a voyage was extremely unlucky.

✦ The reason it is said to be lucky for a black cat to cross your path is that although its evil forces have come close, they have spared you and so you are lucky to have survived.

Witchcraft

Previously revered by many cultures, the cat was persecuted and reviled in medieval Europe for its supposed links with witches and black magic. As early as 962, it was believed that a witch's familiar took the shape of a cat and that cats were evil, dangerous animals with frightening powers. The cat's normal behaviour pattern of coming out at night to hunt for food only increased its reputation for devilry. During the 16th and 17th centuries, thousands of women were charged with witchcraft and executed and many cats were destroyed with them.

The beckoning cat

Cats have a temple consecrated to them in Japan – the 18th-century temple of Gotoku-ji. Legend has it that even though the monks in this temple were starving, they shared their food with cats. One day, some rich Samurai were passing and were beckoned inside by a cat. A terrible storm began and the Samurai took shelter for a while. One later returned to study with the monks and gave the temple a fortune. A small cat shrine was built and the cats buried there are represented by the 'spirit cat' at the heart of the temple. Around the altar are a great many model cats, each with a paw raised in a beckoning gesture. Images of a cat with one paw raised are still a popular lucky charm, known as the *maneki-neko*, or beckoning cat, in Japan.

Bastet

Bastet, the sacred cat goddess of Ancient Egypt, was a popular deity. She was believed to give protection in childbirth and against bodily dangers, such as poisonous animals, infertility and illness. She also protected newborn babies and children and was goddess of pleasure, music and dance. A huge temple was built at Bubastis, northeast of Cairo, in Bastet's honour and thousands flocked to annual celebrations to honour the goddess. Worshippers offered mummified cats, as well as bronze effigies, and it is thought that millions of cats were mummified and buried in honour of the cat goddess.

CAT TALES

✦ In Europe, cats were once believed to suck the breath from sleeping children. In Russia, however, they believe that if you put a cat in a new cradle, it will drive away evil spirits from the baby sleeping in it.

✦ In Scandinavia, a mythical cat known as the 'Butter Cat', is considered to be a protector and provider – the cats' love of cream became associated with gifts of milk and butter. However, many generations of Englishmen believed that cats had the power to turn milk sour and raise plagues of insects to destroy crops.

✦ In Peru, the Indians of the Quecha tribe fear the Ccoa, a mythical striped cat with glowing eyes. It is said to use the forces of hail and lightning to destroy crops and people.

✦ Sailors used to see any strange cat on board ship as a disguised witch. This is probably an extension of an ancient belief that a witch takes the shape of a cat when trying to raise a storm at sea.

✦ In France, there is a legendary black cat called the Matagot that may come to your door. If a family takes in and cares for the Matagot, it will bring them great wealth.

✦ An ancient Japanese legend tells of a vampire cat that kills beautiful maidens by biting their necks and sucking their blood. The cat then assumes its victim's identity and preys upon her lover.

✦ A Spanish-Jewish legend also tells of a deadly vampire cat called El Broosha that comes to sleeping babies in the night and sucks their blood.

Literary Cats

Cats have strong associations with literature – both as companions for authors and as subjects for their work. Many writers have declared themselves drawn to cats more than any other animals and have been moved to celebrate their beauty and independence in poetry and prose. Aldous Huxley wrote, 'If you want to write, keep cats', and Henry James is said sometimes to have written with a cat sitting on his shoulder. Raymond Chandler had a black Persian called Taki to whom he read the first drafts of his murder stories. French author Colette (above) was a passionate cat lover and wrote many stories about cats. One, *The Cat*, written in 1936, tells of a man who left his wife because she mistreated his beloved pet cat.

The Cheshire cat

One famous cat character is the Cheshire cat in Lewis Carroll's book, *Alice in Wonderland* (1865). The cat is best known for its smile – Alice first sees it lying on a kitchen hearth, grinning widely. Alice later encounters it in a wood, and as she watches the cat gradually disappears, starting with its tail and ending with its grin, which remains for a while after the rest of the animal has vanished. Lewis Carroll may have got the idea of a grinning cat from a particular Cheshire cheese that used to have a smiling cat's face marked on one end – hence the name of Cheshire cat.

One of the best known of all cat stories is Puss in Boots. It was written in the late 17th century by French lawyer Charles Perrault, who also wrote Cinderella, Sleeping Beauty and Little Red Riding Hood to amuse his children. The story, based on a traditional folktale, tells of a young man so poor that he decides to eat his cat and wear its skin. But instead, the cat persuades him to make it a pair of boots and a pouch to carry and promises good fortune. The stylishly attired cat catches a rabbit and presents it to the king as a gift from his master, who he introduces as a marquis. The king's beautiful daughter and the 'marquis' fall in love and marry. Puss in Boots retires from rodent-catching and becomes a famous and important figure. This legend of a cat that brings good fortune to its owner is found in many countries, including Denmark and Italy.

Cruel, but composed and bland,
Dumb, inscrutable and grand,
So Tiberius might have sat,
Had Tiberius been a cat.
MATTHEW ARNOLD, POOR MATTHIAS,
1885

FOSS

— ◆ —

Cats do not need to be beautiful to be loved. Victorian artist and humorist Edward Lear made his rather bloated, startled-looking cat with a stumpy tail into a famous cartoon character. When Foss arrived in Lear's home in 1871, a servant cut off his tail because he believed that if a cat left its tail in a house it would never stray from there! Lear so loved his cat that when he decided to move house he had one built that was an exact replica so that the cat would settle in with minimum distress. Foss died aged about 14 and had a full burial in Edward Lear's garden.

He has many friends,
laymen and clerical,
Old Foss is the name of his cat:
His body is perfectly spherical,
He weareth a runcible hat.

EDWARD LEAR, NONSENSE SONGS, 1871

yours affly,
Edward Lear,

My cat "Foss." which his tail is "far too short."—

When I play with my cat, who knows whether she isn't amusing herself with me more than I am with her?

MICHEL EYQUEM DE MONTAIGNE,
ESSAIS, 1571

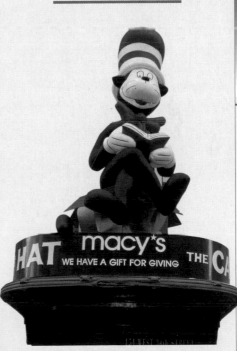

Crazy cat

Just over forty years ago, Dr Seuss (the pen-name of American author Theodor Seuss Geisel) wrote *The Cat in the Hat* – the biggest-selling children's book in the English language. The zany cat has charmed millions of children and adults with his striped hats, mad antics and rhyming stories.

Cats & Art

The supple, attractive form of the cat, combined with its haughty independence, have made it a natural subject for artists since Ancient Egyptian times, when cats featured in many wall paintings and sculptures. Cats have lived as closely with artists as they have with writers and have appeared as subjects in their own right or as part of larger compositions. Artists as diverse as Leonardo da Vinci, Rubens and Andy Warhol have painted cats.

Today, cats also feature in films, advertisements, even on postage stamps, and cats like Tom in the Tom and Jerry cartoons are among the most popular cartoon creations.

Early cat illustrations
Although cats were not as popular in Ancient Rome as they were in Egypt, feline images do feature in some Roman art, such as relief sculptures and mosaics. A particularly fine mosaic (right) was discovered at Pompeii, showing a spotted tabby attacking a pigeon.

CATS IN ADVERTISING
◆

The use of animal images in advertising has long been popular. A pet cat has universal appeal and may be used to convey a feeling of domesticity and comfort; a big cat, such as a tiger, suggests power and strength. Cats have, of course, always featured in advertising for their own foods (see page 242), but they have also been linked with a wide range of other products. The use of a cat on the Black Cat cigarette pack, for example, subtly associates the brand with the black cat's reputation for good luck. One of the most famous illustrators of cats was French artist Théophile Steinlen (1859–1923), whose advertising posters (left) featured cats that were elegant and stylish while still remaining family pets.

Postage stamps
More than one hundred countries have issued stamps featuring cats. There is even a 'Cats on Stamps Study Unit' in the USA. The first cat stamp appeared in 1887 in Germany and showed a cat with a fish in its mouth. The first modern cat stamp was issued in 1930 in Spain to commemorate the historic transatlantic flight made by Charles Lindbergh. Lindbergh's black cat Patsy went with him on the first leg from San Diego to New York, and her image graced the stamp issued in honour of the flight.

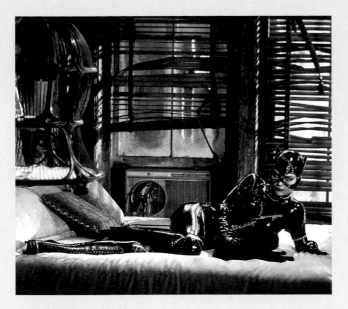

Cats on film

One of the most famous feline characters on film is Catwoman, portrayed most recently by Michelle Pfeiffer (left). Like Batman in the same film, Catwoman can change from a normal person into a part animal/part human with special powers when the need arises. Catwoman is clever, beautiful, sensuous, and independent – a perfect combination of woman and animal.

Cats have seldom had starring roles in the style of Lassie or other famous screen dogs, probably because they are more difficult to train. Many have, however, had small parts in memorable films. Notable examples include Blofeld's cat in the James Bond series and spacewoman Ripley's cat in the film *Alien* (above).

CARTOON CATS

◆

◆ Krazy Kat, a cheeky black moggie, was the first-ever cartoon cat. Born in 1910 in the USA as a Hearst newspaper strip character, Krazy Kat moved to the movie screen in 1916 and was popular well into the 1930s.

◆ In the 1920s, Felix the cat (far right) was even more popular than Charlie Chaplin. He was designed as a resourceful hero – a generous, fearless and optimistic individual. He starred in 80 films and the sheet music to his theme song *Felix kept on*

Walking sold millions. Felix the cat appeared in the first ever 'talkie' cartoon and was the first moving image to be seen on television in an experimental test broadcast in 1928.

◆ In 1939 MGM introduced the *Tom and Jerry* cartoons, featuring a cat and mouse (left) that loved to hate each other and engaged in endless, ever more inventive battles. The creation of Fred Quimby, William Hanna and Joseph Barbera, the warring twosome won seven Oscars in 18 years.

FELIX
ANNUAL

ADVENTURES OF THE FILM CAT

Useful Addresses

General Organizations

Blue Cross
Shilton Road,
Burford,
Oxfordshire OX18 4PF
Tel: 01993 822651
Web site:
http://www.thebluecross.org.uk/

British Veterinary Association
7 Mansfield Street,
London W1M 0AT
Tel: 0171 636 6541
Web site: http://www.bva.co.uk

Cats Protection League
17 Kings Road,
Horsham,
West Sussex RH13 5PN
Tel: 01403 61947
Web site: http://www.cats.org.uk/

Cat Survival Trust
Marlind Centre,
Codicote Road,
Welwyn,
Hertfordshire AL6 9TV
Tel: 01438 716873

Feline Advisory Bureau
Taeselbury,
High Street,
Tisbury,
Wiltshire SP3 6LD
Tel: 01747 871872
E-mail: fab.fab@ukonline.co.uk
Web site:
http://web.ukonline.co.uk/fab/

People's Dispensary for Sick Animals
(PDSA)
Whitechapel Way,
Priorslea,
Telford,
Shropshire TF2 9PQ
Tel: 01952 290999

Royal Society for the Prevention of
Cruelty to Animals (RSPCA)
The Causeway,
Horsham,
West Sussex RH12 1HG
Tel: 01403 264 181
Email: publications@rspca.org.uk
Web site: http://www.rspca.org.uk

Wood Green Animal Shelters
Kings Bush Farm,
London Road
Godmanchester,
Cambridgeshire PE18 8LJ
Tel: 01480 830 757

Breed Associations

Governing Council of the Cat Fancy
4–6 Penel Orlieu
Bridgwater,
Somerset TA6 3PG
Tel: 01278 427575
Web site:
http://ourworld.compuserve.com/
homepages/GCCF_CATS/

National Cat Club
The Laurels,
Rocky Lane
Wendover Dean,
Buckinghamshire HP22 6PR

Internet Cat Club
Web site: http://www.netcat.org

*There are clubs and societies for almost
every breed of pedigree cat. A full list may
be obtained from the Governing Council of
the Cat Fancy, but here is a selection for
some of the most popular breeds.*

Abyssinian Cat Club
Alwyne, 15 Cranhurst Lane
Witley,
Godalming,
Surrey GU8 5RA
Angora Breed Club

26 Essex Road
Enfield,
Middlesex EN2 6UA
Balinese and Siamese Cat Club
Holly Tree Cottage, Clacton Road
Horsley Cross,
Manningtree,
Essex CO11 2NR

Blue Persian Cat Society
104b Llandaff Road
Cardiff,
Glamorgan CF1 9NN

British Shorthair Cat Club
Ty Gwyn,
Llawr-y-Glyn
Caersws,
Powys SY17 5RH

Burmese Cat Club
Southview, Landmere Lane
Edwalton,
Nottingham,
Nottinghamshire NG12 4DG

Colourpoint Cat Club
21 Fairhaven Road,
Southport,
Merseyside PR9 9UJ

Exotic Cat Club
3 Longburgh Close
Hoole,
Chester,
Cheshire CH2 3TA

Maine Coon Cat Club
12 St Josephs Road
Handsworth,
Sheffield,
South Yorkshire S13 9UA

Oriental Cat Association
76 Valley Road
London SW16 2XN

CAT – THE
COMPLETE
GUIDE
*Useful
Addresses*

250

Further Reading

Semi-longhair Cat Association
4 Lynton Avenue
Boston Spa,
Wetherby,
West Yorkshire LS23 6BL

Shorthaired Cat Society
Highridge, Parsonage Hill
Somerton,
Somerset TA11 7PF

Siamese Cat Club
Fistral, 10 Noak Hill Close
Billericay,
Essex CM12 9UZ

Periodicals

All About Cats
Suite C,
21 Heathmans Road
London SW6 4TJ

Your Cat
Apex House,
Oundle Road
Peterborough,
Cambridgeshire PE2 9NP

Cat World
Avalon Court,
Star Road
Partridge Green,
West Sussex RH13 8RY
Web site: http://www.catworld.co.uk/

Books

Bessant, Claire
How to Talk to Your Cat
Smith Gryphon (Blake Publishing)

Bessant, Claire and Neville, Peter
The Perferct Kitten
Hamlyn

Clutton-Brock, Juliet
The British Museum Book of Cats
British Museum Publications

Cutts, Paddy
Identifying Cat Breeds
The Apple Press

Edney, Andrew
RSCPA Complete Cat Care Manual
Dorling Kindersley

Fogle, Dr Bruce
The Encyclopedia of the Cat
Dorling Kindersley

Morris, Desmond
Cat World
Ebury Press

Tabor, Roger
Understanding Cats
Charles Stanley

Tabor, Roger
Cat Behaviour
Charles Stanley

Viner, Bradley
A–Z of Cat Diseases and Health Problems
Ringpress

Viner, Bradley
The Cat Care Manual
Stanley Paul

CAT – THE
COMPLETE
GUIDE
*Further
Reading*

251

Index

Credits

Photograph sources

Abbreviations
b bottom
c centre
l left
r right
t top

Page 1 John Daniels; 2–3 Tony Stone; 4–5 Ardea/John Daniels; 6–7 Tony Stone/Thomas Peterson; 8–9 NHPA/Laurie Campbell; 10 tl Tony Stone/Kevin Schafer, tr Tony Stone/James Martin, b FLPA/Terry Whittaker; 10–11 Stockmarket; 11 t Ardea/Ferrero/Labat, b Tony Stone/Daryl Balfour; 12 t FLPA/K Delport, c & bl FLPA/Terry Whittaker, br Tony Stone; 12–13 FLPA/Panda; 13 l Robert Harding/Franz Lanting, r Tony Stone; 14 FLPA/David Hosking; 14–15 Animals Unlimited; 16 Warren Photographic; 17 t FLPA/E & D Hosking, cl Ardea/John Daniels, cr FLPA/Foto Natura, b Animals Unlimited; 18 tl Ardea/Ferrero/Labat, tr Ardea/E Dragesco, b Tony Stone/B Dittrich; 19 t Ardea/John Daniels, b Cats Survival Trust; 21 Ardea/John Daniels; 22 FLPA/Yossi Eshbol, 23 Ardea/John Daniels; 24 l FLPA/Gerard Lacz, r FLPA/Foto Natura; 25 l FLPA/Gerard Lacz, r Ardea/Jean Paul Ferrero; 26 l Ardea, 26 r – 27 Ardea/John Daniels; 28 FLPA; 29 t Ardea/John Daniels, b Ardea; 30 t Warren Photographic/Jane Burton, b FLPA/F. Coppola; 31 tl Warren Photographic/Jane Burton, tr FLPA/Gerard Lacz, cr Ardea/C Martin Bahr, br Warren Photographic; 32 Ardea; 33 l Ardea/John Clegg, r Warren Photographic; 34 – 35 t Ardea/John Daniels, b FLPA/Foto Natura; 36 Warren Photographic/Kim Taylor; 37 Animals Unlimited; 38 l Animals Unlimited, r FLPA/Gerard Lacz; 39 FLPA/David T Grewcock; 40 Ardea/John Daniels; 41 t FLPA/Gerard Lacz, 41 b – 42 l Ardea/John Daniels, r Ardea; 43 t Warren Photographic/Jane Burton, b Animals Unlimited; 44 tl Warren Photographic/Jane Burton, tr Ardea, b Warren Photographic/Jane Burton; 45 t Ardea/John Daniels, b Warren Photographic/Jane Burton; 46 Ardea/John Daniels; 47 t Warren Photographic/Jane Burton, b FLPA/Gerard Lacz; 48 FLPA/W Rohdich; 49 l Warren Photographic, r FLPA/H D Brandt, b Ardea/John Daniels; 50 t Warren Photographic/Jane Burton, b FLPA/Gerard Lacz; 51 t FLPA/Tony Hamblin, 51 b – 52 b Warren Photographic/Jane Burton; 53 Ardea; 54 t Ardea/John Daniels, b Warren Photographic/Jane Burton; 55 l FLPA/Silvestris, 55 r – 56 t Warren Photographic/Jane Burton, 56 b Animals Unlimited; 57 l FLPA/C Mullen, r Ardea/ John Daniels; 58 t Ardea/Ian Beames, b FLPA/R Tidman; 59 Ardea/John Daniels; 60–63 Warren Photographic/Jane Burton; 64 t Ardea/John Daniels, 64 b – 65 Warren Photographic/Jane Burton; 66 t FLPA/Panda, b Ardea; 67 Marc Henrie; 68–69 Stockmarket/H Reinhard; 70 FLPA/Silvestris; 71 FLPA/Gerard Lacz; 72 l Ardea/ John Daniels, r FLPA/David Dalton; 73 t Ardea/John Daniels, c Ardea/Jean-Paul Ferrero, b FLPA/Gerard Lacz; 74 t FLPA/Leo Batten, b FLPA/Silvestris; 75 t Ardea /John Daniels, b Ardea/Jean-Paul Ferrero; 76 t RSPCA Photo Library/Geoff Langan, 76 b – 77 t Animal Photography/Sally Anne Thompson, 77 b Sylvia Cordaiy/Monica Smith; 78 t Warren Photographic/Jane Burton, c Ardea/John Daniels, b FLPA/Gerard Lacz; 79 t Warren Photographic/Jane Burton, b Tony Stone /Pal Hermansen; 80 t Warren Photographic/Jane Burton, b Ardea/John Daniels; 81 Animal Photographic/Sally Anne Thompson; 82 Warren Photographic/Jane Burton; 83 t FLPA/T Bastable, 83 b – 84 t Warren Photographic/Jane Burton, 84 b FLPA/Silvestris; 85 t Warren Photographic/ Jane Burton, b Pet Magazine/Emap; 86 FLPA/ Silvestris; 87 t FLPA/Foto Natura, b Trip/Anon; 88 t Ardea/John Daniels, 88 bl – 89c bl Your Cat/Emap, 89 b – 90 t Warren Photographic/ Jane Burton, 90 c Your Cat/Emap, b Animal Photography/Sally Anne Thompson; 90–91 Team Media; 91 tl, tr & br Your Cat/Emap, bl Warren Photographic/Jane Burton; 92 l FLPA/ N Newman, r FLPA/Gerard Lacz; 93 Warren Photographic/Jane Burton; 94 t Trip/C Ellison, b FLPA/W Rohdich; 95 t FLPA/Gerard Lacz, b Animal Photography/Sally Anne Thompson; 96 t Solitaire/Angela Rixon, b Warren Photographic/Jane Burton; 97 t Tony Stone/ Timothy Shonnard, b Solitaire/Angela Rixon; 98 t Warren Photographic/Jane Burton, 98 b Your Cat/Emap; 99 t – bc Warren Photographic/ Jane Burton, 99 br Solitaire/Angela Rixon; 100 Solitaire/Angela Rixon; 101 tl Warren Photographic/Jane Burton, tr Sylvia Cordaiy, b Trip/Viesti Associates; 102 t Tony Stone/ Laurence Monnerer, b Bubbles/Frans Rombout; 103 t Tony Stone /Laurence Monnerer, b Bubbles/Jaqui Farrow; 104 t Your Cat/Emap, bl Sylvia Cordaiy, br Your Cat/Emap; 105 t Your Cat/Emap, b Solitaire/Angela Rixon; 106 l FLPA/Gerard Lacz, r Tony Stone/Terry Vine; 107 Tony Stone/Laurence Monnerer, b Warren Photographic/Jane Burton; 108 t Ardea/John Daniels, 108 b – 109 t Warren Photographic/ Jane Burton, 109 b Solitaire/Angela Rixon; 110 t Tony Stone/Frank Siteman, b Ardea/Ian Beams; 111 t Ardea/John Daniels, b Sylvia Cordaiy/Eddy Mayhew; 112 – 113 t Warren Photographic/Jane Burton, 113 bl Solitaire/Angela Rixon, br Ardea/ John Daniels; 114 Solitaire/Angela Rixon; 115 Animal Photography/R T Willbie; 116 Solitaire/ Angela Rixon; 117 Tony Stone/Peter Code; 118 t, Stockmarket, b Sylvia Cordaiy/Monica Smith; 119 tl FLPA/J & P Wegener/Foto Natura, tr Solitaire/Angela Rixon, b Ardea/John Daniels; 120–121 Ardea/Yann Arthus-Bertrand; 122 t FLPA/ Foto Natura, b Solitaire/Angela Rixon; 123 t FLPA/Gerard Lacz, b Warren Photographic/ Jane Burton; 124 t FLPA/David Hosking, c Warren Photographic/Jane Burton, b John Daniels; 125 l Warren Photographic/Jane Burton, r Sylvia Cordaiy/James de Bouverlalle; 126 t Tony Stone/S Lowry, bl Ardea, br Bradley Viner; 127 Warren Photographic/Jane Burton; 128 t Science Photo Library/EM Unit, CVL Weybridge, b Solitaire /Angela Rixon; 129 Bradley Viner; 130 Ardea/John Daniels; 131 FLPA/R Bird; 132 t Warren Photographic/Jane Burton, 132 b – 133 Bradley Viner; 134 t Warren Photographic/Kim Taylor, b Warren Photographic/Jane Burton; 135 Bradley Viner; 136 t Ardea/John Daniels, b Bradley Viner; 137–138 Warren Photographic/Jane Burton; 139 l FLPA/Gerard Lacz, r FLPA/Martin B Withers; 140 t Trip/H Rogers, b Solitaire/Angela Rixon; 141 Warren Photographic/Jane Burton; 142 t & c Bradley Viner, b Solitaire/Angela Rixon; 143 Bradley Viner; 144 t FLPA/Life Science Images, b Warren Photographic/Jane Burton; 145 Ardea/J L Mason; 146 t Tony Stone/ Dale Durfee, b Warren Photographic/Jane Burton; 147 Tony Stone/Claire Hayden; 148–150 Warren Photographic/Jane Burton; 150–151 Animals Unlimited; 151 tl Ardea/John Daniels, tr Animals Unlimited, b Warren Photographic/ Jane Burton; 152 t Ardea/François Gohier, c Animal Photography/Sally Anne Thompson, b FLPA/David T Grewcock; 153 tl Animal Photography/R T Willbie, tr Ardea/John Daniels, b FLPA/David T Grewcock; 154–155 John Daniels; 156 t Marc Henrie, b Chanan Photography; 157 t Solitaire/Angela Rixon, b Chanan Photography; 158 t Animals Unlimited, 158 c – 159 c Marc Henrie, 159 b Animal Photography/Sally Anne Thompson; 160 t Marc Henrie, c Warren Photographic/Jane Burton, b Animals Unlimited; 161 l Marc Henrie, r John Daniels; 162 t Animals Unlimited, b Solitaire/ Angela Rixon; 163 t Animals Unlimited, b FLPA/ Gerard Lacz; 164 Animals Unlimited; 165 t Solitaire/Angela Rixon, c Animals Unlimited, bl Ardea/Jean-Paul Ferrero, br FLPA/Gerard Lacz; 166 – 168 t Animals Unlimited, 168 b Solitaire/ Angela Rixon; 169 FLPA/Gerard Lacz; 170 t Ardea/Eric Dragesco, b Animals Unlimited; 171 Solitaire/Angela Rixon; 172–174 Animals Unlimited; 175 t Ardea/Yann Arthus-Bertrand, b FLPA/Gerard Lacz; 176 t Animals Unlimited, b John Daniels; 177 t – c Animals Unlimited, b John Daniels; 178 Animals Unlimited; 179 t FLPA/Gerard Lacz, c Marc Henrie, 179 b FLPA/ Gerard Lacz; 180 t & b Animals Unlimited, c John Daniels; 181 t Animals Unlimited, bl John